Loren Eiseley's Writing across the Nature and Culture Divide

ENVIRONMENT AND SOCIETY

Series Editor
Douglas Vakoch

As scholars examine the environmental challenges facing humanity, they increasingly recognize that solutions require a focus on the human causes and consequences of these threats, and not merely a focus on the scientific and technical issues. To meet this need, the Environment and Society series explores a broad range of topics in environmental studies from the perspectives of the social sciences and humanities. Books in this series help the reader understand contemporary environmental concerns, while offering concrete steps to address these problems.

Books in this series include both monographs and edited volumes that are grounded in the realities of ecological issues identified by the natural sciences. Our authors and contributors come from disciplines including but not limited to anthropology, architecture, area studies, communication studies, economics, ethics, gender studies, geography, history, law, pedagogy, philosophy, political science, psychology, religious studies, sociology, and theology. To foster a constructive dialogue between these researchers and environmental scientists, the Environment and Society series publishes work that is relevant to those engaged in environmental studies, while also being of interest to scholars from the author's primary discipline.

Recent Titles in the series

Loren Eiseley's Writing across the Nature and Culture Divide, by Qianqian Cheng

The Saving Grace of America's Green Jeremiad, by John Gatta

Art and Nuclear Power: The Role of Culture in the Environmental Debate, by Anna Volkmar

Contesting Extinctions: Decolonial and Regenerative Futures, edited by Luis I. Prádanos, Ilaria Tabusso Marcyan, Suzanne McCullagh, and Catherine Wagner

Embodied Memories, Embedded Healing: New Ecological Perspectives from East Asia, edited by Xinmin Liu and Peter I-min Huang

Ecomobilities: Driving the Anthropocene in Popular Cinema, by Michael W. Pesses

Global Capitalism and Climate Change: The Need for an Alternative World System, Second Edition, by Hans A. Baer

Loren Eiseley's Writing across the Nature and Culture Divide

Qianqian Cheng

LEXINGTON BOOKS
Lanham • Boulder • New York • London

Published by Lexington Books
An imprint of The Rowman & Littlefield Publishing Group, Inc.
4501 Forbes Boulevard, Suite 200, Lanham, Maryland 20706
www.rowman.com
86-90 Paul Street, London EC2A 4NE

Copyright © 2023 by The Rowman & Littlefield Publishing Group, Inc.

All rights reserved. No part of this book may be reproduced in any form or by any electronic or mechanical means, including information storage and retrieval systems, without written permission from the publisher, except by a reviewer who may quote passages in a review.

British Library Cataloguing in Publication Information Available

Library of Congress Cataloging-in-Publication Data

Names: Cheng, Qianqian, 1988- author.
  Title: Loren Eiseley's writing across the nature and culture divide / Qianqian Cheng.
  Description: Lanham : Lexington Books, [2022] | Series: Environment and society | Includes bibliographical references and index. | Summary: "This book offers a coherent synthesis of Loren Eiseley's works, showing how the naturalist and poet fosters readers' ecological consciousness by arguing against artificial divisions between humans and the environment"-- Provided by publisher.
  Identifiers: LCCN 2022033579 (print) | LCCN 2022033580 (ebook) | ISBN 9781666902471 (cloth : alk. paper) | ISBN 9781666902488 (epub)
  Subjects: LCSH: Eiseley, Loren C., 1907-1977--Criticism and interpretation. | Human ecology and the humanities. | LCGFT: Literary criticism.
  Classification: LCC PS3555.I78 Z626 2022 (print) | LCC PS3555.I78 (ebook) | DDC 818/.5409--dc23/eng/20220921
  LC record available at https://lccn.loc.gov/2022033579
  LC ebook record available at https://lccn.loc.gov/2022033580

∞™ The paper used in this publication meets the minimum requirements of American National Standard for Information Sciences—Permanence of Paper for Printed Library Materials, ANSI/NISO Z39.48-1992.

To my mother and father.

Contents

Acknowledgments ix

Abbreviations xi

Introduction 1

PART I: SPLIT BETWEEN SCIENCE AND THE HUMANITIES 5

Chapter 1: Scientific Influences and Poetic Influences 7

Chapter 2: Eiseley's Critique of Science 27

Chapter 3: Solution—Writing at the Intersection 61

PART II: A FRACTURE IN TIME 85

Chapter 4: Time Traveling: Science and Imagination 87

Chapter 5: Resolution: Lessons of the Past 103

PART III: HUMAN AND ANIMAL SPLIT 135

Chapter 6: Familiarity and Similarity 137

Chapter 7: Animals as Mysterious Others 159

Chapter 8: Reconciliation of the Split 181

Conclusion: A Writer for the Twenty-First Century 199

Bibliography 201

Index 205

About the Author 209

Acknowledgments

My first debt is to Loren Eiseley, this important American nature writer and scientist, whose thoughts have given me such pleasure to investigate and to transmit.

I feel grateful to the China Scholarship Council for the grant they awarded me to support my PhD study at Toulouse beginning in 2012. The fact that my project on Loren Eiseley was selected by them indicates the national demand for the younger generation to do research in the domain of the environmental humanities and contemporary American literature. I would like to address thanks to the University of Toulouse-Jean Jaurès and its libraries, especially the Bibliothèque Universitaire Centrale, Centre de ressources des Langues, and the Centre de ressources Lettres Arts Philosophie. My laboratory Cultures Anglo-Saxonnes has provided great help with my research, including offering me the scholarship to visit Lincoln, Nebraska, America in 2014, which allowed me to complete the documentation for my thesis.

Special thanks should go to Professor Tom Lynch, who kindly wrote me an invitation letter for the visiting scholar project. During my stay at the University of Nebraska–Lincoln (UNL), Professor Lynch gave many helpful suggestions about my research. He kindly offered me the "Loren Eiseley walking-driving tour" and advised me to visit Morrill Hall at UNL that displays the saber-tooth tiger bones discovered by the 1932 expedition that Eiseley was engaged in and upon which he wrote the poem "The Innocent Assassins." Thanks are due to UNL libraries: C. Y. Thompson Library at the east campus, and Love Library at the city campus. I worked at the University Archives and Special Collections department in the basement of Love Library, which houses the "Loren C. Eiseley Collection." The archives associate, Josh Caster, helped me with my data collection. Also, I want to thank the Bennett Martin Public Library in the city center of Lincoln. In the Jane Pope Geske Heritage Room of Nebraska Authors there, I had access to many collections about Eiseley, especially "The Gale E. Christianson Collection of Eiseley Research Materials." The former Heritage Room curator, Mrs.

McGowan, helped me with my research. She also gave advice about visiting the Nebraska State Capitol, where there is a bust of Loren Eiseley and the Loren Corey Eiseley Branch library. UNL Professor of Composition Randall Snyder was kind enough to send me by email his composition "Night Country: an Eiseley meditation" (mp3) and the introduction of his orchestral piece "Two Places In South Lincoln," based on addresses by Eiseley and Weldon Kees.

Thanks to the invitation of Professor Lynch, I attended Loren Eiseley's 107th Birthday reading at Meadowlark in September 2014. There I encountered the president of the Loren Eiseley Society, Bing Chen, who later agreed to my interview with him at his office at the University of Nebraska–Omaha. The following books were also kindly offered to me: *The Innocent Assassins* by Polly Wimberly, member of the Loren Eiseley Society and granddaughter of Lowry C. Wimberly; *Artifacts and Illuminations: Critical Essays on Loren Eiseley* by Professor Lynch; *The Loren Eiseley Reader* by Bing Chen; *The Lost Notebooks of Loren Eiseley* offered by Mrs. McGowan. In the front pages of these books they all wrote down encouraging words for my research. Quotations from the poem "A Tropical Swamp at Midnight" in *The Lost Notebooks of Loren Eiseley* appear with the kind permission of the Trustees of the University of Pennsylvania. Since 2019, Dr. Chen kindly invited me to attended Loren Eiseley Public Forum meetings on Zoom, through which I participated in stimulating talks on Eiseley's works.

Thanks also go to other doctors and professors who have helped me articulate my ideas about Eiseley through lectures at conferences, particularly Professor Scott Slovic, Professor Françoise Besson, Professor Nathalie Cochoy, Professor Michel Petit, Professor Richard Kerridge, and James R. Goebel.

This book wouldn't be possible without Professor Wendy Harding. She has guided me through my PhD research as my thesis supervisor. Thanks to her knowledge and wisdom, my journey in studying Eiseley has been very interesting and rewarding. She has continued to encourage my thinking and writing about Eiseley.

I depend on and profit enormously from the lasting and strong support and love from my parents, my sister and brother, and my lovely daughter. With them, I read, ponder, and write with belief in and respect for humanity and nature.

Abbreviations

Works by Loren Eiseley Cited in the Book in Alphabetical Order

AKA	*Another Kind of Autumn* (poetry)
ASH	*All the Strange Hours: The Excavation of a Life*
BMD	*Francis Bacon and the Modern Dilemma*
DC	*Darwin's Century: Evolution and the Men Who Discovered It*
FT	*The Firmament of Time*
IA	*The Innocent Assassins* (poetry)
IJ	*The Immense Journey*
IP	*The Invisible Pyramid*
LN	*The Lost Notebooks of Loren Eiseley*
NA	*Notes of an Alchemist* (poetry)
NC	*The Night Country*
ST	*The Star Thrower*
UU	*The Unexpected Universe*

Introduction

This book is above all an investigation of Loren Eiseley's unique ability to reconcile the domains of literature and science and thus to overcome the divisive mindset of modern Western culture. Eiseley is an unusual writer, exceptional among his contemporaries and the literature and science tradition. He is very original because he breaks with the established worldview and he relates to other worlds of knowledge and nature.

First of all, he is a scientist who writes critiques on science. During Eiseley's time the traditional scientific methodology emphasized the significance and precision of experimentation, and of course this demands a professional laboratory attitude in which scientists remain emotionless and detached from their relationship with other lives. However, the traditional scientific method too often makes people see living beings as only experimental objects. Science is viewed as the way to solve all of our problems. Everything in nature is seen as being put there to dissect and dissolve in scientific ways. In this sense it cuts man off from the natural world. As an alternative to the technocratic image of the scientist, Eiseley ponders nature with the feeling of awe like the Romantics, who emphasize the individual's emotional connection with nature, except that Eiseley's awe is informed by scientific knowledge as well as poetic sentiment. Reconciling the split between science and art can solve the problems inherent in the overreliance on science. That's the reason Eiseley emphasizes the importance of merging science and art; he himself is a practitioner who reaches this reconciliation through writing. This also explains why he expresses his admiration for poetry, quotes from various writers, some of whom are naturalists, some are not, and why he moves to writing poetry that expresses his naturalist's view of the world.

Secondly, Eiseley sees strangeness in the normal, and with his mind's eye he studies strange situations where others might not notice anything odd. He records the strangeness of how humans split themselves from other animals and cut off the bond with nature. He points out that man is "a creature who has abandoned instinct and replaced it with cultural tradition and the hard-won increments of contemplative thought" (UU 7). Is it true that man-made cultures divide humans and more-than-humans? What does Eiseley think of the differences and similarities between humans and other animals? In order to discuss subjects like the relationships between instinct and culture, genetic and ecological effects, and cultural influences, Eiseley devotes much of his writing to personal anecdotes that reveal the relations between humans and other animals. He talks about his childhood innocence and love and humanity's forgotten brotherhood with our animal kin. And he tries to make people become aware that humans are just part of nature like other life forms. Still he insists on the uniqueness of humans and confronts them with their responsibility for their behavior in nature. He insists that what is important in defining man's humanity is the sympathy he can have with other life forms. He anticipates the current discussion on ecocriticism and multidisciplinary animal studies, notably represented by Donna Haraway. Also he emphasizes the significance of the human brain that renders our minds and hearts capable of changing our view of the natural world.

Thirdly, Eiseley often focuses on the past, writing about the intellectual ancestors who impressed him. He has read widely, especially on subjects touching on science and nature. He presents the different worldviews he finds there, comparing them to the modern world of his own time. Eiseley connects these older worlds of knowledge and understanding across space and time, exploring the inner worlds of men of genius. Also, as an archeologist Eiseley learns from his activities of discovering and collecting fossils. Fossils are products of time, evidences of evolution, revealing the history of the natural world. Knowledgeable in studying fossils, Eiseley has the chance to ponder time, and thus tries to confront modern people with the importance of history, and the past—the mirror of the future. He might be placed in the twentieth century when he writes about time; however, he successfully interprets time by projecting himself backward and forward through his archeological activities and his scientific training and more importantly, his own wisdom accumulated through his reading and reflection. Eiseley is a time-conscious modern—like a prophet he foresees the future and he anticipates the consequences of the modern era. He anticipates the discussion of the present era as the Anthropocene, the idea promoted by modern scientific experts and commentators including French philosopher, anthropologist and sociologist of science Bruno Latour. Eiseley's writings intend to awaken modern people's ecological consciousness. In his essays Eiseley reflects on human evolution and the past and future role of science with a visionary and poetic imagination. How did man-apes become man and how did man become so powerful? What mysteries can be found in space and time and the evolution of humans and nonhumans? Uniting science and the humanities, he makes profound connections between the past and the future.

The important characteristic of Eiseley's writing is his manner of combining a philosophy of humans and nature with storytelling. In other words, he derives his interpretations from the anecdotes he uses to let the readers see in his way. The narrative style and the use of the first-person pronoun bring readers into his world. Eiseley is good at perceiving the similarities between two things, and metaphors or analogy is one obvious technique of his writing. He uses the technique of allegory to connect humans and animals. Also, his imagination helps him move back and forth through time, and he can visualize things that no one ever sees. Though he discusses serious topics like humanity and animality in his essays, now and then he reveals a sense of humor.

Combing through most of Eiseley's published books, including his three poem collections and posthumously published *The Lost Notebooks of Loren Eiseley*, my project tries to make a coherent synthesis of Eiseley's works. Some critics already realize the significance of Eiseley's poetry; however, more attention still goes to Eiseley's prose. While I explore the prose writings at length, my book also tries to show how interesting and important Eiseley's poems are. In Eiseley's writings, the line between poems and prose gets blurred: logical discourse transforms into poetry and expository prose becomes poetic. Eiseley's prose often has poetic qualities, making it a challenging but eminently worthwhile reading experience. Compared to prose, poetry is usually more condensed and more intellectually challenging; indeed, Eiseley's poems contain multiple layers of meaning. Usually we can better understand Eiseley's poems by observing his prose and vice versa. Although his poetry is close to prose, and prose close to poetry, each method of writing possesses particular qualities that are different from the other. We will see that each is not replaceable by the other and an appreciation of his writing would not be complete without exploring both. Eiseley is difficult to read and to understand fully immediately. He demands that readers make connections between ideas and his anecdotes, images, and metaphors. In other words, Eiseley's writings ask the readers to participate in the search for understanding.

Perhaps some readers or critics still regard Eiseley more as a literary writer than a scientific expert on environmental problems or animal life. Unlike primatologist and ethologist Frans de Waal, who analyzes and records daily primate behavior, Eiseley does not focus on facts about the natural world. He expresses his philosophical and ecological ideas on man and other animals mostly through recounting his encounters with animals in both natural and man-made settings. Since the stories contain fictional and metaphysical elements, his more pragmatic colleagues may not take his thoughts seriously. Indeed, naturalists' works are still being marginalized in the scientific world. Nevertheless, his philosophical thoughts on humanity and animality can be linked to relevant discussions of the same topics by French philosophers Jacques Derrida or Gilles Deleuze. This book emphasizes the poetic, philosophical, and scientific side of Eiseley's works. His reflections may be brought on by sudden perceptions, which actually are difficult to obtain and precious for a writer; still, it would be inappropriate to say Eiseley does not make analyses, because his attentive observations and perceptive awareness of his surroundings bring scientific results to his conclusions. Eiseley possesses a very original way of talking about man, nature, and the animal life, and this book will try to explore that originality.

PART I

Split between Science and the Humanities

Chapter 1

Scientific Influences and Poetic Influences

Eiseley was aware of the "bipolar division between the humanities and the sciences, which C. P. Snow has popularized under the title of the two cultures."[1] But this twentieth-century writer reveals that the awareness of this split is not found only in his contemporaries' writings; Eiseley attributes the idea to earlier writers like Francis Bacon and Henry David Thoreau, whom he believes to have been prophetic in discerning this "modern" division.

From the 1950s to the 1970s while Eiseley taught at university, disciplines were specialized and interdisciplinarity was not widely practiced. However, Eiseley does not confine himself to investigating his subject through the lens of the discipline in which he was trained; he blurs the lines between the professional and the personal, admitting to "feelings" about and "acquaintance" with his subjects of interest (NC 139). Though trained by the traditional scientific method and installed in his career as a scientist, he turns aside from "the narrowly defined scientific article" (LN 76). He ventures into philosophy or even metaphysics, combining physics, biology, poems, philosophy, and romantic stories. He is a "man of wide-ranging intellect,"[2] whose work and thought touch multiple subjects.

When Eiseley writes of the history of science, in some ways he is interested in producing a manifesto advocating a wider concept of science. Eiseley gives an imaginary dialogue between the voice of science and another voice that speaks for the human mind: "'This is your star,' says science. 'Accept the world we describe to you.' But the escaping human mind cries out, in the words of Chesterton, 'We have come to the wrong star. . . . That is what makes life at once so splendid and so strange. The true happiness is that we don't fit. We come from somewhere else. We have lost our way'"[3] (BMD 80). Eiseley cannot blindly "accept the world" that science claims to "describe," for he is conscious of something missing from the mechanical way in which twentieth-century science reports the world. He contends that life is "splendid and so strange," and science cannot exhaust all the mysteries within life. Eiseley is interested in what science cannot explain and what remains mysterious.

One mystery that attracts him is the human brain, precisely because its possibilities are unlimited and unpredictable. The mind is overwhelmingly emphasized in Eiseley's writing. He says, "Man's mind, like the expanding universe itself, is engaged in pouring over limitless horizons. At its height of genius it betrays all the miraculous unexpectedness which we try vainly to eliminate from the universe" (BMD 78). Scientists still ponder on the human mind. And the unexpectedness of genius is one among many marvels that proves science cannot or should not try to exhaust all mysteries.

Besides the scientific training he gained in universities, Eiseley's wisdom comes from reading the work of former geniuses. He reads and is influenced by both scientists and artists. In addition to his more personal collections of essays and poems, like *The Night Country*, *All the Strange Hours: The Excavation of a Life*, or *The Invisible Pyramid*, which Eiseley wrote purposefully for a wider audience and where his readers can comfortably profit from his imagination and his fictional or nonfictional anecdotes, Eiseley wrote books on Francis Bacon and Charles Darwin. Besides featuring the two men in their titles, the books cite a number of other important influences, in particular Gilbert White, Henry David Thoreau, and Alfred Russel Wallace, so these volumes shed light on Eiseley's thinking and writing: the scientific and literary geniuses are stars to him. They all had an important influence on him and all obtained their prominent achievements by crossing disciplinary fields, not being stuck in a single discipline.

In writing of these geniuses, Eiseley is presenting their different worlds or perhaps the different dimensions they saw in their worlds: Bacon's second world, Darwin's established world, White's natural world, Wallace's spiritual world, and Thoreau's two worlds: "existent and potential nature" (ST 224). Eiseley is trying to understand and explain, to reveal the truth and the deception. Meanwhile Eiseley connects and compares their worlds to his own world. His intellectual talent of freely crossing time and space is executed superbly in his writing. Our time can benefit from his efforts in observing and contemplating the differences and similarities between past and present. Eiseley's modern world does not necessarily refer only to the twentieth century; it is also ours and that of future generations. We can say that Eiseley, following the model of his ancestors, is a brave time-voyager, a creative scientific discoverer, a romantic literary man, and a true poet.

1.1 EISELEY'S SCIENTIFIC FOREFATHERS— BACON, WHITE, DARWIN, AND WALLACE

The Modern Age of Discovery

Restricted within a confined world dominated by old methods and ideas, Bacon and Darwin were courageous to break into the new worlds that their writings established. Bacon was trying to escape the old way of thinking— medieval, theologically oriented logic—through his works, particularly *The Advancement of Learning* and *Nouvum Organum*. He emphasized observation and proposed "the experimental method in science" (BMD 4). Bacon "saw his efforts not as primarily theoretical but as a necessary prelude to experiment" (BMD 33). Eiseley emphasizes that Bacon's observations on "changes in plants" with its "evolutionary overtones was made before the nature of fossils was properly understood and before the length of geological time had been appreciated" (BMD 46–47), which explains the difficulty Bacon had facing the opposition of the Elizabethans who "lacked the words and concepts to deal adequately with events remote in time or hidden behind the outer show of visible nature" (BMD 57). This is why Eiseley admires Bacon's sense of time and speaks of him as time-voyager.

Pioneers in any field, especially those working across disciplinary lines, have difficulty being accepted. Another case in point is Gilbert White, a man who saw beyond the confines of his era. In his introduction to *The Natural History of Selborne*, Bertram Windle characterizes White's age as "one of an artificial character, when little real interest was felt in natural objects." Because of the artificiality of his society, "White had to strike out a line for himself," and thinkers like him "suffered, not merely from isolation in their pursuits, but ran the risk of being looked upon as lunatics, whose harmlessness rendered them objects of pity or derision."[4] Eiseley wants to protect himself and others from the scorn to which predecessors like White may have been subjected, for he "must have been looked upon as little better than an imbecile for wasting his time in watching a tortoise, and concerning himself about the comings and goings of the swallows."[5] Windle points out, in fact, that White's observations were those of a genius, for people in his age never noticed the complexity of the natural life surrounding them. Thanks to White, they at last saw in astonishment another new world.[6]

When Eiseley thinks back to Darwin's voyage on the *Beagle*, he sees Darwin's "five years in the great solitudes, shut out by the wall of illiteracy or prejudice from the possibility of being able to talk freely with his companions" (DC 160). And according to Darwin's son's words, during Darwin's late life, he was still characterized by the "aloof and lonely habits," taking "winter morning walks in Kent—walks taken so early that he used to meet the foxes trotting home at dawn" (DC 160). This anecdote echoes with Eiseley's well-known essay "The Innocent Fox," in which the naturalist recounts how he played with "a small fox pup" near its cave at "the worn timbers of the hulk beside which I sheltered" (UU 208–9). Finally he chose to quit the little fox because "the adult foxes would be already trotting home" in the early dawn (UU 210). This story reveals how Eiseley momentarily escapes his loneliness and partakes in the innocent natural world as simply as a creature, a life. Although the event probably occurred, Eiseley's imagination was surely touched by the earlier anecdote of Darwin's loneliness and his encounter with foxes in the early winter morning.

Intellectual isolation is what Eiseley finds in Wallace's life too. He says, "Modest and solitary by nature, Wallace, unlike Darwin and Huxley, left no scientific descendants to speak for him" (DC 296). Eiseley, who himself is childless, takes the role of Wallace's descendant and explains his ideas. Briefly Eiseley mentions how Wallace was "born into modest economic circumstances," having "little in the way of educational advantages," however, acquiring early "a taste for nature," and reading eminent works that "made a profound impression upon him," spending his youth collecting data in nature, and suffering from illness to originate his groundbreaking ideas (DC 291). All these details are actually similar to Eiseley's own life story. Indeed, it is precisely "while recovering from a respiratory illness that led to temporary deafness"[7] that he conceives *Darwin's Century*, where he talks about Darwin and Wallace.

Bacon ushered in the "dawning age of science"; White's writings "have become part of the general corpus of scientific knowledge";[8] Darwin changed humanity's view of its own history with his evolution theory; and Wallace considered questions about the history of man that science still cannot answer satisfactorily. In discussing these four scientist-naturalists, Eiseley emphasizes their exceptional genius in discovering realms of knowledge that were unexplored in their times. They always glimpsed more than their fellows; they were pioneers who achieved something their ancestors had not attained. Eiseley insists that they not only crossed space but also time. In seeing the world in a way that no one before them had ever seen it, they were like prophets. They saw the future in their mental eyes, and they devoted themselves to going beyond the boundaries of the old, confined world and the past.

Eiseley's Reevaluation of His Predecessors

Eiseley claims the four not only as ancestors but also as kindred spirits—men in whose personal and intellectual lives he found common traits. They are like mirror images to him. He picks up aspects similar to his own experiences from the lives of those men and indirectly compares himself to those four geniuses.

In speaking about them, he tries to defend himself and reveal his exceptional ideas on the philosophy of science. The first common trait shared by them and Eiseley is their passion for science. Then, like his great ancestors Eiseley was committed to what we would now call interdisciplinarity. Like them he believed that scientific knowledge had a connection with moral philosophy. He insists that Bacon was a philosopher and historian as well as a scientist: "He had, as I shall indicate, a clear grasp of the importance of the history of ideas, and in this respect once more forecast a field of thought which is only now receiving the attention it deserves" (BMD 32). This "field of thought" is Eiseley's field and the basis for his nature writings—it is a field that combines the science of anthropology with history and philosophy. Fortunately, when Eiseley taught anthropology in the University of Pennsylvania "anthropology was becoming a respected discipline; professional students were increasing in number" (LN 75). His relatively new professional field was quite long in being accepted. Eiseley is thus conscious of the difficulties facing new ways of thinking.

Eiseley even goes so far as to contend that Bacon was an anthropologist because of his observations of "men and custom" (BMD 33): "Long before the rise of anthropology as a science, he had seen the social dynamic involved in cultural change and divorced it from simplistic explanations based on biology" (BMD 37). Eiseley bases this claim on Bacon's writings about the importance of human culture, drawn from a wide variety of examples. Bacon perceived "the role played by culture in controlling the otherwise uninhibited behavior of man" (BMD 39). Eiseley quotes a passage from Bacon's *Novum Organum*, emphasizing Bacon's claim by putting it in italics: "'*this difference* [between the civilized and the barbarous] *comes not from the soil, not from climate, not from race, but from the arts*'" (BMD 38). This reverence for the arts makes Bacon more congenial to Eiseley than his own scientific colleagues who insist on the importance of biology alone, while ignoring the social considerations. In Eiseley's interpretation, Bacon discovered a world hidden to his seventeenth-century contemporaries, but visible to the twentieth century: "this new universe is, in reality, what the modern anthropologist calls the world of culture, of human 'art' with all its permutations and emergent quality" (BMD 37). For Eiseley, Bacon's insistence on the importance of human culture exempted the great man from the racist prejudice that was to infect science in a later age: "Bacon had already curtly dismissed the racist doctrines that have hovered like an inescapable miasma over following centuries" (BMD 38). In making this claim, Eiseley neatly exonerates himself from the suspicion of racism that tinged the discipline of anthropology.

The important point that Eiseley emphasizes is that the past and the history of anthropology and biology are knitted together. Eiseley indicates that Bacon's essays combined "the social and the biological sciences" rather than splitting the two. His "system of induction" could be applied in discovering both the natural and the cultural world (BMD 35), which implies that at the very first moment of establishing the scientific method, there wasn't a split. Bacon was still a Renaissance man, in spite of his modernity, and Eiseley clearly regrets the narrowing of perspective along with "the rise of a professional jargon" (BMD 35) that comes with the modern age of specialization.

According to Eiseley, the tendency toward specialization in his particular field grew during Darwin's age: "coincident with the development of the evolutionary philosophy has been the rise of anthropology as a science" (DC 337). His book on Darwin attempts to place the theory of evolution in its intellectual context in order to show how the dialogue among different fields led to breakthrough scientific insights: "In reality biological and anthropological thinking have influenced each other and have been part of the same intellectual climate for a long period of time" (DC 337). Turning to his own field of specialization, Eiseley finds analogies: "between theoretical developments in the biological world and events in anthropology" (DC 341); for example, "the holistic, organismic approach which finally emerged in biology when the intricacy of inner co-ordination and adjustment began to be realized has, once more, its analogue in the social field" (DC 344). The two seemingly separate disciplines turn out to have things to learn from one another.

To advocate the pursuit of a more holistic mode of enquiry, Eiseley finds it necessary to revive Bacon's emphasis on the equal importance of the spiritual and material worlds and the necessity of language as a mode of exploration. As both a product of culture and a medium of art, language is as important to science as its technological innovations: Some "men fail to recognize that mere words can sometimes be more penetrating probes into the nature of universe than any instrument wielded in a laboratory" (BMD 34). In Eiseley's interpretation of Bacon's ideas, literature and art are just as vital in approaching the natural world, including our human world, as laboratory techniques. He values the role and the importance of the humanities in approaching the world, opposing a broader vision to the rigid, single-minded view that science can solve all problems and terminate all the mysteries of the universe. The ever-widening split that he witnessed between science and the humanities is a source of worry for him.

Facing the Mystery of the Brain

Eiseley's main concern is about humans and humanity: the nature and mind of man. He is much occupied with the discussion of the brain throughout his essays, probably because it was an important and popular scientific subject in the modern era. Eiseley points out: "All through the nineteenth century the brain as the most mysterious of human organs had been under examination.

It was then, as it is now, 'the greatest enigma of modern science'" (DC 314). He finds it mysterious how humans developed their mental capacities. In this context, he has praise for Alfred Russel Wallace, the English naturalist and contemporary of Darwin, who investigated this problem: "In the arguments which arose upon the subject of man, his animal relationships, his uniqueness or lack of uniqueness as various writers saw the story, the position of Alfred Russel Wallace came to differ markedly from that of Charles Darwin and most of his followers. . . . [And] certain of Wallace's observations were more perceptive than most of the writers of his own day" (DC 290). For Eiseley, the most important issue Wallace investigated is the question of the rapid development of the human brain.

Wallace suggested that "'higher agencies'" caused the rise of man and the development of his brain. As Eiseley points out, "Since this hypothesis removed the issue to the domain of metaphysics, it was not taken seriously in science" (DC 316–17). Wallace tried to go to metaphysics to answer questions to which Darwin failed to give a genuine answer, but he was destined to be dismissed as unworthy of scientific study. And "slowly Wallace's challenge was forgotten and a great complacency settled down upon the scientific world" (IJ 85). Eiseley states, even today "ironically enough, science, which can show us the flints and the broken skulls of our dead fathers, has yet to explain how we have come so far so fast, nor has it any completely satisfactory answer to the question asked by Wallace long ago. Those who would revile us by pointing to an ape at the foot of our family tree grasp little of the awe with which the modern scientist now puzzles over man's lonely and supreme ascent" (IJ 93–94). Eiseley investigates "man's lonely and supreme ascent." Not only dismissing the close relations between humans and apes but also minimizing their differences demonstrates a lack of respect for the mysteries of the living world. In Angyal's view, Eiseley's thinking in this matter was influenced by both Bacon and Wallace: "Eiseley presented his own views of man's cultural evolution and his distinctiveness as a creature bound by time and memory—views strongly influenced by Francis Bacon and Alfred Russel Wallace."[9] Continuing in that tradition, Eiseley ponders the questions raised by his great predecessors, and he admires their wisdom. His own meditations on the human brain focus on the bonds between humans and animals, the mystery of the ways these evolved over time, and how memory comes into being.

Art as the Way to Approach Nature

The naturalists that Eiseley praises have changed the ways in which humans approach nature, Bacon in particular: "more than any other man of his epoch, [he] recognized . . . the unexploited power of humanity, not just to *live* in

nature, but to create a new nature through the right use of human reason—
'that which,' as he expressed it, 'without art would not be done'" (BMD 56).
Man's attention to the living world became one of the modern avenues to
art, just as art became a way to accede to nature. In *The Natural History of
Selborne*, Gilbert White illustrates how to look at, how to feel and how to
know the natural world. White's letters in *Selborne* reflect a form of empiri-
cism. He observes and reflects on what surrounds him and tries to make his
readers aware of the implications of these observations. He renders the natural
world in a vivid manner: "His simple style and the pictures of the life of the
time . . . rendered his work part of the permanent literature of the country."[10]
One of the things that Eiseley and his forebears achieved is to inspire wonder
for the nature of life. Each presented his original version of the natural world.

Indeed, Eiseley manages to change the angle of vision of common men
toward the natural world. In "Art as Technique," Viktor Shklovsky declares
that "The technique of art is to make objects 'unfamiliar,' to make forms
difficult, to increase the difficulty and length of perception because the
process of perception is an aesthetic end in itself and must be prolonged."[11]
Eiseley's writing uses this technique in order to make common things
strange, especially in discussions of the relationship between humans and
other-than-humans. Through his discussions of wild and domestic animals
and his meeting with animals in both the human world and the natural world,
he reveals their closeness to humans as well as the mysterious aspects that
humans can never fully understand.

Eiseley learns from White how to pay attention to the natural world, and
he emphasizes how both his scientific predecessors and he himself have
benefited from White's literary influences. He notices that Darwin was a
beneficiary of the influence of both Bacon and White. He observes and goes
on to point out that Darwin's studies of pigeons may have been inspired by
White's writing:

> Though Darwin is generally claimed by the scientists, it is worthy of note that
> he did not remain uninfluenced by the literary tradition in natural history which
> is so strong in England. He was a devoted reader of Gilbert White. . . . There
> is little doubt that he received the initial stimulus for his earthworm studies
> from *The Natural History of Selborne* (1789) and his debt may be even more
> extensive. It has not been generally remarked by students of Darwin's *Variation
> of Animals and Plants under Domestication* that in 1780 White expressed to his
> friend Pennant the opinion that the small blue rock pigeon is the ancestral pro-
> totype of the domestic varieties of this bird. This hypothesis, greatly elaborated
> by Darwin as part of his marshaling of evidence bearing upon evolution, occurs
> in both the *Origin* and in his later treatise upon domestication. (DC 13–14)

Eiseley discovers the buried hints that even Darwin scholars failed to emphasize, which reveal the direct and indirect influence of White on Darwin.

Besides acknowledging what Darwin owes to White, Eiseley expresses his own debt. He admits: "My later reading would have to be strongly divided between both literature and science as well as the works of the great literary naturalists, such as Gilbert White's *Selborne*, Thoreau's journals, and the several works of W. H. Hudson" (LN 144). An inherent similarity between White and Eiseley is that both talk about the living things around them and both try to make people think about the presence of nature even in daily life. Like White, Eiseley tells of his encounters with living beings and shows his feelings about them. There are, of course, differences between the two attentive naturalists: when Eiseley writes *The Invisible Pyramid*, he moves on to abstract ideas, philosophy and metaphysics, while White's *Selborne* is closer to scientific observation. In this sense, Thoreau is the more likely literary model for Eiseley.

Darwin and White show similar artistic qualities, particularly in revealing wonder and passion toward the living world in their writing about natural history. Eiseley speaks of Darwin as "a master artist . . . [who] entered sympathetically into life." And offering evidence, like a dramatist Eiseley describes this imaginary scene to his readers:

> As a young man somewhere in the high-starred Andean night, or perhaps drinking alone at an island spring where wild birds who had never learned to fear man came down upon his shoulder, Charles Darwin saw a vision. . . . None of his forerunners has left us such a message. . . . None, it may be added, spoke with the pity which infuses these lines: "*If we choose to let conjecture run wild, then animals, our fellow brethren in pain, disease, suffering and famine—our slaves in the most laborious works, our companions in our amusements—they may partake of our origin in one common ancestor—we may be all melted together.*" (DC 351–52)[12]

By staging Darwin's insight in the romantic setting of an Andean mountain or an island spring, Eiseley prepares the readers for a revelation. Indeed, Darwin offers a very impressive perception about the relationship between humans and nonhumans. Though this passage gives credit to Darwin's genius, White prepared for this insight in a sense. As Donald Worster points out: "Beyond the human order, that is, White glimpsed the larger community of man and nature: 'All were parts of one organic whole, which was the countryside, his own but a section of the universal.'"[13] Both White and Darwin saw the world "all in one," seizing the connectedness of living beings. So does their intellectual inheritor—Eiseley. Among many things to learn from Darwin and his century, there is one important lesson that Kenneth Heuer points out in his editorial commentary in *The Lost Notebooks of Loren Eiseley*: "The matter of evolution contributed vastly to Loren's sense of unity in existence, to his capacity to love life in all its shapes and forms" (LN 80). Thus the theory of evolution enriched Eiseley's capacity to relate to the natural world.

Also Eiseley emphasizes how the four naturalists' passion for natural history and nature inspired their thoughts; in doing this, he successfully speaks for himself—his love for the living world makes him a perceptive naturalist. The naturalist's artistic side helps him to carry out his scientific mission. Like his intellectual forebears, Eiseley "had a sympathetic understanding of nature, of birds and insects" (LN 4). What's more, he loved art and took care to make sure that his books were aesthetic objects: he "had a great appreciation of art, and his later books were illustrated by artists with whom he worked closely" (LN 9). Through words and images, Eiseley opens to his readers the natural world that coexists with the human world.

A Continuum from Past to Present

Eiseley proclaims Bacon as one of the founders of modern science, and places him in a continuum that reaches to Darwin and beyond (BMD 12). Eiseley remarked that Bacon's encouraging the continuity of learning and the logic of induction contributed to one of the most important discoveries—the evolutionary theory. "In the end Darwin himself was to write, 'I worked upon the true principles of Baconian induction'" (BMD 47). Also, Eiseley mentions what Bacon suggested about the northern domination of peoples from the south: "Darwin made use of precisely this same idea, extended on a broader evolutionary scale, to account for the frequent dominance of northern faunas over southern ones" (DC 10). But of course the successors take their perceptions beyond the limits of their predecessors. Eiseley admits that for sure, he intends not "to derive Darwin's biology from Bacon, but to give at least a glimpse of the antiquity of some of the ideas which needed only to be developed and elaborated in order to take a legitimate place in an evolutionary system of thought" (DC 11). Eiseley discovers these correspondences in the same way as he unearths the buried fossil treasures in his work as anthropologist. He wants only one thing as a reward: to give more credit to Bacon's creative power in participating in the theory of evolution and thereby to demonstrate the continuity of scientific thought. Starting from this point, he expresses his opinion about the way to wisdom: great ideas come into being when they are nurtured by multiple intellectual resources, from the past and the present.

Eiseley explores scientific knowledge and philosophical thoughts in the works of his four scientific forefathers, especially emphasizing the humanistic side of these former naturalists. In evaluating them in this more generous framework, Eiseley shows the values and qualities he himself also owns. Today, we see the importance of Eiseley's contribution to both science and literature as a scientist who wrote poetic essays on science and nature for the general public; he is a philosopher and historian of science more than an experimental specialist. Like his eminent predecessors, Eiseley tries to give his readers a wider view of what science is and what it is for. The naturalist's artistic side helps him to carry out his scientific mission. Hence a consideration of Eiseley's literary inspirations is in order.

1.2 LITERARY INSPIRATIONS—THOREAU AND OTHERS' WORLDS

Thoreau and "Existent and Potential Nature"

Thoreau combines personal observation with philosophical thoughts just as Eiseley does. Thoreau often begins with quotes, and then engages with the ideas of former geniuses. Eiseley's editor Kenneth Heuer recalls that after Eiseley's early works were accepted by *Harper's*, "over the years the author's voice grew increasingly assertive, his vision increasingly clear. He became a master nature writer on the order of Henry David Thoreau, for whom nature encompassed human nature" (LN 79). Unlike some writers who hide their influences in order to stress their own originality, Eiseley acknowledges his models, using their ideas as a springboard for his own reflections.

In his consideration of transcendentalist ideas in *The Star Thrower*, Eiseley notes that "in the first volume of his journals . . . the young Thoreau ventures 'On one side of man is the actual and on the other the ideal.'"[14] Eiseley then goes on to observe that "these peculiar worlds are simultaneously existent. Life is bifurcated between the observational world and another more ideal but realizable set of 'instructions' implanted in our minds, again a kind of Platonic blueprint. We must be taught through the proper understanding of the powers within us. The transcendentalist possessed the strong optimism of the early Republic, the belief in an earthly Eden to be created" (ST 228–29). One senses Eiseley's attraction to this idealistic mode of thinking in the positive vocabulary he uses to describe it; it is a means to "escape the ugly determinism of the real" (ST 228). The advent of "the Darwinian world of change" brought a dimmer view of human possibilities: "the Platonic abstract blueprint of successive types has been dismissed as a hopeful fiction" (ST 229). Though "the Darwinian circle" that focuses on the reality in nature dismisses the transcendental thinkers' view of ideal nature, Darwin's "own version of the ideal" that "all things will progress toward perfection" seems also inadequate to fully explain nature. Moreover, it offers little to inspire humans to make their world better, since it "offers no immediate hope that man can embrace" (ST 229).

Disliking the pessimism of neo-Darwinian thought, Eiseley critiques their view of man's animality as limited. He prefers to imagine a much more dynamic model of the individual and the species: "man is in process, as is the whole of life. He may survive or he may not, but so long as he survives he will be part of the changing, onrushing future. He, too, will be subject to alteration. In fact, he may now be approaching the point of consciously inducing his own modification" (ST 230). The idea that humans as well as the biosphere are in the process of becoming, which accords with the thought of the twentieth-century philosopher Alfred North Whitehead, is scattered throughout Eiseley's writings. Eiseley finds in the transcendentalists the source of this more celebratory attitude to nature: "Thoreau, like Emerson, is an anticipator, a forerunner of the process philosophers who have so largely dominated the twentieth century" (ST 224).

Eiseley emphasizes the accurate reflection of nature and man that Thoreau obtained from his minute observations of the world around him. Thoreau could see the mystery in nature and the potential forces within it. Eiseley argues, "The world is perhaps vaster than [Thoreau] imagined, but, even from the first, nature was seen as lawless on occasion and capable of cherishing unimaginable potentials. That was where he chose to stand, at the very edge of the future, 'to anticipate,' as he says in *Walden*, 'nature herself.' . . . He viewed us all as mere potential; shadowy, formless perhaps, but as though about to be formed" (ST 231). Eiseley praises the role of Thoreau in foreseeing the oncoming future: "Thoreau, as is evidenced by his final journals, had labored to lay the foundations of a then unnamed science—ecology. In many ways he had outlived his century. He was always concerned with the actual, but it was the unrolling reality of the process philosopher, 'the universe,' as he says, 'that will not wait to be explained'" (ST 234). Though in his middle years Thoreau experienced the time when "the scientist in him was taking the place of the artist" in order to search the reality in nature, he continued to believe that there are unexplainable things in nature (ST 230). Throughout this essay in praise of Thoreau, Eiseley expresses his regret that the writer's early death prevented him from pursuing his inquiry further.

Eiseley suggests Thoreau's unique worldview comes from the fact that he "identifies" with life in nature: "Thoreau preferred to the end his own white winter spaces. He lingers, curvetting gracefully, like the fox he saw on the river or the falcon in the morning air. He identifies, he enters them, he widens the circumference of life to its utmost bounds. 'One world at a time,' he jokes playfully on his deathbed, but it is not, in actuality, the world that any of us know or could reasonably endure. It is simply Thoreau's world, 'a prairie for outlaws.' Each one of us must seek his own way there" (ST 234). The twentieth-century nature writer concludes that Thoreau creates his own world; this world is a unique dimension of the universe that Thoreau draws out of his mental world. To "widen [. . .] the circumference of life to its utmost bounds" Thoreau engages with the real natural world, reflects upon it and, in writing about it, produces out of the contact between himself and his environment a new world for readers to enter. What's more, Eiseley emphasizes that each man "must seek his own way there," which indicates that readers may earn their own worlds in engaging both Thoreau's texts and their environment with their minds and hearts.

"The Mind as Nature": Landscapes of Laymen and Geniuses

As the title of his essay "Mind as Nature" indicates, Eiseley expresses his idea that the mind is like nature itself. He emphasizes the mystery and multifariousness in nature, and the similar aspects in one's mind: "Both space and mind conceal latent powers beyond which we cannot penetrate. We know only that the human mind, like the universe itself, contains the seeds of many worlds" (LN 143). In this essay, Eiseley elaborates this idea by discussing "certain literary figures with whose works [he] happen[s] to be reasonably familiar" to reveal "the odd landscapes and interiors that have nurtured" the "nature of genius" (NC 203). It is a good opportunity to see how Eiseley's literary inspirations influence him.

As discussed earlier, Eiseley admires Thoreau's "own white winter spaces" (ST 234), and he explores this world further together with those of other eminent literary men. Eiseley uses the metaphor of "map" and "landscape" to illustrate the journey (physical and mental) that the literary writers make. He is drawn to their "great creative landscapes in the literary field": Thoreau's "inner forest" that " influenced the lives of thousands of people all over the world and, it would appear, through succeeding generations"; Nathaniel Hawthorne's "interior geography through which even the modern callous readers venture with awe"; Hudson's map of "the vast Patagonian landscape"; Antoine St. Exupéry's "flyer's vision of the little South American towns," Herman Melville's Pacific, or Arthur Machen's "vision of London" (NC 207–8). Like great scientists, these literary men present "the new geography" (NC 208) which refers not only to its literal meaning of real places (mountains, forests, cities, continents, or seas), but also to the inner world that they draw for readers.

It is clear that Eiseley feels attracted to past literary geniuses because of their creativity. He says, "As an evolutionist I am familiar with that vast sprawling emergent, the universe, and its even more fantastic shadow, life.

Stranger still, however, is the record of the artist who creates the symbols by which we live" (NC 202). A scientist/evolutionist like Eiseley possesses scientific knowledge about the universe or the evolution of life, yet he is largely attracted to the strangeness the artist evokes through contact with the natural world. He declares in another essay that "there is a natural history of souls, nay, even of man himself, which can be learned only from the symbolism inherent in the world about him" (NC 148). Eiseley reveals that like plants and animals, man himself and his soul also have a natural history, and to study it one has to look for the symbolism drawn from "the world about him" to make the mental world that reflects the natural world.

Eiseley is not unaware that common men also possess their inner landscapes. These places are alternatives to the dull world of work. He suggests that "many of us who walk to and fro upon our usual tasks are prisoners drawing mental maps of escape" (NC 204). When escape from the material universe cannot be achieved, one can turn inward. However, Eiseley shows that certain individuals possess landscapes that others cannot enter because they keep silent. Unlike those men who are voiceless, "some of the men with maps in their heads do not remain mute. Instead, they develop the power to draw the outside world within and lose us there. Or, as scientists, after some deep inner colloquy, they venture even to remake reality" (NC 206–7). Eiseley admires the literary men's capacity to express their inner worlds, which not only allows others to immerse themselves in their thoughts but can also change the real world. Eiseley observes that such literary men often conduct "intense self-examination" and it is "in this supremely heightened consciousness of genius the mind insists on expression. The spirit literally cannot remain within itself" (NC 216–17). Here again, Eiseley insists on the spiritual dimension of human beings' response to the world: the material sciences are not enough; by fertilizing reality with their unique vision, writers expand the universe for other humans.

Eiseley is impressed by the artist's self-examination and points out that it is frequently the artist who serves as a guide: "the unfortunate soul who forced us into self-examination." "The unfortunate soul" refers to the artists and the geniuses who are "unfortunate" because of their restless, lonely state of meditating. They risk persecution by "the custom-bound, uneducated, intolerant man [who] projects his fear and hatred upon the seer" (NC 209). The quality that the artist strives to transmit to man and even the civilization of his time is the self-awareness of "our own insignificance and vanity" (NC 209) in the vast universe, which certainly displeases certain men who hold the thought that "'man is the center of interest and measure of importance'" (NC 208). So in expanding the physical world by creating mental worlds, the geniuses Eiseley reveres risk their own comfort. Often, like Thoreau, they are misunderstood in their own time and only appreciated in the years after their deaths.

Eiseley not only reveals the past nature writers' genuine contemplation of the universe and man's place in it; he also seeks to transfer their wisdom to the future generations. We can see that Eiseley emphasizes the significance of man's self-examination: "If all knowledge is of the outside, if none is turned inward, if self-awareness fades into the blind acquiescence of the mass man, then the personal responsibility by which democracy lives will fade also" (FT 146). In Eiseley's words, only by cultivating his inner life can man realize both his individual and social responsibilities.

Genius and Teacher

Eiseley finds images of his own life in those many artistic literary men: "their loneliness has been my loneliness; their poverty I have endured; their wasted days have been my own. Even their desolate islands, their deserts, and their forests have been mine to tread. Unlike them I cannot speak with tongues, unlike them I cannot even adequately describe my wanderings. Yet for a brief interval as a teacher and lecturer I have been allowed to act as their interpreter" (NC 220). Eiseley regards himself humbly as a layman who "cannot speak with tongues," who serves as a foil to the greatness of these literary men; on the other hand, he may be suggesting that his place in the scientific community does not provide him the freedom to express his inner thoughts. Eiseley bemoans the fact that the practice of science in the university has not really caught up with the implications of new findings in science and biology:

> Our faith in science has become so great that, though the open-ended and novelty-producing aspect of nature is scientifically recognized in the physics and biology of our time, there is often a reluctance to give voice to it in other than professional jargon. It has been my own experience among students, laymen, and scholars that to express even wonder about the universe—in other words, to benefit from some humble consideration of what we do not know, as well as marching to the constant drumbeat of what we call the age of technology—is regarded askance in some quarters. I have had the vague word "mystic," applied to me because I have not been able to shut out wonder occasionally, when I have looked at the world. (NC 214)

Nature is much more "open-ended and novelty-producing" than the technocrats admit. Despite being referred to disparagingly as a "mystic," Eiseley emphasizes the importance of awareness of self as well as of things beyond our knowing. He suggests that the scientific colleague who forces him to explain himself "was unaware, in his tough laboratory attitude, that there was another world of pure reverie that is of at least equal importance to the human soul" (NC 214). Eiseley's other world offers a place where the writer explores his own experiences and emotions, where "I am trying to write honestly from my own experience. I am trying to say that buttercups, a mastodon tooth, a giant snail, and a rolling Elizabethan line are a part of my own ruins over which the weeds grow tall" (NC 223). This other world is born out of explorations in books as well as nature.

In Eiseley's eyes, because they are charged with the task to "mold the future in the minds of the young," teachers need to go beyond the narrow restrictions imposed by their disciplines. They need to "transmit . . . the aspirations of great thinkers" (NC 211). He takes as his inspiration Dewey's thoughts about the importance of the great books that assist teachers in their mission: "of transmitting from these enrichers of life their wisdom to the unformed turbulent future, of transforming reflection into action consonant with their thought, then some of their luminosity must encompass our minds; their passion must, in some degree, break through our opaque thoughts and descend to us" (NC 219). Hopefully, the teacher will get inspiration from the "luminosity" and "passion" of the geniuses. Since "the more imaginative and literate" (NC 208) may accept the geniuses who invent a new geography, as Eiseley argues, it is then the intention that the messenger of the genius—the teacher—should avoid being "rigid, dogmatic, arrogant" (NC 219). Eiseley extends this expectation to the whole society, "if society sinks into the absolute rut of custom, if it refuses to accept beneficial mutations in the cultural realm or to tolerate, if not promote, the life of genius, then its unwieldy slumbers may be its last" (NC 213). In his suggestion, a society's continuation depends on its remaining humanistic, kind, and tolerant to the geniuses or the potential ones.

Concerning the young generations, Eiseley argues that while transferring the wisdom of the geniuses, a teacher should foster the potential of his students, looking out for "those darker, more uncertain, later-maturing, sometimes painfully abstracted youths who may represent the Darwins, Thoreaus, and Hawthornes of the next generation." Eiseley is aware from personal experience that people "mature in many ways and fashions" (NC 211). Eiseley emphasizes the potential power in the young who may not fit traditional standards or models of success (NC 211). He asks: "Has not Saint Paul said that there are many kinds of voices in the world and none is without signification?" (NC 220). Also, he focuses on the potentialities and multifariousness of the mind. He shows his confidence in individuals, inspired by Melville's words: "'I somehow cling to the wondrous fancy, that in all men hiddenly reside certain wondrous, occult properties . . . which by some happy but very rare accident . . . may chance to be called forth here on earth'"; and like Melville, Eiseley says passionately "I have seen them happen. I believe in them. . . . I believe that the good teacher should never grow indifferent to their possibility" (NC 212). Eiseley has witnessed some marvelous achievements, from either the example of his own insightful thoughts or those of his students. Both Melville and Eiseley choose to believe in the miracles that individuals are capable of: "While I do not believe that the time will ever come when each man can release his own Shakespeare, I do not doubt that the freedom to create is somehow linked with facility of access to those obscure regions below the conscious mind" (NC 218). It is not Eiseley's expectation that each man will become a genius like Shakespeare; however, he wants to make sure they are given the freedom to create and to express their consciousness.

To sum up, Eiseley champions the work of geniuses like Shelley, Shakespeare, Newton, Darwin, Thoreau, or Hawthorne. The thing they share is their ability to inhabit and transmit an original world of the mind: "One thing alone they have had in common: thought, music, art, transmissible but unique" (NC 219). "Unique" refers to the novelty and creativity in their mental or cultural achievements; "transmissible" refers to their talents to express their minds. Another cultural role is important though; teachers need to transmit the wisdom and knowledge of the geniuses to younger generations. For Eiseley, "the teacher is genuinely the creator of humanity, the molder of its most precious possession, the mind. . . . [T]here can be no greater disaster than fail at the task" (LN 118). For him, the teacher is the mind molder, the talent discoverer, and the "sculptor of the intangible future" (NC 200). Eiseley believes that education should be concerned with fostering individuals' self-awareness, so that they are prepared to accept individual responsibilities for shared problems. His hope for humanity resides in the force of individual creativity and morality.

Each individual has his own way to reflect the image of the world he lives within. Though the way each individual sees is personal, our vision is also shaped by the influences that we encounter:

> We see, as artists, as scientists, each in his own way, through the inexorable lens we cannot alter. In a nature which Thoreau recognized as unfixed and lawless anything might happen. The artist's endeavor is to make it happen—the unlawful, the oncoming world, whether endurable or mad, but shaped, shaped always by the harsh angles of truth, the truth as glimpsed through the terrible crystal of genius. This is the one sure rule of that other civilization which we have come to know is greater than our own. Thoreau called it, from the first, "unfinished business," when he turned and walked away from his hut at Walden Pond. (ST 250)

If Thoreau's vision is right and the whole biosphere is changeable, the significance of the artist, the genius, or the great writer lies in changes effected in the existent world by the achievement of the potential world of the mind. Though discouraged by the narrowness of scientific education, Eiseley takes heart by thinking of the contributions made by humanity's great thinkers and writers. He pays tribute to the minds that have influenced his own work, and, at the same time, he follows in their footsteps by transmitting his own imaginings in his poetry and prose.

Eiseley's purpose in writing about these scientific predecessors and literary inspirations can be expressed in what he declares when writing on Darwin: "It is my hope . . . to recapture from the fossil world of documents some glimpses of the living shape of thought as it flows, mutates, and transforms itself from age to age" (DC 4). Words like "transform," "mutate," and "flow," reveal how he understands the continuum of geniuses' intellectual power that helps shape individuals' perceptions and the evolution of the cultural world. The metaphor Eiseley uses suggests how knowledge changes and transmutes in the same ways as living organisms. Like an anthropologist examining a fossil specimen in order to imagine the way extinct creatures lived, he tries to "recapture" the moment in which the great scientific and humanistic discoverers lived. He returns to his predecessors' intellectual world, bringing their valuable thoughts to life again. He traces the history of modern science and the true forces behind its development—the important intellectual powers—showing where they came from and how they have changed.

The importance of these exceptional thinkers lies not only in what they contributed to their own age, but also in the ways that they opened up new vistas into the future. Eiseley marvels at the immense potential for future discovery that the human mind holds: "What we make of Bacon's second world in every human generation lies partly in the unfathomable realm of human nature itself" (BMD 23). Eiseley benefits from communicating with his forebears and encountering the worldviews of literary geniuses. Sensing the split between science and the humanities, he fashions his own version of the scientific world—"a compassionate and humane" one.[15] He acknowledges Thoreau's "'unfinished business'" (ST 250) and knows that Bacon's philosophy is left "deliberately unfinished—not, as he so ably put it, as a belief to be held but rather a work to be done" (BMD 15–16). It is Eiseley's own responsibility and that of those who would follow him to continue the work begun by Bacon, Darwin, Wallace, White, Thoreau, and other geniuses that remains ever "unfinished and open to improvement" (BMD 26).

NOTES

1. Eiseley, "The Illusion of the Two Cultures," 388.

2. This phrase is used by Eiseley to describe Alexander Von Humboldt, who is said to be "a man of wide-ranging intellect" (DC 153).

3. Chesterton's words can be found in XXXVIII, "The Ballade of a Strange Town" of *The G. K. Chesterton Collection [50 Books]*.

4. White, *Selborne*, xiii–xiv.

5. White, *Selborne*, xiv.

6. White, *Selborne*, xiv.

7. Pitts, *Understandings*, 144.

8. White, *Selborne*, xiii.

9. Angyal, *Loren Eiseley*, 54.

10. White, *Selborne*, xiii.

11. Shklovsky, "Art as Technique," 12.

12. Worster also discusses this passage; however, Worster quotes the word *netted* rather than *melted* (Worster 180). And Eiseley in his essay "Science and the Sense of the Holy" cites this paragraph again, however, with "netted" instead of "melted" (ST 187).

13. Worster, *Nature's Economy*, 20.

14. Thoreau, *Journal, Volume 1*, 401.

15. Angyal, *Loren Eiseley*, 63.

Chapter 2

Eiseley's Critique of Science

Science has developed very fast since Eiseley's time. In his essays, Eiseley repeatedly announced that he didn't at all intend to belittle the role of science in the world. Rather, what he criticizes is that in applying scientific findings to the living world, men have denatured our planet and created a world that has become hostile to living things. In other words, it is not science but rather the men who use science wrongly that Eiseley condemns. He hopes that science can coexist in harmony with the humanities, so that modern men will approach the natural world with scientific knowledge as well as artistic and humanistic insights. His wish is that humanity should use its unique gifts—in particular, a highly developed brain—to achieve this reconciliation.

Ironically, man's unique attributes have possibly led him onto the wrong road. At the very first when man's brain had developed enough for him to realize what he could do with a bone as a weapon in his hand, he had also developed his ability to destroy other living things. Eiseley observes, "man, as a two-handed manipulator of the world about him, has projected himself outward upon his surroundings in a way impossible to other creatures. . . . He has always sought mastery over the materials of his environment" (FT 158). The word *outward* may indicate one aspect of modern science's achievements that was particularly pertinent in Eiseley's time—space exploration—and "mastery over the materials" suggests the authority, power, and control that man seeks to gain over his environment. The desire to dominate and the potential to destroy the living world has only broadened in scope, as contemporary society testifies. Eiseley finds it necessary for human beings to rethink their assumptions in order to stop seeing the natural world only from their point of view. Humans think they play the main role on the stage of life and can dominate their surroundings with science, yet these assumptions finally limit what it means to be human. Fortunately, we have the capacity to choose, so we can decide to open our minds to a bigger view of the natural world and to merge the ability to explore and improve the outward world with a more responsible inner world. Particularly, Eiseley proposes that we should approach nature and life with respect and sympathy.

Nowadays science is important and popular, it, as we see from the abundant numbers of students and professors in various scientific fields. The advertising media insist that science offers humanity a better life. In this chapter, I will discuss some of the realities of modern science that the scientist-naturalist wants to explain, what kind of science Eiseley dislikes, and what, in the end, he aims to achieve by criticizing it. His warnings are for his century, but can also apply to the people of the twenty-first century and to future generations. Specifically, in this chapter I deal with two major problems that Eiseley believes modern science has caused. First, he suggests that the scientific method "might be said merely to have widened the area of man's homelessness" (UU 48). Second, he fears that the power harnessed by scientific inventions in modern technology has created an unnatural relationship between human beings and the natural world. Modern man dwells within the material world he has established, as well as his cultural world; the other home, though long forgotten, is nature, the lost environment he shared with other creatures. Now, the danger is that man has become homeless, a confused wanderer; therefore Eiseley investigates how this situation came into being and how humans can be saved from the predicted disaster.

2.1. SCIENTIFIC METHOD—DETACHMENT AND OVERSPECIALIZATION

Objectivity and Detachment

In his book *The Ape and the Sushi Master*, one of the world's leading primate behavior specialists, Frans de Waal, tries to refute the idea that "scientists are supposed to study animals in a totally objective fashion, similar to the way we inspect a rock or measure the circumference of a tree trunk."[1] Emotionless scientists did exist back in the 1950s or 1960s when Eiseley was writing, and objectivity was an important part of the traditional scientific method, under which numerous scientists, including Eiseley, had been trained. In Eiseley's time, under the banner of looking for truths, some scientific practitioners used the guise of objectivity to draw a boundary between themselves and the natural world. They established an asymmetrical relationship between the observers and the objects of observation, even though the other party they faced might be living creatures.

Suspicious of and resistant to the objectivity and detachment that the scientific method requires of the professional, this scientist-naturalist shows sympathy to all forms of life and gets emotionally involved with the life that he encounters. Eiseley realizes that "the austerities of the scientific profession leave most of us silent upon our inner lives," (NA 11) and he is intolerant of this split between inner life and outer exploration. Therefore, he writes essays, and, though timidly, publishes poems, and tells personal stories in both his autobiographical and scientific writings. In this varied body of work, he shares the inner thoughts of a kind man with the combined qualities of a scientist and poet. He offers subjective narrations infused with personal wisdom, rather than only objective scientific reports.

Indeed, Eiseley anticipates modern critiques of objectivity. Donna Haraway, a contemporary theorist of the relations between science and animals, insists that the researcher's political and personal experience should be factored into scientific studies. In her book *Simians, Cyborgs, and Women*, she writes: "Feminist objectivity is about limited location and situated knowledge, not about transcendence and splitting of subject and object. In this way we might become answerable for what we learn how to see."[2] Like Eiseley, she insists on scientists' ethical commitment toward the things they study and the consequences of their findings. Eiseley's writings have certainly been important in furthering the mission of making individuals realize their responsibility and become perceptive scientists who respond actively to the living world.

Eiseley dislikes the pretense of objectivity and detachment in the scientific method because he cannot remain neutral about the things he studies. In *The Night Country*, he contrasts two possible attitudes to living things: detachment or involvement. He narrates a story in the first person, telling about when "I was after the buried treasures that lay beneath [an owl's] nest in the cave floor," "an owl's egg stood in the path of science.... This was a time for decision" (NC 187). "Here in this high, sterile silence ... myself and that egg were the only living things. That seemed to me mean something. At last and quietly I backed out of the cave" and "when I think that the egg became an owl. I had had charge of it in the universe's sight for a single hour, and I had done well by life" (NC 188). Eiseley gets personally involved when facing the owl egg and shows sympathy and respect for the incipient life. He chooses the potential life enclosed in the egg because he values the living world more than the illusory scientific fame brought about by discovering archeological treasures. At the same time, he gives examples of the opposite attitude to this: "I know a primatologist who will lift a rifle and shoot a baby monkey out of its mother's arms for the sake of science" (NC 187)—a brutal illustration of detachment.

Another anecdote Eiseley tells in the first person illustrates his anxiety about practicing the method of objectivity and detachment:

> I was assisting one of my medical superiors in a cadaver dissection.... He took the notion that a living demonstration of the venous flow through certain of the

abdominal veins would be desirable. "Come with me to the animal house," he said. "We'll get a dog for the purpose." . . . Now dogs kept penned together, I rapidly began to see, were like men in a concentration camp, who one after the other see that something unspeakable is going to happen to them. As we entered this place of doleful barks and howlings, a brisk-footed, intelligent-looking mongrel of big terrier affinities began to trot rapidly about. I stood white-gowned in the background trying to be professional, while my stomach twisted. My medical friend . . . cornered the dog. . . . [And] my associate seized him. (ASH 148–149)

In this narration, Eiseley makes the daring comparison between dogs kept for experimental purposes and men in the notorious killing camp. Dogs, like those men, know what is going on. In giving a detailed description of the dog, Eiseley indicates that he regards the dog as an individual; he speaks of it as intelligent. Counting on readers' acknowledgment of the dog's intelligence and sentience, Eiseley imagines the dog making appeals and asking the scientists questions: "'I do not know why I am here. Save me. I have seen other dogs fall and be carried away. Why do you do this? Why?'" (ASH 149). Here Eiseley imagines the voice of the dog and shares the emotion that he attributes to him. He sighs over the fact that "the indifferent class . . . had gained little from that experiment," and "the experiment . . . in my judgment was needless" (ASH 150). In his view, a life was sacrificed needlessly. The cold experimentalists failed to respect the integrity of the living beings perceived by Eiseley. He speaks of his superior as "a kind and able teacher, but a researcher hardened to the bitter necessities of his profession" (ASH 148). Eiseley knows that, once obsessed by the imperatives of objectivity and detachment, an experimentalist who seems a good person in interactions with humans can change to another person who kills animals without hesitation. Is dissecting an innocent living animal necessary just to illustrate a notion?

Science workers may feel that to be professional, one must also be emotionless and detached from the relationship with other lives; but Eiseley disagrees and criticizes the role of objectivity and detachment in producing a cold world in which even the respect for other humans may disappear: "in the modern world the degradation of animals in experiments of little, or vile, meaning, were easily turned to the experimental human torture practiced at Dachau and Buchenwald by men dignified with medical degrees" (ST 193). He criticizes the scientific experimentation that has brought humanity to this cruel state: "it ceases to be objective but rather suggests a deep grain of sadism that is not science" (ST 190). It is no longer an issue about being objective or subjective, it is about being humane or inhumane. Yet Eiseley refuses to turn stray dogs and cats over to the institutionalized carers: "I have never called a humane society because I, too, am an ex-wanderer who would have begged for one more hour of light, however dismal" (ASH 150). He identifies with the homeless animals who simply want to continue existing. He reveals another side of himself and of the true nature of a man—he is simply a creature who clings to life.

A New Attitude toward Laboratory Animals

Throughout his writing, Eiseley tries to blur the boundaries between animals and humans and encourages humans to feel and see like the animals. He takes to its ultimate implications Darwin's insight that humans and animals "may be all netted together" (ST 187). He interprets this comment to mean that: "we are in a mystic sense one single diffuse animal, subject to joy and suffering beyond what we endure as individuals" (ST 187). Eiseley expresses the new outlook upon animals that Singer, Foer, and Haraway (among others) advocate, that animals share with humans the capacity to suffer, and as such they should be protected and respected. Also he proposes that researchers can choose to have a mental attitude of compassionate wonder to reveal the truths of the living world rather than addressing it in mechanical way simply by dissecting it with knives.

Haraway in her book *When Species Meet* says, "My study inhabits one of the major sites where domestic animals and their people meet: the experimental laboratory."[3] Judging laboratories that use animals is a hard issue for scientists and humanists. The excuse that Eiseley knows the experimentalists give for using animals for scientific purposes, unfortunately, most times make them suffer, and the same excuse is made nowadays: "for the social goods of: knowledge-seeking in itself, or applications for human purposes."[4] Although Haraway's critique is more extended and precise, there are some points where Eiseley anticipates contemporary thinking on this issue.

Offering the incident of assisting the cold experimentalist to capture a dog and send him to die for little meaning, Eiseley condemns such inappropriate behavior in cruel experiments with domestic animals: "The cost, it would appear, lies not alone in animal suffering but in the dehumanization of those willing to engage in such blind, random cruelty" (ST 190). For him, the damage done by such experiments is twofold. Not only do animals suffer, but the experimenters lose their humanity. If he has been misunderstood as odd to extend ethics and rights to animals, he should now gain admiration for his speculations. He anticipates works like Peter Singer's philosophical tract, *Animal Liberation* (1975), or Jonathan Safran Foer's 2009 book, *Eating Animals*, defenses of animals that no longer seem so surprising.

Facing the event of taking dogs suffering from hemophilia as patient models in the University laboratory[5] and other cases, Haraway suggests that "breaking the sacrificial logic that parses who is killable and who isn't might just lead to a lot more change than the practices of analogy, rights extension, denunciation, and prohibition."[6] Moreover, she stresses the importance of humans sharing animals' pain nonmimetically, saying, "Sharing pain promises disclosure, promises becoming."[7] The manner of sharing suffering is to respect the other, "looking back, holding in regard, understanding that meeting the look of the other is a condition of having face oneself."[8] These comments correspond exactly to Eiseley's saying, "One does not meet oneself until one catches the reflection from an eye other than human" (UU 24). In his pioneering attack on the cruelty of animal experimentation, Eiseley hopes other men can be awakened by his perception and learn to respect animals, mindful of both their animal past and the present bonds among species.

Regarding other living things in the eyes would be a means of matching the inner world of man, the better nature of humans, to the nature of other species. It would be a way to discover and affirm one's human difference in the discovery of the other. That's the reason Eiseley speaks of the man who has lost this human attraction to other living things as dead: "in science, as in religion, when one has destroyed human wonder and compassion, one has killed man, even if the man in question continues to go about his laboratory tasks" (ST 198). The nature of humans, fostered by the humanities, contains the sense of wonder and sympathy, which the steely experimentalist needs to regain.

Just as Eiseley pities animals' helplessness before the men who probe them with their instruments in order to obtain measurable benefits for humanity, Haraway concentrates on "instrumental, unequal, scientific relations among human and nonhuman vertebrates."[9] She supports her scholar friend's meditations on Whitehead's philosophy "that decisions must take place somehow in the presence of those who will bear their consequences."[10] Haraway argues that in the "wholly humanly-constructed" laboratory characterized by "human power over the animal," the important issue is our choice—what we choose to do.[11] Eiseley, who has been influenced by both scientific and literary writings, sees that man can be many things, can imagine many voices; therefore he suggests that one can choose to become a speculative man who can guarantee a better future for humanity through science by taking a wider view of scientific action. Haraway agrees that "A Whiteheadian proposition" is "an opening to become with those with whom we are not yet. Put that into the dilemma ensuing from killing experimental organisms or meat animals, and the mandatory 'ethical' or 'political' call is to reimagine, to speculate again, to remain open, because we are (reasonably, if we built good abstractions; badly, if we were lazy, unskillful, or dishonest) killing someone, not just something."[12] When an experimentalist becomes more perceptive, and sees who lies under his knife as a living being not as an object, needless killings may be avoided, and the scientist's humanity may be saved.

Eiseley regrets that his scientific associates rely on machines and experiments more than speculation in approaching nature: "with the dawn of the scientific method, he has sought to probe nature's secrets by experiment rather than unbounded speculation" (ST 225). For Eiseley, "life's unbounded creativity" (UU 58) is beyond the grasp of machines whose main advantage is their capacity to duplicate. Probing nature's secrets by experiment is wrong, as is the single-minded pursuit of empirical knowledge at the expense of speculation. As a seer or a philosopher of science, Eiseley believes in approaching nature through both scientific practices and speculation, staying open in order to become wise.

While the sensitive naturalist advocates maintaining a loving, childlike mind when approaching animals, the feminist and scholar on science and animals seeks to know them "in nonanthropomorphic, nonmimetic, painstaking detail."[13] She wants to respect their difference and not project human motives onto them. Both Eiseley and Haraway stress the sentience of animals, which is the very starting point from which they express their love for the creatures they cherish. Then the mystery of life, the alterity of natural life, is the next important issue to explore.

Animate and Inanimate, the Mystery of Life

Scientific analysis is supposed to be governed by precise measurement and carefully controlled data. Things are prone to be defined, explained, and predicted. Eiseley admits sorrowfully, "we are men of precision, measurement and logic; we abhor the unexplainable and reject it" (FT 177). Nevertheless, as a scientist and naturalist he inquires about the truths lying inside nature in his own way. He tries to understand life through his own particular form of observation and speculation, and he believes that a humanistic way of looking at other forms of life can grasp truths that the mechanical way fails to apprehend. One of his genuine perceptions of nature is that "life and time bear some curious relationship to each other that is not shared by inanimate things" (FT 169). Eiseley admires the metaphysical poets as well as the philosophers of science, and in his essays he records exceptional, unexplainable things as well as abstract ideas about science. Often in the encounters with living things that he records in his essays, he believes he witnesses a miracle and he keeps the meaning of his responses and acts to himself, feeling that it is not prudent to report them to his scientific associates, just as the transcendentalist Thoreau made observations that could not be reported to the Royal Society (UU 212). Eiseley inherits the wisdom of Thoreau's transcendentalism as an alternative mental attitude for a man approaching nature.

Eiseley also criticizes the reductionism of some people's dismissal of the complexity of life. In one essay he tells how he "encountered an amazing little creature on a windy corner of my local shopping center. . . . With great difficulty I discovered the creature was actually a filamentous seed, seeking a hiding place and scurrying about with the uncanny surety of a conscious animal" (UU 56). Through such descriptions, he shows the strangeness of a vegetal life making it seem creaturely, at least at first glance. This inspires him to think about the secret of life—how nature creates life. He introduces this seed that moves like a spider as a new possibility for existence: "one of the jumbled alphabets of life" (UU 57). This phrase offers a compelling metaphor for the genetic code that decides the forms of individuals' lives— including humans'. The attentive scientist says that this encounter teaches him something: "We have learned the first biological lesson: that in each generation life passes through the eye of a needle. It exists for a time molecularly and in no recognizable semblance to its adult condition. It *instructs* its way again into man or reptile. As the ages pass, so do variants of the code" (UU 59). He reminds readers that compared to other species, our species is neither the beginning nor the end of natural life. When it comes to genetic codes, the secret of future lives, humans occupy the same stage as other forms of life, and share the same chances for survival. In the naturalist's eyes, man is no more privileged in terms of the life force than other species, including the dinosaurs, the "synapsid reptiles" that have gone extinct: "We refuse to consider that in the old eye of the hurricane we may be, and doubtless are, in aggregate, a slightly more diffuse and dangerous dragon of the primal morning that still enfolds us" (UU 61). In the river of time, man is simply one of multiple possibilities for existence. In this perspective, men are supposed to regard themselves not as dominators of the natural world and other forms of life but as supporting actors in the drama of evolution, prone to be ignored by the stars.

How life first came into form and in which form is mysterious. The genetic code offers the possibility for life to prolong itself far beyond individual existence and to take diverse forms. Man is not master of his destiny; he is the product of genetic replication and mutation. The code is the teacher, not the man. Eiseley's comment is not metaphysical; instead, it comes from his scientific knowledge of evolution. However, rather than making him proud, this knowledge humbles the naturalist. Eiseley demands humans' respect for all life. Indeed, he insists on its miraculous nature. Pondering the change in our understanding of the world made possible by evolutionary science, he makes a plea for an attitude of wonder in regard to the way life constitutes itself out of the chemical constituents in a pile of dust. He asks:

> How natural was man, we may ask, until he came? What forces dictated that a walking ape should watch the red shift of light beyond the island universes or listen by carefully devised antennae to the pulse of unseen stars? Who,

whimsically, conceived that the plot of the world should begin in a mud puddle and end—where, and with whom? Men argue learnedly over whether life is chemical chance or antichance, but they seem to forget that the life *in* chemicals may be the greatest chance of all, the most mysterious and unexplainable property in matter. (FT 172)

This passage encapsulates a sweep of time from even before *Homo sapiens*' distant ancestral origins to the modern astronomer with his sophisticated tools for exploring the universe. For Eiseley, to explain life only in terms of its chemical or biological components is not enough, because life contains mysteries. Indeed "life *in* chemicals"—that is, the capacity of the inanimate to become animate—is itself a miracle.

He relates an anecdote from which he draws an exceptional perception. The countless components that build up the human body, in Eiseley's eyes, are not "odd objects under the microscope" but "tiny creatures" that sacrifice, contribute, lovingly make function "their galaxy, their creation"—the human body (UU 178). This strange insight occurs to him in the most banal of ways: "I caught the toe of my shoe in an ill-placed drain," and fell down and "blood from a gash on my forehead was cascading over my face." Surprisingly, he is concerned less for himself than for the blood that spills out of him: "'Oh, don't go. I'm sorry, I've done for you.' . . . I was addressing blood cells, phagocytes, platelets, all the crawling, living, independent wonder that had been part of me and now, through my folly and lack of care, were dying like beached fish on the hot pavement" (UU 177–178). In telling this anecdote, Eiseley defends his new idea about human nature against "the nineteenth-century evolutionists, and many philosophers till today, are obsessed by struggle. They try to define natural selection in one sense only"—as a struggle for existence on the part of individuals and their species, including man (UU 185). Giving the example of the small parts ["living, independent wonder"] that compound the body and "unknowingly" (UU 178) sacrifice and work together for the organism that the parts cannot see, Eiseley presents the human body as an example of an anti-struggle theory. He tries to make readers escape from the narrow explanation of life provided by the struggle theory and proposes a more cooperative model in its place.

The other meaning of this incident can be extended to the bond between humans and nonhumans because the materials that form the human body include nonhumans. The reminder that humans are made up of other nonhumans makes us aware that we share of life's elements and we are dependent on others for existence. This recalls what Haraway says, "I love the fact that human genomes can be found in only 10 percent of all the cells that occupy the mundane space I call my body; the other 90 percent of the cell are filled with the genomes of bacteria, fungi, protists, and such, some of which play in a symphony necessary to my being alive at all, and some of which are hitching a ride and doing the rest of me, of us, no harm. . . . I become an adult human being in company with these tiny messmates. To be one is always to *become with* many."[14] The final comment corresponds exactly to what Eiseley does in his writings: he proclaims himself to be "a many-visaged thing" (FT 168) and he speaks in many voices. On this point, again Eiseley anticipates the ideas of contemporary ecology.

Overspecialization and Single-Minded

Moby-Dick is one of the books that Eiseley emphasizes in his writing because it "best expresses the clash between the man who has genuine perception and the one who pursues nature as ruthlessly as a hunted animal" (ST 198). Talking about this classic novel in the American literary tradition, he finds the perfect analogy between the perils of modern science and the tragedy of Ahab: "In Ahab's anxiety to 'strike through the mask,' to confront 'the principal,' whether god or destiny, he is denuding himself of all humanity. He has forgotten his owners, his responsibility to his crew. His single obsession, the hidden obsession that lies at the root of much Faustian overdrive in science, totally possesses him" (ST 198–99). The modern scientist is very anxious to unmask the natural world, to try to conquer even the things he does not fully see or understand. Such men have forgotten their animal environment, and ignore their responsibilities as individuals, to their brotherhood—other animals—and to the place where they come from—Earth. Eiseley believes that in forgetting this, man sacrifices the qualities that make him human. He becomes single-minded, obsessed by science and power, and the material comforts they bring. He is too proud not to try to be the dominator. In Eiseley's interpretation of *Moby-Dick*, the novel symbolizes the "two ways of looking at the universe: the magnification by the poet's mind attempting to see all, while disturbing as little as possible, as opposed to the plunging fury of Ahab with his cry, 'Strike, strike through the mask, whatever it may cost in lives and suffering'" (ST 200). Clearly, as readers can see, Eiseley likens himself to the perceptive man, Ishmael, who exemplifies the poet's mind; while the opposite type of human, the modern scientist, is the like the monomaniacal Captain Ahab, ready to destroy the world in the pursuit of a narrow goal.

In resorting to poetic language and literary references, Eiseley wants to help readers see the bigger picture of the natural world and to reveal the reasons he criticizes science and technology. He castigates the drive for power that makes the scientist ready to sacrifice at any cost in spite of the suffering it might cause other individuals and the damage it might do to the environment. When the single-mindedness of Ahab gets expressed in scientific world, it is not just a ship, but the whole planet that is at risk.

For a long time man has not been content to be just a toolmaker; he wants to pursue all knowledge. However, Eiseley worries that man's moral development has not kept up with his ever-increasing understanding of the universe. He declares: "because we know more about time and history than any men before us, we fallaciously equate ethical advance with scientific progress in a point-to-point relationship," and we assume that having knowledge equates with having wisdom (FT 159–60). However, neither is a proper assumption for Eiseley, who realizes "the dangers of narrowing human nature to a 'single vision.'"[15] Though Eiseley does not intend to belittle the role of science in human development, there is a problem he has to point out—the conflict between rapidly developing knowledge of the physical world and the forgotten humanities. When exploiting the material world becomes the single aim, people are more interested in making quick profit from scientific knowledge. Thus, a danger appears: "we become too much concerned with the formalities of only one aspect of the education by which we learn" (UU 49). Why does only scientific knowledge seem worthy of learning, while diverse natural knowledge is offered by hidden teachers in the natural world, ready to grasp by perceptive students? Eiseley meditates on the Bible story of Job[16] and suggests that when humans cannot understand or perceive God's words, it does not mean "God failed to manifest Himself" (UU 49). Divine expression can be found in the soaring hawk, the rain, and the snow—in other words, the teachers in nature. Even if man fails to see, hear, or understand the messages they can bring, it does not mean that natural knowledge is not worthy of learning. Eiseley, as a nature writer and professor of anthropology says, "Sometimes what we learn depends upon our own powers of insight" (UU 49). Man has choices and plays an active role in his own learning. Contemplation of the natural world can bring "some quite remarkable, but at the same time disquieting, knowledge" (FT 169). Thus, when scientists search for knowledge, the knowledge that can be found beyond the benches of the classroom or the laboratory deserves their attention.

The tendency to value only scientific knowledge was getting worse in Eiseley's era; he observes, "Recently it has been said by a great scientific historian that the day of the literary naturalist is done, that precision of the laboratory is more and more encroaching upon that individual domain" (BMD 94). Along the road of progress, it seems that the moderns have lost the ability to balance the values of science and literature. Thus, Eiseley takes on the responsibility to awaken his readers to this unbalance and show them the significance of learning from the natural world. In Eiseley's essay "The Hidden Teacher" he finds teachers concealed in the living world of nature. The lesson he learns from a spider who does not respond at all to him when he "touched a strand of the web" (UU 50) with his pencil, is that the spider inhabits her own universe, confined by her limited senses. Though she is able precisely to sense the wind, the rain, or her prey, she is indifferent to the vibration of the thread caused by the man-made pencil point. Eiseley concludes that all living creatures, whether spiders or humans, inhabit a world that is "limited or finite" (UU 51). When meditating on the reason for the spider's ignorance of him, he comments, "Spider was circumscribed by spider ideas; its universe was spider universe. All outside was irrational, extraneous, at best, raw material for spider" (UU 50). In that sense, he finds it not that different from the universe of men, who are "too content with our sensory extensions," "reaching forward into time with new machines, computing, analyzing," and making no allowance "for the unexpected" (UU 54). In this analogy between the spider universe and the human world of advanced technology, he critiques those who are obsessed with their machines and who reject the mysteries beyond the man-made world.

Also, when Eiseley occasionally hears the boastful pronouncement that humans can turn nature into their garden if they wish, this "mistaken judgment," this arrogant single-mindedness, may be the reason that he feels the urgency to conduct his particular form of nature writing. This may be why he develops techniques of writing to create strangeness and mystery. He believes that "modern man, who has not contemplated his otherness, the multiplicity of other possible men who dwell or might have dwelt in him, has not realized the full terror and responsibility of existence" (BMD 95). The perceptive naturalist and poet realizes that man is not single and fixed, but that he has the potential to change. In opening man's mind and heart to his multiple possibilities, Eiseley wants to alert us to the dangers of human potential as well as the benefits. He worries that single-minded modern people living in their limited world are only concerned with using knowledge for domestic comforts or for weapons. He would like science to work toward the "second world" that Bacon imagines in *The New Atlantis*. He denounces modern man's lack of vision:

> Our ethics are diluted by superstition, our lives by self-created anxieties. Our visions have yet to equal some of his nobler glimpses of a future beyond our material world of easy transport, refrigeration, and rocketry. The new-found land Bacon sighted was not something to be won in a generation or by machines alone. It would have to be drawn slowly, by infinite and continuing effort, out of minds whose dreams must rise superior to the existing world and shape that world by understanding of its laws into something more consistent with man's better nature. (BMD 14)

This reflection ends with the exhortation for humanity to do better, to reach further ("dreams must rise"). Eiseley knows that current problems of science, its mechanical view of the world and its separation from nature, need to be changed. He wants to inspire his readers to have faith in reality, to respect nature, and to dream of how to make the world better. It is not that we don't have enough scientific knowledge, but we need individual perception and sensitivity to see a fuller picture of the world. In this quest, the mind plays an important role: "man inhabits a realm half in and half out of nature, his mind reaching forever beyond the tool, the uniformity, the law, into some realm which is that of mind alone" (BMD 83). The way out of the trap of the limited spider's view of the universe is to find "this [genius artistic and humanistic] rare and exquisite sensitivity to guide us, [without it] the truth is we are half blind. We will lack pity and tolerance not through intent, but from blindness" (BMD 87). Eiseley continues to repeat in his essays that knowledge does not equal wisdom and that perception needs to be enhanced by imagination.

To conclude, Eiseley does not reject all scientific practices as a whole; rather, he passes judgment on particular methods and practices in the science world. Scientific fields are complex and missions are different, but Eiseley's philosophy can and should still be very valuable to contemporary scientists when so much of the world's future seems to depend on the decisions made by the various voices in the public forum. The modern science world needs to reflect carefully on the reductionism that the mechanical scientific method, with its emphasis on objectivity, detachment, and overspecialization, imposes on the human mind. Otherwise, once men lose respect and sympathy for other living creatures or lose wonder and curiosity for nature and life, they are taking the risk of losing what it is to be human. Seeking the mysteries of life and looking back down his evolutionary road, man should be very cautious about displaying too much arrogance in imagining that the purpose of all creatures is to serve humanity. After all, humans are bonded together with nonhumans in many tangible and intangible ways. To avoid falling into the trap of being single-minded, modern men need to combine artistic and scientific approaches toward the world they interact with; perhaps humanity can be saved thereby. By working to prevent the extinction of other species, humans are also protecting against the extinction of humanity. The naturalist, scientist, and literary man warns modern men that without a fuller awareness of the implications of their actions, they can hurt or destroy others: humans, nonhumans, even all of nature.

2.2. SCIENTIFIC AUTHORITY AND THE DESTRUCTIVENESS OF TECHNOLOGY

Mysteries and Metaphysical Ideas

Science makes the world explainable, but Eiseley thinks that scientific explanations can only go so far. He remarks, "I know that the word 'miraculous' is regarded dubiously in scientific circles because of past quarrels with theologians. The word has been defined, however, as an event transcending the known laws of nature" (FT 171). He proposes that "nature itself is one vast miracle transcending the reality of night and nothingness"; so are human individuals (FT 171). He believes there are mysteries that should be approached with wonder and reverence as well as with the inquiring mind.

Eiseley's essay "Science and the Sense of the Holy" focuses on the problem of reductionism in modern science. The title of the essay echoes Rudolf Otto's book, *The Idea of the Holy*, first published in German in 1917. Actually, Eiseley's particular interest in this famous book is its emphasis on mysteries: "It cut across denominational divisions and spoke to all those concerned with that *mysterium tremendum*, that very awe before the universe which Freud had sighed over and dismissed as irrational" (ST 189). Otto has his own explanation of "*mysterium tremendum*": "It has its wild and demonic forms and can sink to an almost grisly horror and shuddering. . . . [A]nd again it may be developed into something beautiful and pure and glorious. It may become the hushed, trembling, and speechless humility of the creature. . . . In the presence of that which is a *mystery* inexpressible and above all creatures."[17] This certainly corresponds to Eiseley's personal way of describing his encounters with mysteries and there exist two mindsets: he feels horror and fear, and also he feels love, beauty, and joy. But these personal responses are absent from the reductionist's attitude.

The power of the holy in the world is best expressed by a word chosen by Otto, the "numinous." In Otto's analysis, this power can be experienced through the emotions: "the nature of the numinous can only be suggested by means of the special way in which it is reflected in the mind in terms of feeling."[18] The sense of awe or of the uncanny alerts one to the presence of the numinous.[19] Meditating on the relation between science and the numinous, Eiseley concludes that because of the reckless scientific exploration of the world, humans risk losing their awe of the unknown. Mystery has become something to be explained away by the scientist. Eiseley compares the men of the past to those of the present; in particular he contrasts their different attitudes to mysteries. He wishes to bring back to modern science the ancient wisdom that held awe for nature, for nonhumans, and for the numinous.

In his essays and poems, Eiseley actually practices cultivating "the sense of holy"; in particular, he tells individual stories (not necessary his own, real incidents), and the themes mostly show perceptive men gaining wisdom through unexpected, mysterious experiences. Rather than striving to eradicate ambiguity and achieve certainty, Eiseley makes an appeal for respect and awe for the unknown. He believes in fostering the sense of "the 'other' of which Rudolf Otto spoke, the sense beyond our senses, unspoken awe" (ST 192).

In his essays Eiseley narrates encounters and events that resist rational explanation, and instead demand poetic and philosophical meditation. He believes that from the beginning it has been the nature of man to confront the unfamiliar with wonder and awe:

> Ever since man first painted animals in the dark of caves he has been responding to the holy, to the numinous, to the mystery of being and becoming. . . . All this is part of the human inheritance, the wonder of the world, and nowhere does that wonder press closer to us than in the guise of animals which, whether supernaturally as in the caves of our origins or, as in Darwin's sudden illumination, perceived to be, at heart, one form, one awe-inspiring mystery, seemingly diverse and apart but derived from the same genetic source. (ST 189)

It may seem surprising to link Darwin's abstractions about evolution to prehistoric cave paintings, but this connection reveals Eiseley's conviction that both art and science can offer responses to the mystery of life. Although life takes many forms, it comes from the same mysterious origin. In spite of the modern conviction that twentieth-century man has advanced so far that he no longer recognizes his kinship with his cave-dwelling ancestors, Eiseley recognizes that his sense of awe in some of the encounters with animals makes a bridge in time that reaches back to man's origins and ancestors.

Power Drawn from Nature and Dark Sides of Men

Eiseley is concerned that scientific knowledge has been misused in the twentieth century. He looks back to Bacon to show where humanity has taken the wrong direction. Eiseley is less concerned with revisiting Bacon's body of work than with entering into a dialogue with the early modern writer. Published in 1962, *Francis Bacon and the Modern Dilemma* is a kind of manifesto in which the twentieth-century writer exposes his concerns about his own age and professes his beliefs about the responsibilities he assumes as an intellectual. Bacon's writings are the starting point for a reflection about the problems facing science in the atomic age.

Eiseley speaks of Bacon as a "time-voyager," a seer, and one "who opened for us the doorway of the modern world" (BMD 5). As a founder of modern science he imagined a future where man controlled the powers latent in the natural world: "He had envisioned man's power to change and determine his own destiny. Scientifically, he was one of the first to grasp the latent novelty that could be drawn out of nature" (BMD 20–21). The power drawn out of nature is largely presented by modern technology, which Eiseley acknowledges as the great intellectual achievement of modern men: "Western man, with the triumph of the experimental method, has turned upon the world about him an intellectual instrument of enormous power never fully exploited by any previous society" (IP 91). Twentieth- and twenty-first-century men have gained power from nature that their predecessors could only have imagined. But Eiseley also observes that science has been elevated into an absolute value that threatens to replace other forms of understanding: "there is a widespread but totally erroneous impression that science is an unalterable and absolute system. It is supposed that other institutions change, but that science, after the discovery of the scientific method, remains adamant and inflexible in the purity of its basic outlook" (BMD 81). He urges his readers to study the motivations behind scientific inquiry.

Eiseley deplores that the quest for power rather than truth motivates scientific research, and particularly that government funding goes to projects that could augment the influence of those who hold political power. The reliability of science, Bacon's scientific method, has not changed while "the motivations behind it have altered from century to century" (BMD 81). Bacon hoped to build a better world for humanity, while his twentieth-century descendants hope to control the world:

> The rise of technology gave hope for a Baconian Utopia of the *New Altantis* model. Problem solving became the rage of science. Today problem solving with mechanical models, even of living societies, continues to be popular. The emphasis, however, has shifted to power. From a theoretical desire to *understand* the universe, we have come to a point where it is felt we *must* understand it to survive. Governments expend billions upon particle research, cosmic-ray research not because they have been imbued suddenly with a great hunger for truth, but for the very simple, if barbarous, reason that they know the power which lies in the particle. If the physicist learns the nature of the universe in his cyclotron well and good, but the search is for power. (BMD 81–82)

Eiseley worries about what future might befall the world if science is motivated only by human interests and by the urge for power. With the help of science, man has knowledge of time and space that no predecessor has had before and he has done things that no predecessor has imagined doing before. The naturalist worries about the dark side of the new men who approach the living world without the light of wisdom or the soul. He admits that different periods of science show varying trends; however, he worries about the directions the discipline has taken, pointing out that minds can turn the brilliance that led to the invention of electricity, greater speed, or new means of communication toward constructing destructive weapons. Neither using power to gain authority over others, nor to advance material conditions can ensure spiritual contentment or moral development. Thoughtfully, he says, "Science can be—and is—used by good men, but in its present sense it can scarcely be said to create them" (BMD 83). Though he does not define what good men are, at least Eiseley makes it clear that science as a tool can be used by various kinds of people: good or bad, and developing or using science does not improve moral life. He knows well the danger that power can bring when it gets into the wrong hands: "with understanding arise instruments of power, which always spread faster than the inventions of calm understanding. The tools of violence appeal to the fanatic, the illiterate, the blindly venomous. The inventions of power have grown monstrous in our time" (IP 92). And Eiseley tries to analyze the nature of man to reveal what leads modern men in the wrong direction along the road of science and technology.

Eiseley is especially concerned with the danger and destructiveness of powerful weapons in the hands of arrogant men. In a passage that refers obliquely to the Cold War, he dramatizes the achievements of modern science and the danger that it represents:

> I switch off my reading light for a moment and a knob manipulated by my hand brings from the ends of the earth threat and counterthreat. . . . Men speak to each other now like the wrathful God of the Old Testament, threatening to make of their enemies' countries dust and a habitation for owls. The threats are real, the power, torn from nature, lies exposed in human hands. The voices pass, faintly contending, on their way to the vast silences of space. (BMD 24)

By not mentioning the radio that he manipulates and only referring to "a knob [that] brings [voices] from the ends of the earth" Eiseley underlines the mysterious, almost magical power of modern technology. Men have the power formerly wielded by "the wrathful God of the Old Testament" and they use it to dominate and control. Thinking of the deathly weapons that threaten the earth in his own time, Eiseley remembers with pain Bacon's appeal that knowledge be directed toward "the uses of life" (BMD 24). Eiseley takes Bacon as his model; like the sixteenth-century scientist, Eiseley knows and warns that misusing the "power torn from nature" will expose his generation to condemnation: "We . . . are now ourselves to be judged" (BMD 24). The language is biblical in tone, fitting the writer's sense of impending doom.

Instead of criticizing the scientific advances of the past, Eiseley is more concerned about his age and future generations. The dangers that worried

Bacon threaten Eiseley's world even more. In their rush toward the future, scientists have not paid enough attention to the past, and without it they risk creating "the world of artless, dehumanized man" (FT 130). The most important quality that Eiseley wants to preserve for a world of increasingly mechanical science is a respect for traditional human values. Eiseley remembers that a young man once proposed solving the problem of overpopulation by killing everything else except humans, thus freeing all the earth for man's use (FT 128). Today, overpopulation is still a serious global problem and variants of the young man's remarks still can be heard in the public forum. Eiseley judges that within the young colleague's remark, "pity had vanished, life was not sacred, and custom was a purely useless impediment from the past" (FT 128). The young man ignores the values that distinguished human beings in the past, revealed even in the evidence found in Neanderthal sites that the dead were given offerings and the handicapped cared for (FT 108–9). Eiseley worries that this lack of moral responsibility is too widespread among his scientific colleagues.

Technological Changes and Cultural Traditions

Modern criticism of industrial science is often about "the dissonance of excessive and rapid change" (BMD 74) caused by and after the Industrial Revolution. The risks that humans took for technological progress resulted in many things that are beyond human control. One of the unfortunate consequences is that "man's industrial wastes and destructive experiments increasingly disrupt and unbalance the world of living nature" (BMD 75). Eiseley's great concern is that men's power to damage the earth threatens both human life and the environment that sustains it. The living world without man, says Eiseley, "is essentially a stable universe," whose "inhabitants are intensely concentrated upon their environment" (FT 121); but things changed with the technological advances achieved by science. "The stability of nature on the planet . . . is threatened by nature's own product, man" (FT 128). For Eiseley, the scientists, newcomers to the planet, were excited to discover new things in nature, already known to other forms of life that have always lived within nature and under its law and kept continuous contact with nature as an old acquaintance (FT 122). With technology, humans interfere with nature, causing unnatural changes to the life forms that exist within it and in harmony with it. Changes in the human world are constantly accelerating, whereas until now, changes in the natural world have "alter[ed] with the slow pace of geological epochs" (FT 122). Human practices cause serious problems for other forms of life, as well as for man himself.

In *The Firmament of Time*, Eiseley lists three consequences of "the technological revolution." First, social advances have failed to keep step with the ever-accelerating course of technological progress (FT 133). Second, machines mobilize a growing amount of man's attention. For Eiseley's generation it is the car and the "flickering screen" of the television (FT 134), and his insight is borne out by the present generation's preoccupation with computer screens and smartphones. Finally, Eiseley bemoans the existence of "a type of man who is not human. He no longer thinks in the old terms; he has ceased to have a conscience. He is an instrument of power" (FT 135). In *The Unexpected Universe*, he repeats the opinion that he is witnessing the birth of "a new type of humanity," quick at mathematics, but "self-centered and contemptuous" (UU 58). He thus distances himself from the achievements of modern science, a surprising attitude for a practicing scientist. Eiseley's strange manner has its purpose—to make modern man, who takes for granted a life aided (or largely controlled) by ever-advancing technology and machines, see the strangeness of this new development that makes man himself, aided by technology, alien.

Modern people expect changes, and Eiseley speaks of his age as one that has turned away from the past: "We in the western world have rushed eagerly to embrace the future. . . . We profess little but the new and study only change" (FT 117–18). Unlike the stable older times, modern society changes so fast that: "many of us are now living in an age quite different from the one into which we were born" (FT 133–34). Driven by the innovations brought about by technology and machines are the ethical adjustments (or maladjustments) that concern Eiseley most. He observes that the Western ethic is moving "toward conformity in exterior observance and, at the same time, toward confusion and uncertainty in deep personal relations" (FT 121). Although this remark has to be placed in the context of the McCarthy era, it reveals his awareness that Westerners lack clear moral direction in response to change. While everybody looks to outer space for man's future, Eiseley suggests that men look inside: not to examine themselves with the eye of science to evaluate men's personalities or explain evil behaviors (FT 130) but to look at the earth under our feet, the nature we live within and the morality inside our hearts.

In traditional cultures, there was not such a marked division between art and technology. For example, for the Cree of the northern forest or the Montagnais-Naskapi studied by Eiseley's teacher Frank Speck, "the tool had largely been forged in the human imagination. It consisted of the way man had come to organize and relate himself to the sum total of his environment" (IP 59). These people were indifferent to technological improvements offered by the American government, or even their Eskimo neighbors (IP 57–58). Eiseley concludes these woodsmen were different tool-users from the type represented by modern men, because they were attached to their cultural traditions and to the natural world:

> This world view was comparatively static. Nature was sacred and contained powers which demanded careful propitiation. Modern man, on the other hand, has come to look upon nature as a thing outside himself—an object to be manipulated or discarded at will. It is his technology and its vocabulary that makes his primary world. If, like the primitive, he has a sacred center, it is here. Whatever is potential must be unrolled, brought into being at any cost. No other course is conceived as possible. The economic system demands it. Two ways of life are thus arrayed in final opposition. One way reads deep, if sometimes mistaken, analogies into nature and maintains toward change a reluctant conservatism. The other is fiercely analytical. Having consciously discovered sequence and novelty, man comes to transfer the operation of the world machine to human hands and to install change itself as progress. A reconciliation of the two views would seem to be necessary if humanity is to survive. (IP 59)

Eiseley lists strong contrasts between traditional and modern cultures; while the former rely on their own powers, the latter depend on machines and technology; while woodsmen are grateful for all the necessities nature provided, modern men greedily take things from nature. These woodsmen seem less interested in the mechanical extensions and material comforts that the innovators are committed to. These two opposite views of the natural world represent two kinds of mind and soul.

Eiseley asks readers to reconsider the prevailing view that man is the dominant hero of the stage of the living world and that "the world was man's niche. All else would live by his toleration—even the earth from which he sprang" (ST 196). Taking an evolutionary perspective, Eiseley has a sense of humanity's insignificance: "Measured against the duration of time and the power of natural forces, his efforts to master nature seem puny and ephemeral."[20] Man's superb brain originated in lowly places and life forms. He has benefited from nature's elements in developing his brain. He should not see the natural world as centering on humanity; other living and nonliving beings do not exist only for his comforts. In talking about human insignificance, Eiseley's purpose is to make man see further than the span of his own life or of a few generations. Looking back at man's evolutionary origin helps man understand he should live with nature and share the planet with other living things.

If man has some distinction that sets him above other life forms, it is that "he is at heart a listener and a searcher for some transcendent realm beyond himself" (UU 55). Humans can use their specialized brains, summoning their imaginations to see beyond their senses, to transcend their limits, and also to see and live within a natural world, not just a human world. The continuing conviction that *Homo sapiens* is the central hero in the story of the planet derives partly from modern man's scientific achievements—the result of human intelligence.

With their reliance on new technologies, modern men have become, in Eiseley's words, "the world eaters" (IP 53). They have abandoned their individualism for a life of easy satisfaction: "If life is made easier it is also made more dependent. If artificial demands are stimulated, resources must be consumed at an ever-increasing pace. As in the microscopic instance of the slime molds, the movement into the urban aggregations is intensified. The most technically advanced peoples will naturally consume the lion's share of the earth's resources" (IP 63–64). With this daringly reductive comparison of humans to "slime molds," Eiseley tries to shock his readers into an awareness of how modern man behaves in cities. Men use their mechanical extensions like machines to gain material comforts, and gain ease by drawing power from nature—they forget that they totally depend on the environment that they are destroying. The problem is that men are consuming nature at a rapid pace, and there is a lack of balance between the time and energy devoted to pursuing only scientific knowledge and developing technology and the time spent to gain knowledge about life and to consider moral responsibilities. The illusion that humanity dominates the natural world just makes the situation worse.

Eiseley's Pessimism About the Modern World and Optimism about the Natural World

As an anthropologist, Eiseley knows that when he targets science for causing waste and destructiveness to the environment, actually it is men that are being criticized. Eiseley expresses his sadness and anxiety about this situation in his poems and essays. In a poem from his collection *The Innocent Assassins*, the act of planting seeds becomes a desperate measure and a form of protest. "Desperate I Walked" records a man's state of mind when he finds no place in the urban landscape to plant the thistledown seed being carried in his hand. The speaker is anxious about the chance of a wild thing like the thistledown seed to live in the man-made environment. He describes a landscape shaped by and for humans with "car lots, highways / . . . pruned hedges [and] formal gardens" (IA 25). Actually, earlier in the 1950s ecologist Leopold expresses similar concern about highways, remarking "a widespread temptation to build new and often needless roads."[21] In Eiseley's poem, the "delicate, suburban gardens" offer no refuge for the tiny seed, since any wild growth would be "quickly weeded" (IA 25). The speaker is ironic about the human-centered selection of living things in these gardens, an unnatural selection that leads to the elimination of many species. His anxiety becomes universalized in the poem, when the speaker describes himself as "the last knowing man / carrying the last vital thing" (IA 25); "the last knowing man" referring to the Latin term for the species *Homo sapiens*. Thus the speaker is potentially the last human in a world where life forms have been suppressed by his own species. The repetition of "last" emphasizes the terminal state of wildlife in the man-altered world and the desperateness of the speaker's mood. We can link this sentiment with those that Eiseley expresses elsewhere in speaking of the modern condition: "I was a man trapped in the despair once alluded to as the utterly hopeless fear confined to moderns—that no miracles can ever happen" (ST 55). The miracles, mystery, and dreams that he wants all come from nature.

For Eiseley, man is too confident in his ability to make his world. Men's industrial activities extend into an environment shared by wildlife, and eventually cause the extinction of wild species. Men are careless or too willing to sacrifice wildlife for economic or political concerns and its loss too often goes unrecorded. That task falls to the naturalist.

In his essay "The Innocent Fox" in *The Star Thrower*, Eiseley testifies to examples of wildlife getting eliminated by the modern human world: "in blundering, good-natured confidence, the last land tortoise had fallen to the new expressway. None of his kind any longer came to replace him. A chipmunk that had held out valiantly in a drainpipe on the lawn had been forced to flee from the usurping rats that had come with the new supermarket" (ST 55). For rhetorical effect Eiseley exaggerates the terrible results of humans' reckless and irresponsible behaviors, claiming that the "new expressway" has destroyed forever the "last land tortoise," a casualty that serves as a representative of the widespread man-made extinction of animal species. Eiseley's feelings of sadness and desperation are understandable, since as a caring observer he knows well the extinction of species being caused by events in the modern world.

In "Desperate I Walked," the outcome of human intervention is not so sad; at last the speaker finds an old wall whose crumbling condition makes it a potential home for the thistledown seed—the last "wild chance" (IA 25) to grow. The poem ends with a reflection offered to the reader: "what have we done, / how have we come to this" (IA 26). The personal pronoun changes here from "I" to "we" and the questions that the speaker ponders are offered to humanity at large. The speaker is saddened to find that the former home for wildlife no longer exists (IA 25). The continuity that previously occurred by natural means now needs human intervention. Still, humans can act in a positive way to make up for the role of nature. Someone has to take responsibility for rewilding the environment, to act as a guardian or even a parent. The speaker's role can be interpreted as a parent and the seed, a child—a connection thus being built between two life forms. In the end, to find a place for the seed is for the man to find a place for himself, in other words, to make the environment more livable.

In another poem, "The Leaf Pile," the speaker's identification with another being is even more obvious. The naturalist observes something stirring in the leaf pile, an "indescribable grey muzzle" (IA 23). The word *muzzle* usually refers to the snout of an animal; it does not apply to humans. Nevertheless, the poem takes a strange turn when the speaker affirms: "it is my own" (IA 23). Since it is impossible to see the muzzle and own it at the same time, the lines bring together the human and the animal in a stroke of the imagination. In fact, the naturalist abandons his usual scholarly stance, characterizing his observation as "indescribable" and resisting prying into the animal's territory—"I shall not investigate" (IA 23). Instead he opts for subjective empathy.

At the same time, Eiseley does not abandon his scientific understanding in this poem; he draws on his knowledge of the way the mind senses odors (the relation between the nose and brain), and how the human brain has evolved all the way from the "reptile past" (IA 23). In acknowledging identity with the creature in the leaf pile, Eiseley finds an original way to recall the evolutionary road of human beings. He says, "Smelling autumn I have resurrected / what has slept a long time" (IA 23). The thing that "has slept a long time" may refer to the memories of the natural world, or to the sharper olfactory senses that modern man's ancestors once had. "It is my own" is his announcement of man's connection with his animal past; the speaker admits his kinship with other life forms. Through the behavior of "smelling autumn," he recalls the similar qualities that man and animals can share. The poem encourages readers to enjoy nature in sensuous ways: to "breathe" autumn, to "savor the earth," to "nuzzle the leaves" (IA 24). These behaviors create connections with wildlife.

In both these poems, Eiseley expresses hope for resurrection after the winter sleep, which shows another dimension of his ecological ideas. In many essays he is also fond of talking about death and life in the winter, especially in snowstorms, and the reason may be that winter symbolizes death—the ancient fear of early man as well as other animals. To resurrect living things from the dead is the naturalist's hope: either to protect the life of endangered species that are seriously threatened by technology's waste and environmental damage or to bring the vigor of wilderness to man-made environments like the cities, or to bring back the memories of the natural world to modern men who have forgotten their animal past. Since Eiseley realizes that to restore wilderness to the human world, human intervention may be necessary, he perpetuates a hobby that dates back to his youth: carrying a seed when he walks in nature. He speaks as if he knows the seeds' thoughts: "they were endowed with a preternatural knowledge that at some point we would lie down and there they would start to grow" (NC 69). Here Eiseley suggests that other life forms will surely outlive humans and humans will come to an end as a species. In his view humans are not as important as they believe themselves to be in the natural world.

Wasteland and City-Dump Philosopher

Besides criticizing the foundation of modern science—the scientific method—Eiseley also concentrates his analysis on the effects of science: what science imposes on the natural world. In his essays and poems, Eiseley analyzes the waste caused by modern technology. "[A]n affluent civilization was consuming its resources at an ever-increasing rate. Air and water and the land itself were being polluted by the activities of a creature grown used to the careless ravage of a continent" (IP 69). He declares: "Modern man, the world eater, respects no space and no thing green or furred as sacred. The march of the machines has entered his blood. They are his seed boxes, his potential wings and guidance systems on the far roads of the universe" (IP 70). Eiseley gives the figure at his time, "over a billion pounds of trash are spewed over the landscape in a single year" (IP 64), and nowadays the problem has only become worse. Eiseley's concern is therefore prophetic, "in these few elementary facts, which are capable of endless multiplication, one can see the shape of the future growing—the future of a planet virus *Homo sapiens* as he assumes in his technological phase what threatens to be his final role" (IP 64). Characterizing man as both the virus and its eventual victim, Eiseley foresees an ecological apocalypse caused by human science and technology.

Man's insatiable desire for technological progress and the lack of concern for other forms of life threatens his own continuation. In an episode from *The Star Thrower*, Eiseley describes how he spies flashes of light at a distant dormer window of an old house. At first he is excited by the spectacle and imagines that a great scientific experiment is in progress: "it pleased me to think that the mad scientists, as I came to call them, were engaged, in their hidden room, upon some remarkable and unheard-of adventure" (ST 56). The intervallic blue man-made flashes sustain his expectation of a Frankenstein-like miracle of "revivifying flesh or leaping sentient beyond it into some unguessed state of being" (ST 56). However, one rainy night the flashes disappear forever. Disappointed, Eiseley compares this episode to the situation of science of his time. He fears that all the work may result in a gloomy end, and man as the creator will finally make his escape silently, leaving just a load of waste that makes no sense. He makes this extrapolation from his archeological investigations of cultures that have disappeared: "I had once stood in a graveyard that was a great fallen city. It was not hard to imagine another" (ST 57). In the long run, the thrilling creations of technology will end in the graveyards of history.

Not only does he sigh over the waste produced by scientific experiments, but also he worries about other sights that seem to augur the end of civilization. In *The Unexpected Universe*, Eiseley narrates how he once, out of curiosity, got off the train before his stop and found "a perpetually burning city dump." The sight recalls visions of Dante's Inferno: "on the borders of hell. . . . One could imagine ragged and distorted souls grubbed over by scavengers for what might usefully survive" (UU 27). Obviously Eiseley connects the great trash burning at midnight to the imagery of hell in religious depictions and he expresses his shock and fear at the way the city deals with man-made "product[s] of the urban world" (UU 39). The scenes in the burning city dump provoke strange feelings and macabre associations. Eiseley connects "the flames and the dangling wire" he sees there to "an air crash years ago and the identification of the dead" (UU 28). He must have participated in this task related to the crash, for he says, "Anthropologists get strange assignments" (UU 28). The attendant forking through the waste to be burned growls in his ear: "'Even dead babies sometimes turn up. From there.' He gestured contemptuously toward the city and hoisted an indistinguishable mass upon his fork" (UU 27). In the attendant's descriptions, the waste coming from the city and of course from the city dwellers is unimaginably horrible; the "indistinguishable mass" could even be human body parts. Eiseley recalls having to reconstitute a mutilated human body: "I had once fitted a seared and broken skullcap over a dead man's brains . . . peering into the scorched and mangled skull vault" (UU 28). The images that he offers to readers are abject. The careful detail with which he describes this recalls the scenes in slow motion in horror movies. Although for Eiseley, the mangled skull vault is "like a beautiful, irreparably broken machine" (UU 28), the horror of death is certainly brought home to his readers.

If Eiseley is deeply pessimistic about the fate of humanity, he still believes "something is still undetermined in the human psyche" (IP 56) and the future is open. He mentions "a story by Don Stuart entitled 'Twilight'" (IP 125), in which the risk of extinction of humanity is imagined. In Eiseley's interpretation of the story, he emphasizes the tragedy of man who has "lost the will and curiosity to seek any further to transcend himself" (IP 126). He wonders at the ending of the story when the protagonist programs curiosity and hope to machines, "whether the time voyager had produced the only possible solution of the final decay of humanity—that is, the transference of human values to the world of imperishable machines—or, on the other hand, whether less reliance upon the machines might have prevented the decay of the race" (IP 127). Borrowing the setting of the story, Eiseley expresses his proposal for saving humanity: either to combine science (machines) with the humanities (wonder and hope) or rely less on machines.

Eiseley's optimistic hope that humanity could avoid its current race toward extinction depends on other kinds of men, or rather other aspects of man's nature. He believes that salvation lies in returning to the natural world.

The Ecological Implications of Eiseley's Thought—Connections to Rachel Carson and Aldo Leopold

Eiseley's growing consciousness about the dangers to the planet is certainly nourished by the ideas of important contemporaries like Rachel Carson and Aldo Leopold, whose books *Silent Spring* and *A Sand County Almanac: And Sketches Here and There* were manifestos for a new relation to the American land. Their work responds to the damage that modern technologies have done to the environment and proposes more ethical attitudes toward the land and its other-than-human inhabitants.

Rachel Carson, in her *Silent Spring*, provided evidence of the damage done to nature by pesticides, in particular DDT:

> Carson assembled enough facts to show why the more persistent chemicals must be restricted, but her deeper message was the need for ethical change, away from a spirit of conquest and toward a respect for all forms of life and an acknowledgment of our dependence on them. "The 'control of nature,' she wrote, 'is a phrase conceived in arrogance, born of the Neanderthal age of biology and philosophy, when it was supposed that nature exists for the convenience of man. . . . It is our alarming misfortune that so primitive a science has armed itself with the most modern and terrible weapons, and that in turning them against the insects it has also turned them against the earth."[22]

Carson's observation about the potential dangers of science is also the message of Eiseley's writing—he gives a similar warning, especially through his personal stories. A long-time admirer of Eiseley's books, Carson wrote to her fellow author that she enjoyed his "thesis . . . so beautifully developed" and she thanks Eiseley for "reminding us of that wonderful passage in Thoreau . . . [and] too, the bit from Jefferies."[23] Like Eiseley, Leopold responded to the problem of industrialization in modern society, especially industrial-scale farming, and regretted the numerous species that were the victims of overexploitation. In proposing ethical attitudes to all living things, both Carson and Leopold appealed to the emotions and consciences of their readers in response to the threat of species extinctions. Attuned to their ideas, Eiseley is greatly concerned with this particular ecological disaster: the disappearance of wild things. All three naturalists appeal to their contemporaries to respond to the problem. Eiseley says sadly, "Western man's ethic is not directed toward the preservation of the earth that fathered him. A devouring frenzy is mounting as his numbers mount. . . . Man is now only a creature of anticipation feeding upon events" (IP 69). Not only is he worried about overpopulation problems, but also he fears men's dark inner world, particularly their unreasonable desire for power. He believes that the solution to ecological problems such as the extinction of wildlife species, the proliferation of man-made waste, and the growing damage to the environment is to develop men's inner world, especially their ethics.

Progress and Ethics

In the foreword of *A Sand County Almanac: And Sketches Here and There*, Aldo Leopold presents himself as the kind of person who cannot live without wild things and the book is a collection of essays expressing his delights and dilemmas in existing alongside them. Leopold questions "whether a still higher 'standard of living' is worth its cost in things natural, wild, and free."[24] In criticizing the so-called progress that twentieth-century men value over wildlife, Eiseley engages in the same battle. The two ecological writers present their critiques on men's recklessness and irresponsibility in building their human and cultural world and in looking at nature only as a resource to be exploited. When commenting on the relation of scientific progress to morality, the two writers agree that these values are not synchronized. Leopold worries that mechanized man has broken his cultural ties to the land in valuing it only for its utilitarian yield: "that land is a community is the basic concept of ecology, but that land is to be loved and respected is an extension of ethics. That land yields a cultural harvest is a fact long known, but latterly often forgotten."[25] Eiseley also criticizes the modern tendency to see science and technology as a priority that diminishes ethical considerations. Both argue that modern society emphasizes economic growth and material comforts too much and fails to maintain a healthy ecosystem. Both want to bring ecological ideas to the forefront of modern society's agenda, urging that "a shift of values can be achieved by reappraising things unnatural, tame and confined in terms of things natural, wild and free."[26] The situation will improve only when men rethink their relation to the land and make room for the esthetic and ethical considerations.

Both nature writers compare evolutionary changes to the man-made changes in modern science and society: "evolutionary changes, however, are usually slow and local. Man's invention of tools has enabled him to make changes of unprecedented violence, rapidity, and scope."[27] The two ecologically minded writers make it clear that men with their machines have made too sudden changes to the natural world. Although their tone is different, they issue a similar warning. Leopold's measured tones contrast with Eiseley's dramatic picture of man as world eater, but he still apprehends the effects of modern man's actions: "man-made changes are of a different order than evolutionary changes, and have effects more comprehensive than is intended or foreseen."[28] Men should consider how nature and life within it can adapt to these abrupt man-made changes. With his field experiences, Leopold can measure the degree of the potential destruction: "the less violent the man-made changes, the greater the probability of successful readjustment in the pyramid [biotic mechanism]."[29] When men treat land more gently, they actually cause themselves fewer problems and tensions.

Hunting, Collecting, and Living

Eiseley and Leopold's ecological ideas also converge on the subject of hunting. Leopold writes from his professional experience, making observations on categories of hunters, as well as writing on his own experience of hunting. In "Thinking Like a Mountain" he explains his conversion from an avid wolf hunter to an advocate of the protection of such important predators. Eiseley narrates several personal experiences with hunters (although it is possible that the stories are fictional), and the main aim is to persuade the hunters to put down the shotgun pointing at living beings, especially endangered species. Leopold criticizes the type of person—"the trophy-hunter"—whose capacity to observe is lost; and thus, "to enjoy he must possess, invade, appropriate."[30] This is also the dark side of hunting that Eiseley wants to reject, as he criticizes "the modern vandal totally lacking in empathy for life beyond his own, his sense of wonder reduced to a crushing series of gears and quantitative formula, the educated vandal without mercy or tolerance, the collecting man that I once tried to prevent from killing an endangered falcon, who raised his rifle, fired, and laughed as the bird tumbled at my feet" (ST 193). The "modern vandal" is what Eiseley criticizes, and hopes this kind of man can finally change his behavior and be inspired by the other kind of man—the far-seeing man "with reverence and compassion in his heart" (ST 193). In dividing mankind into categories, Eiseley runs the risk of being too general; however, he does so in order to make a point. These totally opposite attitudes to life, Eiseley says, are the "the extremes of temperament" (ST 193), thus he is surely tolerant of other kinds of mental attitude among his various readers. Between the reverent person and the unconcerned one, Eiseley makes it quite clear, the division may not be so abrupt as he described, but "there is an invisible line of demarcation, an ethic that science must sooner or later devise for itself if mankind is to survive" (ST 200). Eiseley's observations and prophecies about science ring even truer today than at the time he was writing. The efforts he makes in his writing to bring artistic, ethical, and scientific approaches together could guide humanity toward a more balanced relationship with the environment.

In *The Star Thrower*, Eiseley tells how he once concealed himself "beneath a fisherman's cap and sunglasses" to visit Costabel Beach and discovered the "vulturine activity" of "the professional shellers": "After a storm one can see them hurrying along with bundles of gathered starfish, or toppling and overburdened, clutching bags of living shells whose hidden occupants will be slowly cooked and dissolved in the outdoor kettles provided by the resort hotels for the cleaning of specimens" (ST 170–71). Looking at "the steaming kettles in which beautiful voiceless things were being boiled alive" (ST 173), Eiseley finds greedy madness and mercilessness in this activity of competing shell collectors. It is then he encounters the star thrower, who picks up still-living starfish and flings them back to the sea. The conversation between them is filled with symbols and philosophical and ecological meanings: "'The stars,' he [the star thrower] said, 'throw well. One can help them'". . . . "'I do not collect,' I [Eiseley's speaker] said uncomfortably. . . . 'Neither the living nor the dead. I gave it up a long time ago. Death is the only successful collector'" (ST 172). Putting it in very simple words, Eiseley delivers to his readers the message of the star thrower that one can help save animal lives. Eiseley's idea is that one should collect nothing at all. Living things should be allowed to go to their destiny—to death—in a natural way. Though knowing that the role of star thrower is lonely and the task tremendous, Eiseley decides to "walk against the shell collectors and the flames" (ST 185) and becomes another star thrower; because while "I picked and flung another star. . . . I could feel the movement in my body. It was like a sowing—the sowing of life on an infinitely gigantic scale" (ST 184). This image of the sower recalls the man who carried seeds in his pockets; both men perform a gesture for the purpose of perpetuating life. Eiseley praises "the thrower who loved not man, but life" (ST 185), and expects that men like him can earn the wisdom that the indigenous peoples "had sensed intuitively that man cannot exist spiritually without life, his brother, even if he slays" (ST 185). When Eiseley offers his ecological ideas concerning modern men's hunting and collecting, it is to value and save all life forms, and as he tries to save still-living starfish cast up by the sea and stuck on the sand, he tries to bring back the wisdom long known by traditional cultures and to pass it on to the covetous modern men exemplified by the shellers, to change their minds and to encourage them to gain a proper perception about man's living within nature, alongside other life forms.

Land Ethic: Wilderness-Minded vs Economics-Minded

An intersecting point that Eiseley and Leopold share is the awareness that man, as a member of the land's community, should show love and respect to it. First Leopold makes it clear that "the land ethic simply enlarges the boundaries of the community to include soils, waters, plants, and animals, or collectively: the land."[31] Basically, for Leopold, the land stands for what is generally thought of as nature or the environment. Perhaps he uses the term "land" so as to depart from older ideas about nature and, at the same time, to use vocabulary that is familiar to everyone. Still, he has to redefine "land," dissociating it from the idea of property. He claims that the assumption that land is man's to dispose of is wrong: "the assurance with which we regard this assumption is inverse to the degree of our education."[32] Leopold's innovation lies in his assertion that man should have an ethical relation not only to other human beings, but also to the land: "there is as yet no ethic dealing with man's relation to land and to the animals and plants which grow upon it. Land, like Odysseus' slave-girls, is still property. The land-relation is still strictly economic, entailing privileges but not obligations. . . . Individual thinkers . . . have asserted that despoliation of land is not only inexpedient but wrong. Society, however, has not yet affirmed their belief."[33] He wishes that the whole society develop the land ethic and his writings seek to educate his fellow Americans to get new knowledge and wisdom about their dependence on the natural environment.

Without a proper perspective on the land, people cannot develop this land ethic. Leopold declares that "it is inconceivable to me that an ethical relation to land can exist without love, respect, and admiration for land, and a high regard for its value. By value, I of course mean something far broader than mere economic value; I mean value in the philosophical sense."[34] The problem for Leopold is that educational institutions have not yet furthered a healthy relationship to the environment: "we have more education but less soil, fewer healthy woods, and as many floods as in 1937."[35] When man's choices and behaviors are only based on self-interest, and he only cares for what can be profitable to himself, education needs to work to change mentalities. What is needed is "an internal change in our intellectual emphasis, loyalties, affections, and convictions."[36] For Leopold, mentalities need to evolve toward a broader understanding of the place of other species in the biotic community: "the evolutionary process for an ethic is simply this: quit thinking about decent land-use as solely an economic problem. Examine each question in terms of what is ethically and esthetically right, as well as what is economically expedient. A thing is right when it tends to preserve the integrity, stability, and beauty of the biotic community. It is wrong when it tends otherwise."[37] Though the prescription Leopold offers is simple and wise, he wonders whether men will follow it. He laments that "philosophy and religion have not yet heard of it."[38] This is where Loren Eiseley's writings take up Leopold's cause.

Leopold proposes that men regard themselves not as conquerors but as simple members of a larger-than-human community. This corresponds to Eiseley's idea that one should see oneself as one of nature's people instead of a dominator. Both writers emphasize respect for the land and all life forms. And both predict that the role of conqueror or dominator is self-defeating and self-destroying. Just as Eiseley criticizes men's arrogance in trying to get rid of all mysteries, Leopold finds men are only interested in utilizing the wild things after science has "disclosed the drama of where they come from and how they live."[39] The two essayists refuse simple and reductive explanations of the natural world, in particular the mechanistic view of other life forms and of the world in general. Leopold points out that "the ordinary citizen today assumes that science knows what makes the community clock tick; the scientists is equally sure that he does not. He knows that the biotic mechanism is so complex that its workings may never be fully understood."[40] Both Eiseley and Leopold have a broader vision of the complexity of the natural world and both feel that altered perceptions will help preserve this natural world. Eiseley believes that there will always be mysteries unsolved by scientists; if people were to admit this, the assumption that men can master all that surrounds them would fall of itself.

Like Eiseley, who remains an optimist about the capacity of individuals' minds and the positive changes that men can make to develop the green world, Leopold urges experts in other domains, especially politics and economics, to reach a common understanding and wisdom about the value of wilderness. That's also the reason Leopold encourages all grades of amateurs in wildlife research and explains that the motivation for the amateurs who finally achieve success and recognition is that "they simply realized that the most fun lies in seeing and studying the unknown."[41] Eiseley also encourages the free spirit of individuals in learning and researching nature.

Though there are similarities, Eiseley and Leopold stress different subjects; for example, two of the most important themes in Eiseley's writing are time and space and Leopold emphasizes conservation. While Leopold's writing is very practical, suggesting rules to readers like a handbook, Eiseley's writing is philosophical, offering a deep reflection on earth and the relations between men and animals, which leads his readers to think about what it is to be human and what it means to live in time. He looks at man and space within the long stretch of time. Given the number of Bible stories and philosophical discussions scattered throughout Eiseley's ecological writing, it seems safe to say that Eiseley tries to extend Leopold's ecological ideas to the fields of philosophy and religion. Through his lyrical meditations on man's place in the biosphere, Eiseley seeks to reach out to Leopold's public but also to speak to readers beyond this circle. In sharing his perceptions about man's relation to nature, he hopes to encourage people to become more ecologically minded.

The point of Eiseley's critique of science is to change readers' outlook upon the living world. Reacting against the coldly objective pursuit of knowledge, he advocates approaching nature through the emotions as well as the intellect: "in the supposed objective world of science, emotion and temperament may play a role in our selection of the mental tools with which we choose to investigate nature" (ST 187). Each individual's mindset is important in the way he studies nature. In his writing, "besides straightforward science and contemplative natural history, there is a more personalized scientific literature that reflects a labor of love, where fact and knowledge are balanced by affection."[42] Combining his human capacity to use words in order both to reason and to move, he finds a powerful means of persuasion. He shows that man's instinct and his sensation of his surroundings can work together with his mind and heart. Sensitive to the claims of both science and literature, Eiseley sees how scientific geniuses can change human mentalities. He therefore advocates merging literature and science in order to approach the world in a more holistic way.

Eiseley is saddened by the fact that wildlife is disappearing because of human activities. He regrets that modern men forget or belittle man's animal past and become narrow-minded and arrogant. As an attentive naturalist as well as an archeologist, he comments that "upon this world, life is still young, not truly old as stars are measured. Therefore it comes about that we minimize the role of the synapsid reptiles, our remote forerunners, and correspondingly exalt our own intellectual achievements" (UU 61). He believes that humans may pass away but life will remain. Nevertheless, we humans exist as world eaters. Since men explore, build, and consume in a reckless way, he asks us to view the modern man as a parasite: "Perhaps *Homo sapiens*, the wise, is himself only a mechanism in a parasitic cycle, an instrument for the transference, ultimately, of a more invulnerable and heartless version of himself" (IP 54–55). By belittling the role of man in front of nature, Eiseley reminds us of the lack of wisdom and affection revealed in the impact that our destructive behaviors can have on the natural world. In dealing with the relationship between the rural and urban worlds, Eiseley urges modern men to escape their narrow human worldview by respecting nature and life within it. People should not blindly believe that we are the dominators of the world. We create weapons and machines in order to control and we choose power, ignoring morality in order to pursue material enjoyment and authority over others. Eiseley observes that "in the endless pursuit of the future we have ended by engaging to destroy the present. We are the greatest producers of nondegradable garbage on the planet. In the cities a winter snowfall quickly turns black from the pollutants we have loosed in the atmosphere" (IP 105). He appeals to us to become planet protectors rather than planet eaters, which actually would save humanity from extinction.

Though Eiseley is specific about the points he criticizes about science, and careful about the logic of the essays, his prose is dense, and sometimes it still can be difficult to get his general and abstract ideas immediately. Eiseley is an exceptional writer. He is writing at the intersection of various disciplines and contributing hybrid essays where the Bible stories or the ideas of other philosophers or poet get mixed with his own. When criticizing science, he writes in a visionary way; therefore the next chapter will focus on his writing style—how he manages to criticize science in his double role as scientist and poet.

NOTES

1. Waal, *Ape*, 37.
2. Haraway, *Simians*, 190.
3. Haraway, *When Species Meet*, 84.
4. Haraway, *When Species Meet*, 87.
5. "[T]he course of years beginning in the late 1940s in the laboratory of Kenneth Brinkhous at the University of North Carolina at Chapel Hill" (Haraway, *When Species Meet*, 82).
6. Haraway, *When Species Meet*, 82.
7. Haraway, *When Species Meet*, 84.
8. Haraway, *When Species Meet*, 88.
9. Haraway, *When Species Meet*, 90.
10. Haraway, *When Species Meet*, 83.
11. Haraway, *When Species Meet*, 86–87.
12. Haraway, *When Species Meet*, 93.
13. Haraway, *When Species Meet*, 93.
14. Haraway, *When Species Meet*, 3–4.
15. Angyal, *Loren Eiseley*, 61.
16. "Over two thousand years ago, a man named Job, crouching in the Judean desert, was moved to challenge what he felt to be the injustice of his God" (UU 48).
17. Otto, *Holy*, 13.
18. Otto, *Holy*, 12.
19. Otto, *Holy*, 13–14.
20. Angyal, *Loren Eiseley*, 122.
21. Leopold, *Sand County*, 191.
22. Worster, *Nature's Economy*, 349.
23. Carson, Letter to Loren Eiseley.
24. Leopold, *Sand County*, vii.
25. Leopold, *Sand County*, viii–ix.
26. Leopold, *Sand County*, ix.
27. Leopold, *Sand County*, 217.
28. Leopold, *Sand County*, 218.
29. Leopold, *Sand County*, 220.

30. Leopold, *Sand County*, 176.
31. Leopold, *Sand County*, 204.
32. Leopold, *Sand County*, 205.
33. Leopold, *Sand County*, 203.
34. Leopold, *Sand County*, 223.
35. Leopold, *Sand County*, 209.
36. Leopold, *Sand County*, 210.
37. Leopold, *Sand County*, 224.
38. Leopold, *Sand County*, 210.
39. Leopold, *Sand County*, vii.
40. Leopold, *Sand County*, 205.
41. Leopold, *Sand County*, 185.
42. Angyal, *Loren Eiseley*, 35.

Chapter 3

Solution—Writing at the Intersection

Living and observing the dilemmas of the twentieth century, Eiseley is firstly a scientist who writes critiques of science that challenge common opinions. He looks at science in a new way, romancing the discipline by infusing it with poetry. Rather than accepting the doxa of modern mechanical science, he returns to past thinkers to find new angles from which to view the universe and *Homo sapiens*' place within it. Science's mission is to gain knowledge, to eliminate mystery, while the poetic imagination strives to preserve mystery. Eiseley creates strangeness in his writing, whereas strangeness is what science or scientific writing tries to eliminate. Second, he is a hybrid essayist who brings contraries together in tension. Science and poetry are seen as opposites in academia, but Eiseley brings them into dialogue. He concentrates on multiple matters such as science, time, and nature, weaving his reflections together in stimulating new ways. Eiseley's work illustrates the idea that the most inspiring science writing is not strictly science writing; it can be literary, poetic, and philosophical.

An exploration of Eiseley's writing style illustrates one of the ways in which he works to reconcile the split between science and the humanities. In his own discussions of his writing, one term stands out—his claim to have invented the "concealed essay." Heuer says that during the 1950s when Eiseley taught in universities, "he started to use scientific material in a different way, trying to arouse the interest of the general reader in subjects that fascinated him" (LN 19). He chooses subjective narrations for his prose and poems, and even in very scientific writings, he occasionally provides his personal experiences. Since Eiseley's concealed essays stress personal anecdotes and ideas, autobiography is the first important genre that can accomplish this task. Normally in autobiographical writing, the writer selects memories and pieces them together to create a coherent picture of himself. Eiseley is quite different. He offers us fragmentary and anachronistic memories; he jumps back through the decades, his mind goes back and forth in time, and he links these seemingly disparate incidents by featuring a common object in different scenes.

Eiseley also creates ambivalence in his work, as he mostly uses the first-person pronoun, which encourages readers to regard his autobiographical writings as Eiseley's real-life experience. The fact is, the speaker's account of his experience can be both fictional and lived. Through the ambivalence surrounding the first-person persona, Eiseley reveals the potentiality of looking at the natural world from the angle of a scientist as well as a poet, and being oneself and at the same time being other-than-oneself. Moving from one side to another, from one decade to another, he shows the existence of in-betweens. Moreover, it seems he wants readers to go deeper than what he says and think over what is not said. His writing on science, man, and nature responds and even raises objections to strictly defined scientific writing.

In this chapter I will consider how Eiseley establishes his concealed essay, where his prose and poems present hybridity and intertextuality, how he manages to combine history, geological events, science, and meditation in poetic form and how his writing manifests poetic qualities. His childhood and the paradoxes accompanying it inspire Eiseley's contemplations of the lines that are conventionally drawn between wildness and civilization and good and evil. In other words, I will offer here a picture of how Eiseley's mode of writing works to resolve the split between science and the humanities.

3.1. THE HYBRID ESSAYIST

Fragments of Memories: The "Splintered Glass" of a Life

In *The Night Country* Eiseley records his memories in great detail and relates a number of incidents from his life. Although his fragmentary memories seem to be in disorder, they are assembled in such a way as to give a picture of the individual. Eiseley published his autobiographical book *All the Strange Hours* in 1975, just two years before his death. Pondering how an old man collects his early memories, he reflects that "the act is not one of total recall like that of the professional mnemonist. Rather it is the use of things extracted from their context in such a way that they have become the unique possession of a single life" (ASH 156). He admits that the recall of his life story does not aim for the accuracy of the skillful archivist or historian, but rather seeks to present a highly personal and thus unique view of his life. The images of the passage of time came to him under certain circumstances. That is why he says, "They represent no longer the sequential flow of ordinary memory"

(ASH 156). "No longer" here, especially mentioned in this book that recounts his own life, reveals a dim feeling of helplessness before the passage of time past. Though his life unfolds in sequential order like an ordinary man, at the end of life, he chooses not to collect all the events of the past and retell them as they happened. On the one hand, perhaps he yields to the power of forgetfulness or concealment from oneself; on the other, perhaps he feels that certain moments take on more importance than others in retrospect.

In his autobiographical book *The Night Country*, the memories are dissociated in time but connected thematically. Each chapter has a theme introduced by discourse but Eiseley links them smoothly in a way that allows him to suggest the relation of one anecdote to another. The personal anecdotes are disparate in time and place so that readers are aware of the gaps and disruptions in the text. These anachronistic incidents are fragments of memories. Eiseley once said that his mind could be symbolized by cracked glass, "as someone said of the mind of the English artist and poet William Blake on another occasion, if it was indeed flawed, 'it was cracked so that the light shone through'" (LN 10). This image could also describe how Eiseley's essays and his intellectual world appear to readers. Most of Eiseley's books are collections of different articles and thanks to his "careful and extensive revision and rearrangement of the essays," readers can enjoy finally books of still "a notable unity of theme, tone, and style."[1] Though his essays are scattered like "cracked glass" in his books, they assemble to reflect coherent and beautiful thoughts.

What's more, Eiseley is far from being interested in the restricted sphere of the self, and he combines personal anecdote with reflection on the whole of mankind. He selects memories that permit him to cross over into other worlds. Their importance is not autobiographical in any narrow sense; instead personal memories allow him to connect inner and outer worlds. In fact, the importance of his experiences resides in the way they allow him access to what is alien to him. He is interested in exploring the boundary lines between the civilized and the wild, the present and the past, humanity and animality. Autobiographical books like *The Night Country* are twilight places where those boundaries become indistinct and allow entry into new spheres of experience. The book does not follow the order of a life as lived, but rather creates patterns of thought and memory; it breaks with the usual chronology of autobiography in order to imagine the future, and it records personal experience in order to reflect on the distinctiveness of the human species. Eiseley picks up accidently (at least it seems) pieces of personal incidents and links them together by virtue of a shared subject so that in the end correspondences emerge.

The Concealed Essay

One of Bacon's most important influences on later generations is the essay genre, and, to a certain extent, Eiseley takes Bacon as his model in literary writing on science. Nevertheless, he also innovates the conventional essay form. Given that the essay is a form that usually aims to reveal opinions or facts in a clear and logical manner, his invention of "the concealed essay" is something of a paradox. In his autobiography *All the Strange Hours*, Eiseley explains why he elaborates the form of "the concealed essay"; it begins with an article that he "counted heavily upon" but that was not taken by a prospective publisher, "a scientific oriented magazine." Eiseley therefore decides to modify his mode of writing:

> [S]ince my market was gone, why not attempt a more literary venture? Why not turn it—here I was thinking consciously at last about something I had done unconsciously before—into what I now term the concealed essay, in which personal anecdote was allowed gently to bring under observation thoughts of a more purely scientific nature? (ASH 182)

Eiseley acknowledges also in this book that in his own time, "the personal essay was out of fashion except perhaps for humor" (ASH 182). He therefore faced the problem of finding an audience and developing a new form. Angyal characterizes Eiseley's essay as a paradoxical venture; "what Eiseley accomplished is virtually to invent a new genre—an imaginative synthesis of literature and science—one that enlarged the power and range of the personal essay."[2] Eiseley reveals the world of science through the double vision of a scientist and a poet. Each essay achieves a mix of discourses in which "a personal anecdote introduced it, personal material lay scattered through it, personal philosophy concluded it, and yet I had done no harm to the scientific data" (ASH 183). Eiseley adopts "the concealed essay" as his solution because he is attached to the personal essay and sees the "straitly defined scientific article" as too restrictive (ASH 182). He is trying to find a new way to write essays about science, man, and nature, in other words, to combine science and literature.

The word *concealed* means hidden or not shown. In part, the concealment comes from what is not said—the gaps or cracks in the text from which something not expressed in either science or life writing emerge. Books like *The Unexpected Universe* (1969), *The Invisible Pyramid* (1970), *The Night Country* (1971), and *All the Strange Hours* (1975) best illustrate the idea of the "concealed essay" because in these books scientific discussions emerge out of the personal anecdotes and perceptions.

Eiseley's "concealed essay," first of all, contains a mix of discourses. It ranges back and forth between autobiographical anecdotes recovered from distant memories and from real-time experience, between Native American cultures, mythology, science, and poetry. Second, even though in his autobiographical writings Eiseley talks about selective memories from his past, there are memories that are not revealed and they are hidden from readers as well as, perhaps, from Eiseley himself. Part of him remains concealed; some parts of his narratives are obscure and enigmatic. His essays only give us fragments of his life and they can be difficult to understand. The images and details puzzle readers and compel us to find new coherence and new meaning in them.

Intertextuality

Since the concealment discussed above involves combining different forms of discourse, hybridity is an obvious characteristic of Eiseley's "concealed essay." One form of both hybridity and obscurity can be found in Eiseley's tendency to begin his essays and books with epigraphs. In *All the Strange Hours*, for example, Eiseley begins with an epigraph from Robert Browning's *The Ring and the Book*:

> I' the color the tale takes, there's change perhaps;
> 'Tis natural, since the sky is different,
> Eclipse in the air now, still the outline stays.

The poem "deals with the impossibility of discerning 'truth' because multiple perspectives make impossible a single identifiable truth."[3] That Eiseley puts this epigraph here seems to indicate that the autobiography cannot be regarded as a single true life of the author; its "color[s]" change, and his tales contain more than one point of view. In fact this book blends the autobiographical and the fictional. *All the Strange Hours* is divided into three parts, and before each part, Eiseley also puts an epigraph. For the first part—"Days of a Drifter"—he chooses lines from the epic poem *The Odyssey*: "There is nothing worse for mortal men than wandering" (ASH 1). Thus he links his own travels as a youth (and those of other poor men) to the epic difficulties of Odysseus. For the second part—"Days of a Thinker"—he chooses a quotation from G. K. Chesterton: "One must somehow find a way of loving the world without trusting it; somehow one must love the world without being worldly" (ASH 73). Eiseley encourages people to love the natural world though there is deception within it, and there is violence and death in it. He advocates love and respect for nature and living creatures, including humans, though he fears that "worldly" longing for material comforts has become the main pursuit of the modern science world. Urging love and respect for all the forms of life including humankind seems to go against the detachment expected of a scientist. Chesterton's words express Eiseley's double vision of the world: the attentive scientist has a poetic mind and heart. Finally, in the third part—"Days of a Doubter"—Eiseley comes to the conclusive part of the book where he confronts the divide between science and the humanities as well as man's alienation from the natural world. He begins with lines from Ruland the Lexicographer: "The Alchemical meditato is an inner dialogue with someone who is invisible, as also with God, or with oneself, or with one's good angel" (ASH 219). This epigraph prefaces the part in which he tries to examine his inner self so as to understand his own life and by extension to find meaning in humanity. Eiseley sees himself as an alchemist and his writing as expressing "the eccentricities and diversities of my life" (NA 11).

Epigraphs also appear in other books: two epigraphs for the whole book *The Immense Journey*; one for the whole book and one before each chapter in *The Firmament of Time*; and the same for *The Invisible Pyramid*, *The Unexpected Universe*, and *Darwin's Century*. Eiseley takes a quotation out of its original context and gives it new meaning so that it can serve his own essay; thus, he merges his own perceptions with those of the wise men who have gone before him. However, the other reason Eiseley does this, I think, is that the riddles lying in the texts intrigue him. He continues the tradition of the master essayists who use arcane references. Each epigraph in Eiseley's writing not only guides and instructs the direction of the reflections in the following writings; it also leads readers to broader, ancient wisdom. Once readers begin to search where the quotations come from and what their meaning is, Eiseley leads them to other wise authors, and finally, he links the quotations to his own thoughts. In short, these epigraphs function as literary indications of Eiseley's intellectual journeys as well as guides and links to the themes of Eiseley's discussion.

A Hybrid Autobiographical Persona

The concealed essays employ narratives to move the train of thought along; and it seems pertinent to examine how Eiseley uses the materials for these stories to build up his intellectual world. In the essay "Willy" Eiseley explains his manner of writing the personal essay. He says that the memories are like pictures, "the brain has become a kind of unseen artist's loft" (ASH 156) and "one has just so many pictures in one's head which, after one has stared at them long enough, make a story or an essay" (ASH 161). If memories are visual and they call on the art of description to render them, the writer has to undertake the work of assembling a narrative out of the pictures that come to mind. Although pictures, scenes from the past times, no longer exist in the present, as long as they stay in Eiseley's mind they are available for making a story or an essay. Eiseley's attitude to his memories is like his attitude to all things past; whether human history, fossils, man's animal past, and his own evolutionary road, these multiple subjects need to be considered by the light of the imagination.

Moreover, Eiseley cherishes his impressions drawn from nature more than the scientific knowledge learned in the classroom. Aware of the "heresy" of this attitude for his scientific colleagues, he asks, "why should my dance with a crane supersede in vividness years of graduate study?" (ASH 158). He admits that "on the whole, as I pause to examine this lost studio in my head, the animals outnumber by far the famous people I have met" (ASH 157). There is a kind of humor in this self-revelation because when people narrate their life stories they are usually inclined to mention famous people they know or have encountered. By contrast, Eiseley makes animals the most important pictures in his artistic loft.

The pictures that Eiseley creates hold particular meaning for him; that is why he mentions a particular image and extends his discussion afterward. He does not necessarily refer to real birds or dogs, or relate incidents that have actually happened, but the pictures have to be vivid and convincing. Their effect on readers can be powerful because people have their own particular experiences or memories with animals. Moreover, Eiseley's descriptions can easily evoke either familiar memories or new thoughts. Using personal stories, Eiseley integrates his memories with readers' memories.

Since Eiseley takes the liberty to make stories out of memories from his own angle of view, so the anecdotes related in essays are not always exactly real happenings. As the editor of *The Lost Notebooks of Loren Eiseley*, Kenneth Heuer, comments in reference to Eiseley's notes, "although Loren was always writing about himself, he, like many other creative authors, manipulated the accounts of his life. In his essays, he occasionally invented characters, rearranged events, and composed conversations in search of a larger reality. His intention was not to deceive or falsify, but rather to clarify, and he managed to give reality the vividness of fiction by the way he reported an incident" (LN 76). For example, Eiseley's note on February 17, 1969, reads "Whirlwind, Hurricane, Ravenswood, and Ravencliff, Va. Good town names with possibilities" (LN 183); thus Eiseley accumulates some suggestive place names that can be used later in his essays or poems. Angyal makes a similar observation to Heuer's in discussing how Eiseley creates his essays: "Often Eiseley began with the kernel of an actual field happening and selectively altered or fictionalized it to heighten a mood or tone, or else to emphasize some theme or motif. In such writing, as the incident unfolds natural history gradually becomes a metaphor for personal history as the author probes the recesses in his mind."[4] Though there are many critics who accuse Eiseley of not always telling the truth, I think his poetic license is one of his strong points, because it allows him to follow a train of thought and organize his ideas rather than sticking faithfully to a linear chronology or a journalistic account of experience. The most important element is the effect of Eiseley's imaginative adaptations on the readers. Though imaginative embellishment is part of Eiseley's literary technique, he declares: "It is not, you understand, an hallucination. It is a reality" (FT 167). Eiseley explains that his particular way of representing his experience "is a matter of seeing" (ASH 163); the essayist "sees as his own eye dictates" (ASH 159). Thus, he expresses what he sees through his mental eyes and leads the reader to see what he sees.

The significant personal experiences one recollects reflect key concerns about oneself and one's life. In relating his experiences, Eiseley discovers alternative versions, realizes new truths, or finds the answers to troubling enigmas; in other words, the incidents he chooses work to develop and illustrate Eiseley's abstract ideas. People who criticize Eiseley's stories as false, or who doubt that his emotions about loneliness are authentic, seem to fail to grasp the complexity of the relation between imaginary creation and material reality, and to misunderstand his method of merging literary writings and scientific reports. I think the truthfulness of the incidents is less important than the profound ideas that they carry.

The American poet Howard Nemerov was inspired by Eiseley's essays in composing his own poetry. He understands the originality of Eiseley's way of seeing the world. He wrote to Eiseley saying, "your way of dealing with the world is for me one of the ideas one hopes to learn to think with. . . . (A baby spider is crawling across the page on which I've copied the little poem for you. Parable quite in yr [your] own style. But I shall try not to envelope him)" (LN 220). Like Eiseley, he sees the significance of apparently unimportant things, how the incident of a spider crawling across the paper could offer a parable in Eiseley's style. The personal incidents Eiseley records with other-than-human beings in them often contain encounters with common animals in common places, like a spider on its web in the rain or pigeons in the train station. Almost everybody can experience common encounters like these; however, the encountering is not the point—it has to become the carrier of Eiseley's philosophical ideas. Readers do not have to re-experience the same contact as the subject in Eiseley's writing to have access to his meditation. The point is to follow the speaking subject in the development of his thoughts, to appreciate the ideas that he draws out from the incidents he relates.

One thinks of the autobiographical "I" as the avatar of the author's self, but the French specialist on autobiography Philippe Lejeune has shown in *On Autobiography*, the writer and the narrating "I" are never quite the same. Though Eiseley mostly narrates the essays in the first person, and especially so when he writes the autobiographical books, Eiseley's "I" is not to be taken naïvely for Eiseley himself in real life. This is obvious when a writer writes about his childhood because his much older self is telling about his younger self. It is clear that Eiseley is re-shaping events drawn from memory. In the first chapter of his study, "The Autobiographical Pact," Lejeune defines autobiography as: "Retrospective prose narrative written by a real person concerning his own existence, where the focus is his individual life, in particular the story of his personality."[5] According to this definition, Eiseley's books like *The Night Country* and *All the Strange Hours* do have autobiographical qualities: he writes in the first person and he focuses mostly on his life experiences (particularly those from his childhood). Though the two books fall into the category of life writing, they are not limited to personal autobiography—Eiseley writes about more than his own existence. He meditates on the meaning of life—both the lives of individual human beings and those of other life forms on the planet Earth.

There is a space between the real Eiseley and the "I" in his writings. It is true that in his autobiographical essays he draws on real materials. For example, he uses his wife's real name, Mabel, and his own name, Loren Eiseley, whom he identifies as the "I"; however, some details are made up and thus they are "false." Nevertheless, qualities like observations, sensations, and meditations are Eiseley's personal offerings. Moreover, speaking of the narrator, Eiseley identifies the narrating "I" not only with the real Loren Eiseley, but also purposefully identifies that "I" in a romantic way with other persons or even with animals, like a wolf or a dog.

Besides identifying his narrating "I" with either human or animal others (taking other characters as himself), Eiseley also sometimes takes himself as others. In the essay "The Places Below" from *The Night Country,* Eiseley narrates an episode in which his childhood playmate Rat leads him down into the sewers and almost gets them both killed when water unexpectedly fills the pipes because "a city employee had opened a fire hydrant for testing" (NC 24). In this narrative, the two boys (Rat and "me") experience together the horror of being chased by the running water and potentially overcome by imminent death underground in the darkness. Elsewhere, in an untitled note, Eiseley writes, "You lead your following to the sewers. Into these you disappear" (LN 221). It seems in this note that Eiseley imagines or remembers himself leading his followers (the other child or children) into the sewers, but in the essay he characterizes the narrating "I" as the timid one, and invents a brave animal-like playmate, "Rat," whose fictional name expresses his physical and mental agility. Reading the note together with the essay, we can infer that both the Rat and the narrator are Eiseley. The story thus brings out two sides of a child, indicating a dual mental world in which the self is both adventurous and timid. This fluidity of roles reveals the multiple sides of a man, the many shapes he can take on in his imagination.

As Eiseley frequently uses the pronouns "we" and "you" in his writings, especially in his discussions about humans' responsibilities and the proper view of the natural world, he may be taken for a moralist. I think Eiseley does establish or at least analyze the ideal "I" as the model of a good man who wants the natural world to stay natural, who loves and respects life, and responds to mystery with awe. He adopts a serious tone because he wants his meditations to serve as signposts indicating the road for human beings to follow. His writing and his arguments with scientific authority aim to reorient humanity in a less destructive direction.

To conclude this reflection on Eiseley's hybridity as an essayist, the humanistic and artistic vision in his works gives readers new insight into the relation between science and the humanities. However, his double vision as scientist and literary man makes his works difficult but rewarding to read. Admiring a master of essays like Bacon who "loved obscure and arcane references,"[6] Eiseley also inherits this erudite writing style. Readers can find legends, folk tales, the Bible stories and scientific discoveries and theories in his essays; they seem always to be at hand for the writer when needed. Unlike conventional scientists who give scientific facts and hypotheses, Eiseley tells personal incidents and develops metaphysical ideas. Some things in Eiseley's essays are declared overtly and some are not. The obscure and arcane references are not easy to get immediately. Moreover, Eiseley often evokes multiple topics and links them into deep meditations for readers to digest. This reflection of Eiseley's writing would not be complete without looking at the way it blurs the line between prose and poetry. His poems contain multiple layers of meaning. Thus in the next section I will talk about the way he introduces romantic and literary themes into essays on science and scientific themes in his poems and philosophical prose, and where autobiography and personal reflection enter under the cover of serious scientific considerations.

3.2. ROMANCING SCIENCE

The Poet as Crab

Eiseley has three published poetry collections: *Notes of an Alchemist* (1972), *The Innocent Assassins* (1973), and *Another Kind of Autumn* (1977) and a posthumous book *All the Night Wings* (1979). In his poems, especially *Another Kind of Autumn*, Eiseley usually expresses his emotions and abstract ideas more directly. Science is supposed to be objective and emotionless, but Eiseley is very passionate in his feelings for the world. Although he had started writing poems in his youth, he waited until his late years to publish his poetry, and he explains that he enjoyed them in secret for a long time (NA 11).

It seems Eiseley shares a similar feeling with Thoreau—one of his literary inspirations—because Thoreau "in his early years . . . saw himself as a poet struggling for liberation from a confining world."[7] Eiseley's academic career spans the era when "the austerities of the scientific profession leave most of us silent upon our inner lives" (NA 11). Thus the traditionally trained scientist tries to escape the restrictions imposed by scientific authority and to breathe the freer air of poetry. Poetic forms offer a way out, a form of release, a means to express his inner world. The need to escape the confining scientific atmosphere, especially its standards for objective academic publishing, helps Eiseley overcome his timidity about publishing his poems. Presenting his first volume of poems, *Notes of an Alchemist*, to the public, in its preface he speaks of how "a scientific man has transmuted for his personal pleasure the sharp images of his profession into something deeply subjective" (NA 11). He chooses to reveal scientific truths about the world in ways that are different from those prescribed by science, and to share his thoughts and feelings with his readers. In transferring his meditations to his readers, he does not expect that all of them will feel the same as he does; instead, he believes in the creative power of the individual and is tolerant of personal interpretation, which also reflects his modest attitude as a writer.

Besides justifying self-revelation in the preface of the first poem collection, in his prose Eiseley had already mentioned what it is to be a poet. In *The Invisible Pyramid* Eiseley declares what he thinks a true poet is and what his mission in his time should be. He quotes Thomas Love Peacock's words, saying, "'a poet in our times is a semi-barbarian in a civilized community. . . . The march of his intellect is like that of a crab, backward'" (IP 123). In Eiseley's interpretation of this image, the backward-moving crab becomes a positive symbol of the poet's defense of culture:

> He never runs, he never ceases to face what menaces him, and he always keeps his pincers well to the fore. . . . The true poet is just such a fortunate creation as the elusive crab. He is born wary and is frequently in retreat because he is a protector of the human spirit. In the fruition time of the world eaters he is threatened, not with obsolescence, but with being hunted to extinction. I rather fancy such creatures—poets, I mean—as lurking about the edge of all our activities, testing with a probing eye, if not claw, our thoughts as well as our machines. (IP 124)

Clearly Eiseley worries about the diminishing numbers of true poets in the twentieth century, and he assigns the poet the mission to protect the human spirit against the ravages (both cultural and material) caused by human activities. Eiseley personifies the crab and also describes how poets act in a crab-like manner, like "creatures" "being hunted to extinction," which blurs the line between humans and animals. He gives readers the impression that humans and animals have connections between them that ought not to be ignored. Rather than despising crabs for their "rearguard action and withdrawal" (IP 124), Eiseley admires the virtue in both crabs and true poets—their boldness in refusing to drift with the current—because it takes courage to hold onto the past, while looking at the present and into the future. The true poet, as Eiseley emphasizes, is also a prophet who sees the dangers looming in the future. Those dangers are both environmental and cultural, since "the world eaters" are only concerned with converting the world into consumable materials.

Actually, Eiseley's mission in criticizing science corresponds exactly to what a true poet is supposed to do, to look for values higher than exclusively material goods. He warns men of the danger and damage that machines impose on the earth; and most importantly, he foresees the future and warns men of potential ecological disasters. In trying to bring the humanities into dialogue with modern science, Eiseley becomes the protector of the human spirit. He knows that he will be misjudged, but he is not afraid to be dismissed as strange in choosing to write with the double vision of scientist and poet in order to convey his vision of science, nature, and man.

Another skill and also virtue of true poets is their ability to perceive the things that are of eternal value to humanity:

> They have, in addition, a preternatural sensitivity to the backward and forward reaches of time. They probe into life as far as, if not farther than, the molecular biologist does, because they touch life itself and not its particulate structure. The latter is a recent scientific disclosure, and hence we acclaim the individual discoverers. The poets, on the other hand, have been talking across the ages until we have come to take their art for granted. It is useless to characterize them as dealers in the obsolete, because this venerable, word-loving trait in man is what enables him to transmit his eternal hunger—his yearning for the country of the unchanging autumn light. (IP 125)

Eiseley puts the poet and the scientist (the biologist in this example) side by side and defends the poet's version of life as being equally important or even more important than that of his scientific contemporaries. He looks at poets and scientists in the scale of time and says the scientific observation on "particulate structure" of life is "recent," but speculation on "life itself" is timeless because it is "the country of the unchanging autumn light" that the poet looks for. It seems that poets can escape the restrictions of time and pursue the eternal value of life. With the modern adulation of scientific knowledge, the experimentalists have gained prestige, and the arts of the poets have lost respect and affection; they are seen as "dealers in the obsolete." Nevertheless, for Eiseley, language is what makes man human and nothing can be achieved without it. As Eiseley explains his ideas on poets, actually he also indicates how what he does in his writing fits into the concept of the true poet. The skill Eiseley admires in poets can be also applied to himself—he jumps back and forth through time.

The Untraveled Traveler

Eiesley's scientific explorations around his native environment probably inspired his ideas about time traveling; as he says, "I . . . was born on the Great Plains and was drawn almost mesmerically into its rougher margin, the Wild Cat Hills and the Badlands, where bone hunting was a way of life. . . . As a young man engaged in such work, my mind was imprinted by the visible evidence of time and change of enormous magnitude" (IA 11). He reminds us that "Thoreau, the physical stay-at-home, was an avid searcher of travel literature, but he was not a traveler in the body" (UU 140). Eiseley too is "an untraveled traveler" (IP 124); though he writes about his native environment, he travels through time and space in his imagination. Eiseley learns from other writers that "some landscapes cry out for a story. W. H Hudson found it so of the South American pampas. . . . Charles Dickens, though he achieved wealth and comfort, was haunted by 'the cold, wet, shelterless streets of London.' Thoreau never escaped the canopy of the great eastern forest" (IA 11); the same is true of "White's Selborne, Jefferies's Swindon . . . Emerson's Concord."[8] Paying respect to these literary inspirations, Eiseley writes about locale, the landscape of his boyhood. Lincoln, Nebraska, is the place where Eiseley passed his childhood and youth, where he collected and observed the things of nature. Heuer insists that: "the influence of this landscape on his imagination persisted in his adult writing" (LN 14). Moreover, Eiseley points out that the landscape can reveal more than what is immediately perceptible in the present: "I am powerfully influenced by locale and, being geologically trained, a locale which may be projected vertically in time" (LN 79). He obtains from his own life the raw materials for his essays and poems, which corresponds to his shared belief with Ralph Waldo Emerson that "the great writer is peculiarly a product of his native environment" (IP 124). And there is another inspiration from Emerson as Eiseley demonstrates in speaking of the poet's capacity to make correspondences: "As an untraveled traveler, he picks up selectively from his surroundings a fiery train of dissimilar memory particles—'unlike things' which are woven at last into the likeness of truth" (IP 124–25). Through the fragments of memories he presents—usually "'unlike things'" that seem in disorder—Eiseley leads readers to perceive what it is to be human. In imagining his own destiny, he also intimates that of all mankind.

With pride, a local Nebraska journal speaks of Eiseley as a scientist and naturalist who "contributed to the scientific discoveries in western Nebraska like no other."[9] An important contributor to scientific findings on his native region, Eiseley blends these findings with speculations into poems. He admits, "Bone hunting is not really a very romantic occupation" (ST 144), but with his artistic speculation Eiseley manages to lend it romance.

Overall Eiseley not only practices the missions of the true poet but also the poetic skills; he accomplishes the former by expressing his philosophical ideas in descriptions of lived experience; he achieves the latter by cherishing the English language. Angyal argues, "Eiseley was poetically rather than philosophically minded."[10] Indeed, Eiseley admires poets and worked secretly at his poetry in order to be worthy of the title. As Heuer comments, "Loren is one of the few American nature writers of stature who also published poetry. From this he derived a heightened sense of imagery and cadence, as well as an awareness that the rhythms of prose may draw from but must not emulate the meter of poetry" (LN 164). Indeed, although he writes in free verse, his poems have particular qualities that are different from his prose. Increasingly, he became more comfortable with the role of poet; his friend and editor Heuer observes that "it had become easier for him to give a poetry reading than to prepare a special lecture for the public" (LN 164). The transition from prose to poetry is not necessarily easy, so I will now examine how Eiseley becomes poetic.

Language, Prison, and Poetry

I mentioned earlier that Eiseley uses epigraphs as a writing technique and some of them are extracts from the work of eminent poets. Actually Eiseley often quotes either poems or other literary works to introduce a topic, to illustrate the current discussion, or to make a thoughtful conclusion. This practice hybridizes Eiseley's words with those of other writers, as well as showing Eiseley's affection for poetic language. Eiseley appreciates the almost miraculous achievement of man's invention of language: "long ago he cunningly devised language to reach across the light-year distances between individual minds. . . . They found, fantastic though it now seems, the keys to what originally appeared to be the impregnable prison of selfhood" (IP 125). In poetic words, Eiseley expresses his abstract ideas on language. First he speaks highly of the way language allows humans to communicate from one mind to another, so that each one is not imprisoned in his own thoughts. However, the word *cunningly* indicates a potential danger or a dark side to the power of this invention. His opinion on men's language is a paradoxical one, as he says, "Words are man's domain, from his beginning to his fall" (IP 125). This statement suggests that language allowed the human species to claim a territory—"man's domain"—and, at the same time, to lose one—to "fall" out of nature. Eiseley is not sure whether in finding the key to liberate themselves from the prison of selfhood, humans did not thereby enter into another prison. His essay "The Cosmic Prison" illustrates this idea. Eiseley quotes a saying from a poet to begin the discussion: "'A name is prison, God is free,' once observed the Greek poet Nikos Kazantzakis" (IP 31). Although Kazantzakis is commonly known as a writer and philosopher, Eiseley titles him poet. In doing so he praises the poetic quality of Kazantzakis's essays, novels, and plays, which may reflect his view of himself; Eiseley writes essays but actually can be seen as a poet. Eiseley quotes from Kazantzakis to express his idea about man's unique invention—language:

> I think, that valuable though language is to man, it is by very necessity limiting, and creates for man an invisible prison. Language implies boundaries. A word spoken creates a dog, a rabbit, a man. It fixes their nature before our eyes; henceforth their shapes are, in a sense, our own creation. They are no longer part of the unnamed shifting architecture of the universe. They have been transfixed as if by sorcery, frozen into a concept, a word. (IP 31)

Words are extremely useful to humanity, but they are also limiting since they freeze one's conception of reality into conventional patterns. The cultural world that man defines in language "transforms that universe into a cosmic prison house which is no sooner mapped than man feels its inadequacy and his own" (IP 32). Thus, language can limit man's capacity to understand the mysteries of the universe. The poet's role is to free language from convention by using it in new ways. In facilitating liberty of thought, poetry can then contribute something of value even to scientific culture. Men's limited concepts of other forms of being make men blind to the dynamic possibilities of existence; they fix the limits of knowledge to what has been acquired in the present. The poet opens up time and space; he is a boundary crosser who uses his imagination to break out of the cosmic prison.

Imagination and Analogy

Eiseley's double vision as scientist and poet can be better understood in the light of Edward O. Wilson's essay "The Poetic Species" from *Biophilia*. Wilson offers his concept of the ideal scientist: "both very original and committed to the abstract ideal of truth in the midst of clamoring demands of ego and ideology. . . . [and] their principal aim is to discover natural law marked by *elegance*, the right mix of simplicity and latent power" and "elegance is more a product of the human mind than of external reality."[11] Wilson's observations reveal the same problem with the twentieth century that Eiseley finds: the scientific authorities overemphasize the value of scientific knowledge gained by mechanical experiments; only the imagination can produce theories marked by elegance. Both Eiseley and Wilson call for a science that can reveal the truths hidden within the vast scale of time by deploying the simplicity and potential force lying in the human mind. Wilson claims that "the ideal scientist can be said to think like a poet"[12] and "the great artist touches others in surgical manner with the generating impulse, transferring feeling precisely. His work is personal in style but general in effect."[13] Eiseley is this kind of scientist because, at the same time, he is also a poet. He offers readers personal stories whose surprising images create echoes of his strikingly original perceptions in our minds and hearts.

To regain the passionate wonder for mystery and to jump over the boundary between science and poetry, as well as the boundaries of language and time, men need imagination. Eiseley is disappointed with the lack of imagination shown by the science world of the twentieth century. If scientists had more imagination, they might reflect on whether the objectivity and detachment of the traditional scientific method permit them to see other connections between humans and nonhumans beyond the asymmetrical relationship between the observers and the objects of observation. With more imagination perhaps cold experimentalists could view the living world with compassionate wonder rather than addressing it in a mechanical way. With imagination, modern men might contemplate the mysteries within the universe and escape the trap of over-specialization and single-mindedness so as to see the world from a new and different angle. Perhaps man can recover his original simplicity and openness toward the world, as Eiseley reminds readers, "before act was, or substance existed, imagination grew in the dark. Man partakes of that ultimate wonder and creativeness. . . . [M]an, the self-fabricator who came across an ice age to look into the mirror and the magic of science. Surely he did not come to see himself or his wild visage only. He came because he is at heart a listener and a searcher for some transcendent realm beyond himself" (UU 55). Eiseley reveals the nature of man and the deep meaning of being a human. In his words, imagination helps build humanity's cultural world, and we need it in order to coexist with other forms of life, to transcend ourselves and embrace life.

In a discussion of about humans' cultural world, Eiseley reflects that at a time when space travel occupies people's minds, correspondingly space travel literature is on the increase. Eiseley complains as he reads the space travel books about "the appalling poverty of imagination manifested in our descriptions of the world outside—whether within our universe or far beyond in other galaxies and remote from us by light-years." In these books he finds not only a lack of literary imagination, but also "the lack of grasp of biological principles" (LN 86). Humorously Eiseley says he prefers to stay at home than to encounter the beings found by space travel in the starry systems described in these literary works. Compared to the majority of science fiction works, Eiseley's discussions of man, nature, and science, I think we agree, offer marvels to readers along with reasonable scientific information. Eiseley demands that readers use their imaginations, for example, when he describes events happening in the wilderness, far from human habitation or far back in time, before human memory.

Writing as both a scientist and a poet, Eiseley leads readers to undiscovered terrain; to that effect Eiseley's imagination is the helper, and the means he uses is often analogy. As Wilson states, "The key instrument of the creative imagination is analogy."[14] Eiseley uses analogy and metaphor to make his abstract ideas accessible to readers by linking the unknown or the unexpected to what they already know. Moreover, where the poems deal with issues that are vital to ecological harmony, they use strong language such as superlatives. For example, the poem "Desperate I Walked"[15] goes to the extreme of having the speaker describe himself as "the last knowing man / carrying the last vital thing," (IA 25) to express anxiety about the continuing existence of wildlife in a man-made industrial world. A final point to be made concerning imagination in Eiseley's writings is that compared to prose, poetry is more condensed and more intellectually challenging, and Eiseley's prose often has this poetic quality, making it a challenging but eminently worthwhile reading experience.

Childhood Innocence and Violence

The obsession for discovery in science or literature can often be traced back to childhood. Eiseley is fond of talking about the importance of his childhood experiences in his writings. He tries to reach his readers by describing how he sees and feels, and the strongest feelings often come from his memories of his childhood. For me, childhood is a period before the individual learns from or is influenced by others. Before imbibing conventional thought, social fashion, and time-limited and dominated theories, a child uses his sensations—the pure and original responses of (human) nature—to experience his surroundings. Then these sensory impressions—what he sees, hears, and feels—and how he reacts to them can leave deep impressions and strike him in his later years sometimes even when he tries not to remember.

Actually, one can better understand Eiseley's meditation about his childhood by observing those Romantics who are important in shaping his vision. William Wordsworth is the great influence on Eiseley, and Angyal compares him to the English poet "in his use of memory."[16] In his autobiographical epic poem *The Prelude*, Wordsworth writes about childhood and most importantly the child's reaction to nature. In the opening Book, "Childhood and school-time," Wordsworth describes the great joy of a child who escapes from the city and throws himself into the arms of nature. He describes how he feels freedom, ease, and delight while feeling the influence of the "gentle breeze," "azure sky," "clear stream," and hills.[17] The innocence of childhood is revealed with the image of a child leaving the city to take pleasure in the joyful green world. Among his childhood memories, Eiseley's narration of his escape into nature resembles this description by Wordsworth. It is his first venture into the wild as he secretly hitches a ride on the rear of a tea wagon. He recalls "It was . . . the most marvelous ride I shall ever make in this life"; and during his wagon journey "shafts of light," "the green meadows by the roadside," "the flowers," and "the sky" (NC 9) all give great pleasure to the little child.

In his essay "Willy," Eiseley relates several childhood encounters with animals, two of which are good examples to express his idea about childhood innocence. The first one is that he remembers a redheaded woodpecker that lies stunned by an electrical charge caused by knocking the telephone pole behind Eiseley's house. The child carries the bird to the house and admires his color. In a passage of self-examination Eiseley gives an unassuming explanation as to why this childhood episode remains in his mind, "because it was my first glimpse of unconsciousness, resurrection, and time lapse presented in bright color?" Then the bird furnishes a striking image of the power of memory: "I have never chanced to meet another adult who has a childhood woodpecker almost audibly rapping in his skull" (ASH 157). The anecdote shows how nature teaches things to human beings, for, most importantly, the child learns about the threat of mortality and the healing power of time. Eiseley emphasizes it is his "first glimpse," and he regrets that this experience is so unique that no one else could have the same. I think the experience shows the contrast between innocence and experience; Eiseley shows readers how each is alone in his own experience and gains unique pictures that others do not share, except, of course, thanks to the power of literature. The second example illustrates how he learns that "in the animal world lines of definition are not as severely draw as in the civilized one that we inhabit" (ASH 157). He tells how once, on a visit to a zoo, he accepted the dance invitation of an African crane who practiced dancing in order to find her mate. The detailed description of how he dances seems ridiculous to an adult: "I extended my arms, fluttered and flapped them. After looking carefully up and down the walk to verify that we were alone, I executed what I hoped was the proper enticing shuffle and jigged about in a circle. So did my partner" (ASH 158). Here, Eiseley becomes and acts like an African crane's potential mate. He even checks that they are alone, as if he worried about other competitive candidates for a potential mate, or perhaps he is more afraid about other human beings seeing him. Still, he does call the dancing bird his partner and make efforts to do the mating dance. He believes the bird draws no line between herself and the human in front of her, but actually, it is Eiseley who does not follow the definitions made and accepted in the human world. Both the lines drawn between humans and animals and those distinguishing the sexes seem insignificant, as he admits being "uncertain about the sex role I was playing. Male, female?" (ASH 158).

Meditating on the reasons for his actions in the two incidents and on the way those pictures live in his mind, Eiseley declares, "I think, you know, it is the innocence" (ASH 159). The capacity for responding innocently to another creature lies in the individual's refusal to fall back on conventions when confronting an unexpected, unique experience. Meeting another being innocently has an ethical dimension if we consider that the word implies acting without intent to harm, acting without guilt. It also implies responding to others in the confidence that they pose no threat. The animals respond in this way to Eiseley: the redheaded woodpecker innocently falls into the human world to be restored to life after being knocked unconscious by electricity; the African crane tries to engage a human child in a dance in order to find a mate. These creatures that live within or adjacent to the human world inevitably encounter humans, but they do not demonstrate any fear of the child. Though these are simple episodes, Eiseley offers readers the opportunity to reflect on the relation between humans and other creatures. In my opinion, the childhood innocence Eiseley presents is the life-affirming innocence of nature; it appears simple but the origin of it remains mysterious. Secondly, the innocence Eiseley talks about seems to imply the possibility of communication between animals and human beings. The two birds show the little child the behavior that nature prompts in them, and the child admires and reacts positively and naturally. It is only later in life that adults are cut off from the lives of other animals, in relationships based only on exploitation: "A violent dog-eat-dog world, a murderous world, but one in which the very young are truly innocent" (ASH 159). It seems that Eiseley believes that only the very young approach living things without the intent to harm them.

William Blake may also influence Eiseley's perspective on childhood innocence. In his poem collection *Song of Innocence and Experience*, Blake introduces the reason for writing "Songs of Innocence":

> And I made a rural pen,
> And I stain'd the water clear,
> And I wrote my happy songs
> Every child may joy to hear.[18]

The songs are made for children and aim to praise joy of life. The poem "The Lamb," found in the "Songs of Innocence," poses a child's innocent question about man's and animals' origins, for the nature of creation represents the timeless puzzle for all human beings. In the first part of this poem, the child asks, "Little Lamb who made thee? / Dost thou know who made thee?" and in the second part, he answers his own questions,

> He is called by thy name,
> For he calls himself a Lamb:
> He is meek & he is mild,
> He became a little child:
> I a child & thou a lamb,
> We are called by his name.[19]

The lamb of course symbolizes Jesus, so the poem associates childhood with divinity. The poem stresses the positive aspect of Christian faith by associating it with the natural world, rather than the corrupt urban world of "Songs of Experience." Eiseley's view of innocence also associates it with the child's capacity to interact with animals in a manner that is gentle and harmless ("meek" and "mild"). In dealing with man's relation to nature and other forms of beings in the natural world, Eiseley also opposes the child's innocence to the evil side of human beings, who in their will to dominate the earth, become arrogant, abusive, merciless, destructive, and greedy.

In his essays, Eiseley also analyzes and leads the readers to ponder the question of how man and other forms of life come into being, and what humanity's place within nature should be. Influenced by Darwin's discussion of natural violence, Eiseley's thoughts on childhood do not only center on innocence but also address its dark side. Even as a child he witnessed the evil behavior of children. In *The Night Country* Eiseley relates a memory involving a childhood encounter with wildness. Eiseley tells the story in several scenes. In the first one the little Loren follows a group of shabby older boys to a wide, flat field at sunset. The place is called Green Gulch. The name is suggestive, for it is not so much a gulch as a material divide between man and the wild: "It was a huge pool in a sandstone basin, green and dark with the evening over it and the trees leaning secretly inward above the water. When you looked down, you saw the sky. I remember that place as it was when we came there. I remember the quiet and the green ferns touching the green water. I remember we played there, innocently at first" (NC 5). This description produces a beautiful and tranquil picture of nature. The parallel constructions "I remember . . . " emphasize something folded in his memory. Then the scene gives rise to something repressed: a second picture appears of the children finding a huge old turtle asleep in the ferns and pounding it to death with stones. It is an ugly and cruel scene that shocks the little Loren. The boys then turn to their small companion. They throw stones at him, splash water over his suit, strike him and finally drag him to the road, forcing him to go home alone. The little boy does not know the way home but has to go. The last picture is the small figure walking slowly in darkness, with the wind blowing. In this memory a group of children that come from the civilized world kill a harmless animal. And the older children force the smallest one into a darkness that is both literal and symbolic. He has discovered the wildness of which humans are capable. In fact he has "discovered evil. It was monstrous and corroding knowledge. It could not be told to adults because it was the evil of childhood in which no one believes. I was alone with it in the dark" (NC 6). Though childhood is often linked with innocence, Eiseley reveals that there is violence in the darker side of human beings even as children.

He thus gives a more complete picture of the world, in the same way that Blake presents the counterpart of the lamb in his "Songs of Experience." In "The Tyger," the speaker asks: "What immortal hand or eye / Could frame thy fearful symmetry?" He asks the same question that the child asks in "The Lamb," except that he seems to wonder at reasons for creating a fearful being like a tiger. Especially, he questions the apparently malevolent force of the creator. Rather than the pastoral images of "The Lamb," "The Tyger" uses the imagery of metal and fire, the materials of the Industrial Revolution:

> What the hammer? what the chain?
> In what furnace was thy brain?
> What the anvil? what dread grasp
> Dare its deadly terrors clasp?[20]

Showing the strong contrast between the innocence of lamb and the deadly terrors presented by tiger, the poem asks, "Did he who made the Lamb make thee?"[21] The two poems reveal to the readers that both good and evil, gentleness and violence, life and death exist in nature as well as in the human world, just as in childhood innocence and experience. In Eiseley's writings, those two sides are also shown, and like Blake, he often links the more violent impulses to the power attained from the scientific and technological advances of the modern world.

Loren Eiseley has been variously described as archaeologist, anthropologist, educator, philosopher, poet, and natural science writer. He is a hybrid essayist who mixes the genres and styles of autobiography, fiction, meditation, history, field notes, and poetry. Eiseley's writings correspond to two of the senses of "paradox" in advancing opinions that conflict with common belief and in exhibiting apparently contradictory characteristics. He challenges commonly held views of science, nature, and man and brings science and literature together by expressing his ecological, philosophical, and metaphysical ideas in both essays and poems. He shows that the best science writing is not strictly scientific; it also fertilizes science with imagination.

Through investigating Eiseley's writing style, some of the enigmas in Eiseley's writing become less perplexing. An interest in the author's life writing may be the first thing that draws general readers to him. Quite successfully, Eiseley attracts readers (as well as critics) with this genre. He admits that his autobiography is more "creative writing than a scientific effort," and "'hope[s] to transcend the purely personal by suggesting unusual factors common to the life of man in a universe he is forced, from childhood, to try to understand'" (LN 79). Eiseley collects his fragmentary memories as a creative artist displaying pictures of different times and places in order to see the whole picture of his life as well as mankind's. Autobiographical writing is a good way for him to explore scientific themes. Whether the anecdotes he relates are true or not does not matter; more important is Eiseley's way of describing things to reflect his personal wisdom. Readers are guided by the light within his personal philosophy to walk into his memories and meditations. We fall like Alice into a world of strange adventures and into other dimensions of time and place. With individual effort and contemplation, we can join the fragments of images and ideas to form a fuller picture of human nature.

Eiseley presents his personal feelings in words even beyond words. There are many hidden meanings waiting for readers to explore; the pictures he creates contain unspeakable secrets, and the poetic language carries deep thoughts for contemplation. Eiseley's poems and essays may be difficult to understand at first; however, after delving into his work one can be suddenly enlightened, especially when finding how he mentions the same incident in both poems and essays. One thing needs to be noticed; if we find the same event in the two forms of writing, both are necessary styles in Eiseley's writing because they create different effects thanks to the different qualities that Eiseley knows well and puts to good use. When we consider them together, the diverse fragments of his memories and thoughts can be more revealing than polished wholes because they both reveal and conceal ideas.

Eiseley is a hybrid essayist because his writing can be scientific, for example in his discussions of scientific findings on nature and time, and it can be humanistic when he talks about issues such as the diminishing of human potential through the industrial society, or the doomed fate of innocent but poor lives (humans and nonhumans) used for merciless and mechanical scientific experiments. He becomes metaphysical in interpreting Indian legends and traditional human values; then again, he is eminently literary in infusing his own ideas with those of other poets, philosophers, and nature writers or in fictionalizing his life experience. Above all these characteristics, his writing is exceptional and full of puzzles. He is a writer who writes at the intersection as a true scientist and also a true poet.

A true poet, Eiseley is the protector of the human spirit. He ponders the paradox of mind and body and remains a native writer of a local environment while mentally traveling through time and space in his imagination. He urges men, particularly modern scientists, to escape the limited anthropocentric view of defining and naming their surroundings. This inevitably imprisons them in only a partial human world, while the fullness of the natural world can be seen with both scientific knowledge and an artistic and humanistic view.

As a nature writer whose efforts are devoted to blending science with the humanities, he offers his writings as a solution to the split between the two at a time when "the humanities presence faded quickly"[22] in the environmentalist circles. For this Eiseley was misjudged and was regarded as an outsider by other scientists. But as time passes, "our belief that science alone could deliver us from the planetary quagmire is long dead" and "our hopes are tied to the humanities."[23] Nowadays the concept of the environmental humanities is welcomed and practiced in universities. A combination of the scientific and humanistic approaches to study the natural world has begun to be introduced into universities as a new discipline; this proves that, though shockingly new for his century, Eiseley's writings and ideas actually anticipated the future.

NOTES

1. Angyal, *Loren Eiseley*, 77.
2. Angyal, *Loren Eiseley*, 39.
3. Pitts, *Understandings*, 58.
4. Angyal, *Loren Eiseley*, 14.
5. Lejeune, *On Autobiography*, 4.
6. Angyal, *Loren Eiseley*, 38.
7. Worster, *Nature's Economy*, 99.
8. Angyal, *Loren Eiseley*, 35.
9. Nelson, "Walking," 12.
10. Angyal, *Loren Eiseley*, 57.
11. Wilson, *Biophilia*, 60.
12. Wilson, *Biophilia*, 62.
13. Wilson, *Biophilia*, 62.
14. Wilson, *Biophilia*, 66.
15. See 2.2. Scientific Authority and the Destructiveness of Technology.
16. Angyal, *Loren Eiseley*, 80.
17. Wordsworth, *William Wordsworth*, 35.
18. Blake, *Blake's Poetry*, 19.
19. Blake, *Blake's Poetry*, 21–22.

20. Blake, *Blake's Poetry*, 49–50.
21. Blake, *Blake's Poetry*, 50.
22. Sörlin, "Environmental Humanities," 788.
23. Sörlin, "Environmental Humanities," 788.

PART II
A Fracture in Time

Chapter 4

Time Traveling

Science and Imagination

Long before Eiseley "entered college, he had become aware of the life of past geological periods" and "had never lost his fascination with prehistoric animals" (LN 16–17). Eiseley's imaginative descriptions and scientific discussions of the prehistoric past of humans and other animals are an outstanding feature in his mature writings. Nevertheless, these texts do not just consider the prehistoric past; in them, Eiseley also reflects on the image of modern man and his civilization. This chapter intends to investigate how Eiseley brings his readers back to the ancient past and then forth to the present or even the future, thereby helping us extend our knowledge of humanity and man's place in nature.

If other forms of life accompany humans on the evolutionary road, is man a weaker or stronger creature compared to others? Why did some ancient animals that were physically stronger than man not outlive him? And how did man's brain help him escape the trap of specialization that led to species extinction? Exploring humanity's antiquity, Eiseley argues that man comes from nature but unlike other inhabitants living within nature, he alters nature in order to build his own cultural world. Unfortunately this man-built world has developed in unnatural ways. Man has tried to free himself from the animal past by building a human-centered world where nonhumans are unfairly ignored, hurt, or even pushed into extinction.

He takes it upon himself, as a "changeling"[1] who remembers that origin, to issue prophecies and warnings. Nevertheless, Eiseley emphasizes it is one of the nobler human gestures—caring for others—that first marks a man as human. A prophet and teacher, he reminds us of the survival of man through torrential rains and periods of glaciation. In telling these stories, he urges the twentieth century to see itself through the archeologist's eyes. It is a way for us to imagine the destiny that awaits us as human beings.

4.1. ALIENATION FROM THE NATURAL WORLD—MAN AS OUTCAST

From Fish to Man

Eiseley visualizes the development of *Homo sapiens*, under the influence of Darwin's theory of evolution, in which lower forms of life developed into more complex forms. In the essay "The Snout" from *The Immense Journey*, the first-person speaker recounts a conversation between himself and a friend who reports that in Australia he has seen fishes (at the end of the essay Eiseley shows it is actually the mudskipper) falling from trees. The friend, "one of these Explorers Club people," shows his confusion: "Things ought to know their place and stay in it, but those fish have got a way of sidling off. As though they had mental reservations and weren't keeping any contracts" (IJ 48–49). The explorer represents the point of view that species are fixed and that fishes belong in the water. Fish that fall from the trees seem alien to him, outside the order of nature, and perhaps failing to keep a promise (perhaps to God?) about their role in creation. The friend's qualms provide the impetus for the speaker to pursue a discussion on how to see man's evolution and that of the rest of life. Eiseley's poetic imagination and scientific knowledge allows him to convey his understanding of origin of the species in an original way, and especially to illuminate the immense evolutionary journey that man has made.

Human existence begins dramatically in the distant past, "in all that weird and lifeless landscape," "in the ooze of unnoticed swamps." Humanity "began with a strangled gasping for air" in that hostile environment, but its future was far from being predictable from the inauspicious scene that Eiseley describes. There was only one thing that "could breathe air direct through a little accessory lung and it could walk. . . . The creature was a fish" (IJ 49–50). It is the need for oxygen—the reaching out for air—that drives the fish to walk—the first step on the journey into human form. Like the fish that fall from trees in the explorer's story, the idea of fish walking seems inconceivable. Eiseley certainly wanted to amaze his readers in linking this prehistoric fish to man directly. Eiseley also provocatively uses the word *snout* to describe the breathing apparatus of the various life forms that left the water and proliferated in the swamps. Among many "strange snouts," the creature that is the remote ancestor of humanity escapes "water-failures" and paradoxically "though he breathed and walked primarily in order to stay in the water, he was coming ashore" (IJ 50–51). In his description, becoming man seems to be the opposite goal to the fish's primary purpose. Eiseley makes the story of how the fish walks onto the road to man—the land dweller—interestingly mysterious.

The transition between fish living in the water and man the land dweller in Eiseley's words sounds like a transgression. The departure from the swamp, Eiseley says, "was a monstrous penetration of a forbidden element, and the Snout kept his face from the light.... In three hundred million years it would be our own" (IJ 51). Though Eiseley does not elaborate on the "forbidden element," presumably air rather than water, the image suggests that the transgressive creature risks his life in leaving his familiar territory. A shapeshifter, the Snout violates his natural element and walks out of the waters in order to survive. The word *forbidden* recalls the forbidden fruit eaten by Adam and Eve, who disobey God. Man comes into being when the fish penetrates a forbidden territory; so Eiseley's almost mythical narration of evolution recalls the Bible's account of man's origins. Instead of giving scientific explanations for the steps of evolution, Eiseley makes an imaginative leap and links the image of the walking fish and walking man directly together. Mysterious as the process is, Eiseley here gives it a fabulous dimension, linking it with the journeys of heroic figures, although it is based on the science of anthropology. One may notice that Eiseley capitalized "the Snout," and changes the persona "it" for the Snout to "he" when he begins to refer to the fish as man's ancestor. The creature's departure from water—this uncanny journey—in Eiseley's words "was a stealthy advance made in suffocation and terror, amidst the leaching bite of chemical discomfort. It was made by the failures of the sea" (IJ 54). This statement illustrates the dangers on man's evolutionary road; nature can be terrible and man comes from the failures of water.

The Specialized Human Brain

Following Darwin's theory of natural selection, man the land-dweller comes into being in a struggle with other forms of life: "in the ruthless selection of the swamp margins, or in the scramble for food on the tide flats, the land becomes home" (IJ 55). In this description, man's preference for the land sounds like a retreat rather than an advance, a failure rather than a process to perfection. What then is the nature of man? Eiseley is interested in the question that Darwin posed about the human species—should man be seen as a warrior, "the product of ruthless, competitive forces," or as a "weak-bodied, unarmed primate" (FT 101)? Struggling to justify the theory of evolution, Darwin and his scientific colleagues didn't really know the answer to the question of why a physically weak, almost helpless, creature like man can outlive others.

On this question, Eiseley favors Wallace's view on the evolution of man. In his interpretation, Wallace views man's evolution in two stages: first the physical changes "the product of... natural selection," and then "an evolution of *parts*, specializations promoting certain adaptive ecological adjustments of the individual" (DC 305–6). The first stage conforms to Darwin's theory of natural selection; the second is somewhat different, as it puts other specialized adaptations such as the "seal's flipper or the wing of a bird" on an equal footing with man's "bipedal posture" and free hands (DC 305–6), which indicates a respect for the evolution of all forms of life. Eiseley wants to emphasize how the human ancestor (the Snout) was equal with other early forms of life on the evolutionary road. Man's vital difference lies in another element of life—the second stage of the evolution of man Wallace proposed—the "bodily specialization" that the human brain constitutes (DC 306). Eiseley is not convinced by Darwin's explanation for the rise of the human brain: "a long struggle of man with man and tribe with tribe" (IJ 82), even if it seemed reasonable in his time. Eiseley believes, "something—some other factor—has escaped our scientific attention" (IJ 91). He admires Wallace because he originally "glimpsed this timeless element in man" (IJ 90) and suspected "that the human brain might have had a surprisingly rapid development" (IJ 86). Eiseley proposes his understanding of the development of man's brain. He claims that man's weakness made him dependent on others of his species; "it also involved the growth of prolonged bonds of affection in the sub-human family, because otherwise its naked, helpless, offspring would have perished. It is not beyond the range of possibility that this strange reduction of instincts in man in some manner forced a precipitous brain growth as a compensation—something that had to be hurried for survival purposes" (IJ 92). In order to survive within a hostile environment under pressure from more instinctive animals, man had to develop his own secret weapon—his brain. Affirming his scientific forefathers' studies, discoveries, and discussions on the human brain, Eiseley emphasizes how man's brain allowed him to gain control of his environment. In other words, once "his intellectual powers were strengthened," man was "able to survive on the ground in competition with the great carnivores" (FT 101). The human brain is a more important change than other, more readily observable characteristics, and it allowed him to survive when other big animals became extinct.

As mentioned in the essay, "The Snout," the human brain began in a lowly place. The essence of man's evolution is the growth of the brain, and "the brain had to be fed" (IJ 52); literally the brain and the nerve tissues need oxygen to function. Eiseley compares the different processes of man's brain and that of aquatic life forms—the thin-walled tubes that developed once creatures ventured onto land versus the thicker "solid masses of nervous tissue" of fish in oxygenated waters (IJ 53). Eiseley points out how a different evolutionary path produced the "solid brain," "of insects, of the modern fishes, of some reptiles and all birds. Always it marks the appearance of elaborate patterns of instinct and the end of thought. A road has been taken which, anatomically, is well-nigh irretraceable; it does not lead in the direction of a high order of consciousness" (IJ 53). This discussion of the differences between the brain that humans developed and that of other forms of life underlines the higher order of consciousness attributed to *Homo sapiens*. It confirms Eiseley's argument that man is a changeling, thrust out of nature and its instinctive forms of understanding.

The exceptional nature of the human brain gives man a paradoxical role in the story of evolution, one that eludes some of the scientific theories. Man's brain helps him escape the evolutionary imperative to specialize: "Nature, instead of delimiting through *parts* a creature confined to some narrow niche of existence, had at last produced an organism potentially capable of the endless inventing and discarding of parts through the medium of a specialized organ whose primary purpose was, paradoxically, the *evasion* of specialization" (DC 306). In this interpretation, "Nature" produces a creature that can escape from nature. Whereas other species become more and more specialized, humans escape the trap of specialization that leads to species extinction. Their brain allows them to change with the world and to change their world.

Eiseley gains this view of man by looking at human development through the long stretch of evolutionary time. The present time does not allow one to foretell what modifications will succeed and what will fail: "Who is to say without foreknowledge of the future which animal is specialized and which is not?" (IJ 55). And "it is only now, looking backward, that we dare to regard him [the Snout, man] as 'generalized'" (IJ 56). The uncertainty lies in understanding which specialized feature will be useful in the future. When seen from a narrow perspective, if "we would have thought in water terms," a strange creature like the Snout can be seen as "failure off the main line of progressive evolution . . . scorned by the swift-finned teleost fishes who were destined to dominated the seas and all quick waters" (IJ 56). Man's evolution toward land dwelling would seem to be specialized and doomed to failure instead of "generalized." Eiseley even declares man to be "without doubt the oddest and most unusual evolutionary product that this planet has yet seen" (ST 194). In emphasizing the strangeness in the nature of man and man's evolutionary road, I think Eiseley is trying to change his contemporaries' limited anthropocentric attitude toward nature. If men feel sure of their superiority and feel they are more important, or stronger, or fitter in the race for survival, Eiseley gives them a chill with evidence that other forms of life too solved the problem of adaptation. As he says, "there were many and that they had solved the oxygen death in many marvelous ways, not always ours" (IJ 58). Looking at man's evolutionary road, he sees that we humans are one among many that adapted to a new environment and survived.

Dream Animal

In addition to the question of how man survived the competition with other forms of life that seem biologically stronger than he, there is another question that Eiseley reflects on. If man's developed brain allowed him to find solutions to the challenges of his environment, how did he cope with the changes that his abandonment of intuitive reflexes caused? Eiseley turns away from the idea of man competing against other species and imagines him instead involved in an interior struggle: "Man's competition . . . may have been much less with his own kind than with the dire necessity of building about him a world of ideas to replace his lost animal environment" (IJ 92–93). His reading of Darwin's *The Descent of Man* illustrates his idea that man did fall: "Mr. Darwin. . . . shows that the instincts of the higher animals are far nobler than the habits of the savage races of men" (UU 136). In comparing man with the higher animals, Darwin tried to apply his insights on animal evolution to that of humans; however, he failed to account for this fall from nature into culture. The chaos of man's cultural world sounds out of tune with his theory of life's progress toward perfection.

Eiseley finds helplessness and loneliness in man since he is "bereft of instinctive instruction and dependent upon dream, upon, in the end, his own interpretation of the world" (UU 113). He introduces the legendary cycles of the Blackfoot Indians as a trace of the moment of rupture with the natural world. Speaking of Native American dreams and totem animals, he hypothesizes that once deprived of animal instincts and of nature's instruction, yet still dependent upon their environment, men turned to animals as human helpers and counselors "because they alone remembered what was to be done" (UU 113). Different from cultural man, animals are the real children of nature and thus benefit from nature's instructions and "respond to [the environment] totally" (FT 121). These inhabitants of the universe "reflect their environment but they do not alter it" (FT 121). Only man, in Eiseley's view, constantly tries to alter his environment. The Christian world that modern Western men built took humanity to be above nature, and in Bacon's era, men began to focus only on the power they could exert over nature (FT 138). Man departed further and further from the road on which animals accompanied him; he could not go back because the green forest refuge he has left behind "has been consumed" (FT 139).

Eiseley points out that as a changeling of Mother Nature, man has lost his real home and a return to the past is impossible; that abandoned home no longer exists: "I, like that lost creature, would never find the place called home. It lay somewhere in the past down that hundred-thousand-year road on which travel was impossible" (ST 147). Man becomes homeless and therefore susceptible to nostalgia (from the Greek *algos*, pain, grief, distress, and *nostos*, homecoming), that longing for a lost home.

On the topic of the changeling, Eiseley turns to the transcendentalist Thoreau. In *The Unexpected Universe*, he quotes an extract from Thoreau's *Journal, Volume 2*: "fox belongs to a different order of things from that which reigns in the village,"[2] and he offers his own idea right after it: "Fox is alone. That is part of the ultimate secret shared between fox and scarecrow. They are creatures of the woods' edge. One of Thoreau's peculiar insights lies in his recognition of the creative loneliness of the individual, the struggle of man the evolved animal to live 'a supernatural life.' In a sense, it is a symbolic expression of the equally creative but microcosmic loneliness of the mutative gene. 'Some,' he remarks, 'record only what has happened to them; but others how *they* have happened to the universe'" (UU 140). The last sentence Eiseley quotes from Thoreau is from another book, *Early Spring*.[3] In weaving Thoreau into his text, Eiseley expresses his admiration of Thoreau's perception of nature and he adds his own insight about the creative potential of individual loneliness. He then extends Thoreau's concept of man as an evolved creature that tries to transcend his animal nature and to build a mental and cultural world to his own theory of a mutative gene that produces individual genius. The fox and the scarecrow are for Eiseley figures of outcasts inhabiting "the wood's edge." They are also figures of the poetic imagination standing for those who can respond to the natural world (*"they"* is italicized by Eiseley for emphasis). These outsiders not only record what has happened to them but also their inner experience of the exterior world so that they make an impact upon it—they happen "to the universe." Borrowing Thoreau's words, Eiseley indicates the path to mutual communication between man and the environment; the wisdom of reflecting the natural world through one's inner world.

Homo Sapiens

Another essay, "How Man Became Natural" also gives space for a scientific discussion of the prehistoric past of the human race. Eiseley admits though "the nature of the original animal-man is still a matter of some debate" (FT 109), "man, bone by bone, flint by flint, has been traced backward into the night of time more successfully than even Darwin dreamed. He has been traced to a creature with an almost gorilloid head on the light, fast body of a still completely upright, plains-dwelling creature. In the end he partakes both of Darwinian toughness, resilience, and something else, a humanity . . . that runs well nigh as deep as time itself" (FT 113–14). Thanks to modern science, man acknowledges more about his origin, his animal past; however, to fully understand the humanity of our ancestors, it is important to blend knowledge with imagination. Making unconventional claims about the Neanderthal man, "whom scientists had contended to possess no thoughts beyond those of the brute," Eiseley praises their cultural behavior of burying their dead with ceremonies that suggest their grief. Imagining the meaning of the traces of this ritual activity, he says a "message had come without words: 'We too were human, we too suffered, we too believed that the grave is not the end. We too, whose faces affright you now, knew human agony and human love'" (FT 113). Eiseley imagines hearing these words whispered by the beings who had ceremonies for the dead. He thoughtfully points out the essence of humanity lies in not in physical shape; it is more about the mind and heart: "It is the human gesture by which we know a man, though he looks out upon us under a brow reminiscent of the ape" (FT 113) says Eiseley. It is love that makes a man human. No one can know where this inner light came from, but surely it was not made by man himself (FT 145). There is a force in nature beyond his reach that guides man along the evolutionary road.

Eiseley reads Thomas Browne and quotes his saying "Be not under any Brutal Metempsychosis while thou livest and walkest about erectly under the scheme of Man" as the epigraph for the chapter "How Human is Man?" Walking upright marks the physical change that distinguishes man on his evolutionary path, and his mental capacity, his human intelligence, comes after. Eiseley's choice of this quotation indicates that since man has attained his human form, his mental power should match this physical change; in other words, since man has gained those characteristics that allow him to call himself *Homo sapiens*, he should avoid losing them by acting brutal. If man sees nature as only "something to be crushed, . . . that second order of stability, the cultural world, was, for him, also ceasing to exist" (FT 128). In other words, if human beings view the natural world without sympathy for all life forms, they lose what makes them worthy of being called human, and their cultural world is doomed to vanish along with the natural one.

In conclusion, with immense imagination, Eiseley leads readers back to the primeval swamp where our ancestor the Snout began his transitional road, driven by the vital need of oxygen. Rejecting the idea that man's survival derives from specialization, Eiseley shows readers a new angle of view: compared to other life in the seas, our ancestor the Snout is a failure since he was not fit for life in water, but he adapted in other ways. Man springs from this animal origin. Though it is debatable whether man evolves as stronger than his related animal kin or weaker, it is sure that man draws power from nature to make up for what he lacks compared to other animals armed with fangs or claws. Seen from the perspective of the earth's history, man learns from animals how to survive to fight against darkness, cold, and the unknown in nature. Seeing clearly how man came from nature and established his cultural world, Eiseley emphasizes that it is love for his fellows that makes a man human, though he still carries his animal past physically. Still, Eiseley regards himself as a changeling of Mother Nature because he continues to align himself with the natural world. He opposes himself to other men who try to alter nature and regard it only from a utilitarian point of view. If man insists on remaining detached from the nature from which he sprang, the threat of losing the world that sustains him looms in his future. Eiseley takes his mission to foresee that disaster and to warn humans about it and thus to be a protector of both the human spirit and the environment.

4.2. A NEW JEREMIAD: DREAMS AND PROPHESIES OF DISASTER

A Watery Death

Eiseley offers a personal reflection on a watery death when he describes in *The Night Country* how the young Loren descends underground with a newly found playmate. The narrator is attracted to the boy because of his animal qualities. He is "deceptively slight of build, with the terrible intensity of a coiled spring. His face, even, had the quivering eagerness of some small, quick animal" (NC 19). The boy leads the child Eiseley into a terrifying but fascinating experience in which they go down into the sewer and they are caught in the tunnel when the water fills the pipe. The experience is a brush with the knowledge of death from which the new playmate, whom Eiseley nicknames "the Rat," will extricate him through his skill in negotiating the sewers. In recalling the incident, Eiseley creates a mirror-like structure in which the two boys, face to face, reflect one another, and the older man, remembering, acknowledges his kinship with the rat: "My memory is a rat's memory scurrying with disembodied alacrity through a hollow maze of tubes that exist now only in my head. It turns right and left unerringly. It knows the one way out of a chamber where four black openings yawn simultaneously. Sometimes in that chamber a candle flickers, lighting momentarily another sweat-streaked desperate face" (NC 19). It is not clear whether the "other" face is Eiseley's own or his companion the Rat's. Later he says, "I could see the straining intensity flicker on the Rat's thin face as he turned the candle toward me" (NC 22). Through anaphoric phrases Eiseley links the behavior of an ordinary rat to his own brain and to the boy—the Rat in the recalled story. Are the tubes in his head the labyrinths of the mind or the remembered pipes of the sewer system? The inner and outer spaces are confounded in the telling. What is powerful in this memory is the thrilling loss of identity brought on by the contact with the night world and with the animal. In this personal childhood experience, Eiseley expresses the terror that the watery death brings to small animals like rats and men. When going underground, it is water that takes control, not man.

Another water-related experience inspires Eiseley's contemplation about man's existence in nature and in the vast time scale. In a meditative mood in *The Unexpected Universe*, the speaker looks into a rain pool and draws an analogy between "the occasional spreading ripple from a raindrop or the simultaneous overlapping circles as the rain fell faster" and "the whole history of life upon our globe" (UU 105). He sees the appearance of "the early primates" as something similar to the drops that cause a "wide, sweeping circle" in the puddle, and later, the emergence of "the first men" makes a wider circle, that changes "into a great hasty wave" that swept the mammoths under (UU 105). This analogy offers a quick and comprehensible picture for readers to visualize the natural world before man's emergence and to understand the impact of man's evolutionary road. The passage focuses on the fact that though human beings are initially like little raindrops produced by nature, they have managed to cause massive disasters. Through this meditation, Eiseley infuses a scientific discussion of mankind with his own experience and feelings. Moreover, there is a deeper meaning in the choice of the rain pool to draw this analogy. In his essay "The Angry Winter" Eiseley declares that "for over a million years man, originally a tropical orphan, has wandered through age-long snowdrifts or been deluged by equally giant rains" (UU 98). Through this poetic image that compresses the experience of millennia, Eiseley relates the evolutionary history of *Homo sapiens*: man first appears in the tropical rain forests, and yet survives through rains and snows to occupy practically every space on the earth.

A Snowy Death

Eiseley feels that "illiterate man has lost the memory of that huge snow-fall from whose depths he has emerged blinking" (UU 97). Limited by their inability to imagine the vast time scale of their evolutionary history and with no instruction about the ice age, humans have already forgotten their own history in the blizzard. Eiseley takes it upon himself to remind readers of our past in deep time.

What Eiseley searches for in "the white oblivion of the snow" (NC 227) seems to be indicated in his poem "Why Does the Cold So Haunt Us" in his collection *Another Kind of Autumn*. It is the paradox of life and death the great ice brought that impresses Eiseley. "Today we trace the ice, we learn the temperate zone / once held / gigantic elephants and roving beasts" (AKA 78). The giant beasts of earlier times have disappeared while man remains. Science gives modern man access to the knowledge of that ice age. Through looking back to the ice age, Eiseley shows his readers the full picture of man's place in nature. He warns that the ice will return. Studying deep time gives him an understanding of the future. Eiseley asks the question what has ice with to do with man's history and he answers that "it has, in fact, everything" (UU 107). Cold "accompanied the birth of man" (UU 101), and what's more man is "a survival from a vanished world" (UU 101). In his eyes, "man is the product of a very unusual epoch in earth's history" (UU 98), for "our species arose and spread in a time of great extinctions. We are the final product of the Pleistocene period's millennial winters" (UU 97). The extinction of other species serves as a warning to humanity. If men survived the ice age and witnessed how it could wipe out other species, the cold might once again surprise forgetful men. In poems and essays Eiseley speaks in a regretful tone of man's survival in periods of extreme cold.

A prophet and teacher, Eiseley reminds us of this history. Paying attention to geological history will permit us to relativize the period in which we live: "With our short memory, we accept the present climate as normal. . . . The ice has receded, it is true, but world climate has not completely rebounded. We are still on the steep edge of winter or early spring" (UU 108–9). Here he foretells the planet's warming, but he also warns that the ice "will march back again." The disaster of cold desolation may again strike men who cannot "outthink ourselves" (AKA 78). Eiseley's eyes are focused on a far horizon; in measuring man's place in the vast scale of time he reveals man's insignificance in time. He points out that the Pleistocene episode when man is newly emergent (UU 102) is "insignificant as a pinprick on the earth's great time scale" (UU 103). Looking back to man's escape and survival from one catastrophic episode of the time scale, Eiseley postulates that man also trembles before the vastness in space and time; in spite of science, the comprehension of nature is always beyond man's full reach. He wonders whether humanity is capable of understanding "an intangible abstraction called space-time" or whether we are bound to "shiver inwardly before the endless abysses of space as [w]e had once shivered unclothed and unlighted before the earthly frost" (UU 104). Eiseley links man's ancestral horror of winter with his similar terror of space-time.

Lost Habitat and Small Dreams

One of the ecological disasters this nature writer and archaeologist looks at thoughtfully is the disappearance of wildlife in the industrialized human world. Eiseley once notices a giant slug "feeding from a runnel of pink ice cream in an abandoned Dixie cup" (NC 229) at the suburban shopping center. Creating quite a shocking effect, he draws an analogy between the slug and a creature emerging from the sea onto the shore: "I began to realize it was like standing on a shore where a different type of life creeps up and fumbles tentatively among the rocks and sea wrack. It knows its place and will only creep so far until something changes" (NC 229–30). This comparison obviously corresponds to man's evolutionary road, in which "the Snout" emerges from the water failures. Eiseley connects the image of the giant slug to the image of Crossopterygian—man's long-departed ancestor. Actually, in a certain way, their form does seem alike and the slug can also be both a water and land creature. However, this analogy is quite surprising because the creature from which *Homo sapiens* originated into the modern man who takes pride in his advanced status is linked with a somehow repugnant little creature that man never gives a look at. There is even the hint that this slug that has adapted to man's waste products may transform someday into a new species. Maybe that's why the speaker sees the small area (a runnel stained with dropped pink ice cream) where the slug is feeding as "the wild-rose thickets" (NC 230) that accord with the tropical forests where man's life came into being. Though interested in and caring for small beings like the slug, a bee, and the "scurryings" gathered in the runnel, the speaker knows that as commercial centers like "Wanamaker suburban store" keep on coming, their lives or thousands of other "obscure lives were about to perish" (NC 230).

The essayist tells another story in the first person about one day returning and seeing mud on his carpet—the result of a mouse coming to his apartment and digging into his flower pots. The speaker never sees this mouse; he knows of his passage only from the traces left behind: "I realized I had a visitor" (NC 230). This declaration echoes Thoreau's expectation of a visitor whom he never saw. Here in the fanciful and humorous vein of his famous nature-writing predecessor, Eiseley describes crossing paths with wild creature who seeks its lost green world where flowers are planted in the earth and where it can pleasantly make its hole. Strongly influenced by Thoreau's idea about the spirit within nature, Eiseley says that the mouse dreams of finding a secure home in nature once again: "It was a small dream, like our dreams, carried a long and weary journey along pipes" (NC 232). Here "a long and weary journey" echoes Eiseley's above-mentioned story of his adventure with his childhood playmate "Rat," who leads him down sewers and through pipes risking a watery death, but emerging safe and sound. Comparing the mouse's imagined dream of the earth to man's dreams of exploring the unknown, he observes that both man and mouse undertake "a long and weary journey." The diminutive mouse has a small dream just like man. Both look for a secure home and a place to live freely.

Dreams in Darkness

Dreams are vital to Eiseley since they signify both human and animal aspiration and also the work of the imagination: "great art is the night thought of man" (UU 64). Man's meditations during the night or his dreams nourish his inner world and "they can be interior teachers and healers as well as the anticipators of disaster" (UU 64). Insofar as the imagination can instruct, it can aid the scientist. Eiseley tells of an experience where he once had to crawl toward darkness when he had crept into a cave as part of an archeological exploration: "I lay on my back, finally, and the outside world seemed far away and infinitely wearying as a place to which to return. I was in a room meant for a king's burial" (NC 26). Eiseley's narrator admits he is drawn to the cave by something. Lying in the ancient tomb, he says, "Some in the world of light desire the darkness. I saw that then more clearly than before. The whole infinite ladder of life was filled with this backward yearning. There were the mammals who had given up the land and returned to the sea; there were fish that slept in the mud, birds that no longer flew. Probably also there had been hairy men who wept when fashion tore them from their caverns" (NC 26–27). This imaginary act of lying on the ground like one long dead inspires Eiseley to meditate on ancient man's attachment to place and to the womb-like caves that sheltered him long ago. He emphasizes the historical values of other ways of living as well as modern man's.

Lying in the chamber in the cave is about experiencing death and the past. Another deep underground experience Eiseley provides is about reviving. He relates an anecdote about the time he and his companion archeologist "panic when the air gives out deep within a cave."[4] Experiencing the darkness and threatening lack of oxygen, Eiseley gained an exceptional insight. When he and his colleague finally find the way out: "by the time I stood at the cave entrance I was looking at life, at my companions, at the traffic below on the road, as though I had just arisen, a frozen man, from a torrent of melting ice. I wiped a muddy hand across my brow. The hand was ten thousand years away. So were my eyes, so would they always be . . . I did not find a way to speak" (ASH 109). The experience renders the speaker speechless but plunges him deep in thought. As a man living in the present, he comes to see life as if he had revived after the ice age. The two underground experiences inspire Eiseley to conclude: "the modern world was small, I thought, tiny, constricted beyond belief. A little lost century, a toy" (ASH 109). Looking back at the life-and-death experiences that accompany man's road, Eiseley understands that the modern era is brief and man's achievements, small.

Double-Faced Mankind

Eiseley finds a parable about the destiny of men in a ghost story by Walter de la Mare in which a traveler meets a mysterious stranger on the road "who has about him, though he is clothed in human garb and form, an unearthly air of difference" (BMD 64). The stranger has the other-worldly aura of one of those Greek gods who visits mortals in disguise. He asks for directions and when the traveler points out "the road to town, the road of everyday life," the "person of divinatory powers" rejects it, for he seems to see "in it some disaster not anticipated by ourselves" (BMD 64–65). Eiseley interprets this story as a warning that his compatriots' careless daily life conceals some future disaster, some unseen threat: "The road we have taken for granted is now filled with the shadowy menace and the anguished revulsion of that supernatural being who exists in all of us" (BMD 65). Eiseley is like both the traveler and the seer in de la Mare's story; he implies that everyone should pay attention to "a person of divinatory powers" who sees the future and can prevent humanity from setting foot on the wrong road. Eiseley himself writes about the enigmas he encounters in both literature and in nature. In his poems and essays, he meditates on the strangeness within normal life, for it holds clues to men's destiny.

In a similar vein to this ghost story, Eiseley tells of a quest for "certain curious and rare insects . . . stick insects which changed their coloration like autumn grass." Though this is normal for a naturalist, what he discovers moves the anecdote into the realm of the uncanny: "It was a country which, for equally odd and inbred reasons, was the domain of people of similar exuberance of character, as though nature, either physically or mentally, had prepared them for odd niches in a misfit world" (BMD 91). Here Eiseley draws likeness between insects and people; both have the capacity to change forms. The statement recalls his writings on man's evolutionary journey: physically—from a walking fish to a walking man and also mentally—where man submits to the cruelty of ice and ends by imitating its relentless power (UU 99). Again Eiseley refers to man as a stranger in "a misfit world," a failed water-dweller, and a remnant of the ice age.

When the stormy, wet night falls, Eiseley's speaker gets lost and asks directions of a farmer who is driving two horses in a wagon that rushes by. He has a frightening vision of a "horror-filled countenance" (BMD 92) because with a bolt of lightning he sees the farmer's face is "two faces welded vertically together along the midline" (BMD 93). The speaker realizes that "I saw the double face of mankind. . . . I saw man—all of us—galloping through a torrential landscape, diseased and fungoid, with that pale half-visage of nobility and despair dwarfed but serene upon a twofold countenance. I saw the great horses with their swaying load plunge down the storm-filled track. I saw and touched a hand to my own face" (BMD 93–94). Eiseley extracts the symbol of mankind from this vision of the man with two faces: humanity's animal past juxtaposes modern civilization. Human history is divided between "nobility" and "despair." Thus, Eisleley echoes the "supernatural" story that Walter de la Mare tells and asks the exact same question: "Which . . . is the way?" (BMD 64) for man's future and his culture.

A hundred-year-old anecdote extends Eiseley's discussion on this topic. Two English gentlemen witness an uncontrollable coach running downhill, with a cliff before it. They bet money on the coach going over the cliff, but their waiting comes to nothing. Eiseley compares this story to the situation of modern man: "The lunging, rocking juggernaut of our civilization has charged by. We wait by minutes, by decades, by centuries, for the crash we have engendered. The strain is in our minds and ears. The betting money never changes hands because there is no report of either safety or disaster. Perhaps the horses are still poised and falling on the great arc of the air" (NC 61). His prophetic interpretation of this vision is suspended, undecided, like the horses, between "safety or disaster." He then recounts his own experience of recognizing an oracle. On a midnight train, in the same compartment with Eiseley, the conductor asks a ragged derelict for his ticket. The man then asks to buy a ticket to wherever, which symbolizes for Eiseley the terror of an open-ended universe. Eiseley then meditates on the end of man. Seeking answers, Eiseley brings up his contemplation of nature. He thinks, "in time, nature would be spoken of as the second look of God's revelation. Some would regard it as the most direct communication of all, less trammeled by words, less obscured by human contention" (NC 68) and "nature, the second book of the theologians, would prove even more difficult of interpretation than the first" (NC 68). Although this idea that nature holds a revelation suggests the transcendentalists, for Eiseley the book of nature is less open and direct than the one his American predecessors imagined. Its opacity comes precisely from the fact that it is never stable, it is always moving into the future, into a zone of darkness that is both inspiring and terrifying: "Nature, as I have tried to intimate, is never quite where we see it. It is becoming as well as a passing, but the becoming is both within and without our power" (NC 54). Eiseley lacks the optimism of the transcendentalists, for he has seen how the industrial world that was just beginning in their time has developed. He warns us that "modern man, for all his developed powers and his imagined insulation in his cities, still lives at the mercy of those giant forces that created them and can equally decree his departure" (UU 98–99). He announces his prophecy of disaster for modern men.

To conclude, through the long evolutionary road, *Homo sapiens* is not satisfied to remain only a tool-maker; aided by science, he expands his sensory perceptions so far that he becomes too confident to believe any longer in mystery. Waving goodbye to his animal environment, he establishes his cultural world, his own version of the natural world, and continues to build his web outward in time and space. Eiseley warns that this confidence may be a form of hubris: "Man, I concluded, may have come to the end of that wild being who had mastered the fire and the lightning. He can create the web but not hold it together, not save himself except by transcending his own image. For at the last, before the ultimate mystery, it is himself he shapes" (UU 66). For him, man holds a power drawn from nature that he cannot fully control. What's more, his restless mind—his quest to master all—may bring disaster in the future. Man's road to an unknown future—his escape route from his own confined world—finally means changing himself. But in reaching beyond his limits, in remaking himself, he may no longer be able to live within a green world that respects all forms of life.

A modern archeologist and evolutionist, Eiseley inspires his readers' interests in man's evolutionary path and recalls how man has diverged from his animal antiquity to finally become an outsider, alienated from nature. Eiseley calls humans changelings because they are out of place in the natural world. He believes man has fallen out of nature, and that he now destroys the green world that man as animal depends on but which he has forgotten. The twentieth-century nature writer fears that the only world that wildlife knows (the natural world) is vanishing due to the expansion of the industrialized human world. Eiseley reveals that both man and the small animals seek a secure home and a place to live freely. Man's loss of the green world and the past has brought on a loss of habitats for animals and plants; Eiseley finds that the solution lies in affirming an attachment to place.

Eiseley advocates a return to the green world of nature and the suggestion he provides need not be seen as regressive. Modern men need to perceive the shaman's prophecy of disaster shadowing their path to the future. He warns that the ice will return and "a nature still / as time is still / beyond the reach of man" (NA 22). Eiseley urges the double-faced mankind, whose animal past juxtaposes his modern civilization, to pay attention to the visitors in the guise of various small animals in man-made settings. He learns long ago from a watery near-death experience that in the night world, man can get lost. Animals can serve as men's helpers and counselors—the perception the indigenous peoples grasp through their belief in totem animals.

NOTES

1. As man has alienated himself from the natural world, Eiseley describes him as a changeling, which in English mythology refers to a fairy child exchanged for a human child.

2. Thoreau, *Journal, Volume 2*, 89.

3. Thoreau, *Early Spring*, 326.

4. Angyal, *Loren Eiseley*, 24.

Chapter 5

Resolution

Lessons of the Past

Eiseley observes that the problem of his era is the burden of history people carry behind them and yet neglect to acknowledge: "Our age, we know, is littered with the wrecks of war, of outworn philosophies, of broken faiths. We profess little but the new and study only change" (FT 118). Modern men have become obsessed with the new and hence oriented toward change at all costs, so that "the future has become our primary obsession" (IP 105). In modern technological civilization, science somehow holds out deceptive promises of a bright future to men, and the future-oriented society urges scientists to pursue omniscience, which in Eiseley's view is impossible for any man. Though clearly not wanting "to denigrate the many achievements and benefits of modern science" (IP 105), Eiseley encourages the objective study of the way science is conducted, and he reveals the subtle relationship between the scientific laboratories and industrial business. Even more dangerous to the earth is the lack of balance between scientific pursuits and the rhythms of the natural world.

For Eiseley, America, with its new faith in science and technology and its orientation toward the future, has lost its sense of history and its relation to the past. He ponders the idea that "man . . . is a time-binding animal" (FT 167), meaning perhaps that he governs his life by measuring his existence in time. If this is so, the modern attitude to time changes that mode of being: "The erasure of history plays a formidable role in human experience" (IP 100). Taking the American westward movement for example, Eiseley regrets that the American Indians have had their way of life destroyed and their peoples decimated. The lack of respect for the past has something to do with these upheavals. Still the lure of the frontier myth haunts him. Like many Americans, he cherishes the dream of turning westward into the future: "Why far to the west does my mind still leap to great windswept vistas of grass or the eternal snow of the Cascades?. . . I will tell only because something like it is at war in every American heart of the last of the westering crossing. The net closes; I age, but I still look sidelong for escape" (LN 238). The "war in every American heart" may refer to the conflict between memory and forgetfulness, between an attachment to the past and the call of the future. "The net" refers to the awareness of the limits of individual capacity that comes with age. Science is like youth, confident in its capacity to mold the world to its desires. The humanities teach respect for the past and the lessons it can yield, as well as a sense of the different beliefs held by different peoples. Eiseley discusses the divergent attitudes of traditional and modern men regarding time and nature. The gap between the two visions depends on how much (or how little) their minds and acts demonstrate a sense of time as cyclic and natural. Offering his speculation upon life and death, Eiseley helps modern readers see the meaning of living in mortality as well as living with a sense of infinity. To indicate man's insignificance in time and man's arrogance about the illusion that he lives in the center of the world, he emphasizes the biodiversity in the natural world and stresses the necessity of fostering it. For Eiseley, the future of man is just as uncertain as the continuation of other species.

Since Eiseley advocates that man should learn from the past so as to prepare to live a better future, he discusses the proper way to look at the past. As an anthropologist, he studies the remnants of bygone civilizations: "You try to see what the ruin meant to whoever inhabited it and, if you are lucky, you see a little way backward into time" (ASH 223). The "ruin" refers to the real monuments of departed people, but symbolically it can also refer to lost civilizations or, again, in a narrower sense to an individual's life. Whether talking about an individual's life history or that of all humankind, Eiseley knows it is impossible to "dig into every cistern for treasure" (ASH 223), to exhaust all the material resources. This is why Eiseley chooses to reveal himself through fragmentary memories, as discussed in the preceding chapter. At the same time, the material resources that the scientist can excavate are not enough to perceive the full picture of a people's history; the humanistic angle of view and the romantic imagination are also strongly needed.

5.1. TIME-OBSESSED MODERNS

Future-Oriented and Causal Time

Eiseley draws an analogy between men and their inventions—in particular their civilization. Each civilization can be seen as having a personality. He believes that the West has been the most intensely aggressive "particularly in the last three centuries which have seen the rise of modern science" (IP 103). He explains "When I say 'aggressive,' I mean an increasingly time-conscious, future-oriented society of great technical skill, which has fallen out of balance with the natural world about it" (IP 103–4). Very clearly, Eiseley points out that the twentieth century's problem is that man dreams that with his technology he can build a better, man-controlled world. Eiseley warns that this man-made world is already causing many serious problems, in particular, the conflict between technology and the green world from which he sprang.

Eiseley questions the wisdom of the so-called "Green Revolution" said to have occurred between the 1930s and 1960s. Modern technologies were put into use to solve the problem of providing food for the planet; however, other problems like the reduction in biodiversity of agriculture and wilderness came right after it. Eiseley's skepticism about the success of this phenomenon is quite prophetic: "we are immediately encouraged to believe in a 'green revolution'. . . . [which] even if highly successful, would not long restore the balance between nature and man" (IP 106). Time-obsessed modern man is inclined to believe in his ability to alter the present and create the future with his technologies, but is he able to foresee the consequences of his actions? Eiseley fears that his contemporaries neglect to inquire whether this unnatural man-invented phenomenon destabilizes an ecology that has taken centuries or even millennia to develop. To evaluate what is at stake in the "green revolution," a long-term perspective would be necessary, yet scientists cannot predict its consequences. Eiseley ironizes that: "the social world is stubbornly indifferent to the elegant solutions of the lecture hall, and that to guide a future-oriented world along the winding path to Utopia demands an omniscience that no human being possesses" (IP 106). In the twenty-first century, decades after Eiseley's death, some of the negative effects of intensive agriculture are becoming obvious.

The relentless pursuit of scientific knowledge and the power it represents is "the final culmination of the Faustian hunger for experience" (IP 109). Like Faust, who made a pact with the devil to exchange his own soul for unlimited knowledge and worldly pleasures, modern men aim to pursue material comforts and eliminate all the mystery of the universe. In Eiseley's view, modern society regards science as "a kind of twentieth-century substitute for magic" and the scientists play the role of the soothsayers (IP 105). Pondering the "popular" and "promising" futures guaranteed by scientists, Eiseley compares modern men's obsessive faith in science to the desperation of the sick: "contingencies multiply at a fantastic rate and nations react like fevered patients whose metabolism is seriously disturbed" (IP 106). All the possibilities described by scientists tempt modern men to put their faith in the promised wonders. Eiseley holds back, however, believing that the scientist "does not possess marked political power, yet he has transformed the world in which power operates." His role as seer brings with it "dangers and exacerbations" (IP 106). We already know that science and technologies driven by political power and other types of human power threaten disaster not only to humanity and modern civilization but also to the whole planet.

Instead of treating science as magic, Eiseley urges the objective study of its structures and institutions.[1] He studies the relationship between science and the industrial society. He observes the subtle process of how scientific research gets involved with business in the society of consumption: "With the passage of time and the growth of the urban structure, funds for research and development take up a far greater proportion of the budget of a particular industry. . . . [T]he laboratory and its priesthood take an increasing share of the profits as they become a necessity for business survival" (IP 104). Industrialization and urbanization cannot develop without scientific research; their innovations depend on the scientist in his laboratory. Thus, increasingly, scientific research demands the lion's share of industrial profit. An objective view of the links between scientific and commercial interests would lift the cloak covering the scientist-soothsayer with his magic of technology.

The problem that Eiseley points to in twentieth-century Western civilization is that man pursues only short-term goals: "The attempt to leap forward into the future or grudgingly to accept the fleeting moment as the only abode of man is particularly a phenomenon of our turbulent era" (IP 111). If man sees "the fleeting moment" as his "only abode," he will exploit the earth that sustains its inhabitants. It is no coincidence that man the time effacer becomes also the world eater. Brushing aside the importance of the past in understanding the future is a form of willed ignorance. Both historical time and geological time—deep time—give a sense of perspective that is lacking in modern society. Cutting oneself off from the past means cutting oneself off from human culture: "We have abandoned the past without realizing that without the past the pursued future has no meaning, that it leads . . . to the world of artless, dehumanized man" (FT 130). Without an awareness of where they have come from, humans are de-natured, no longer human.

Eiseley points out that modern man focuses only on his technological time and ignores the vastness of what he calls "earth time." Even though the time effacer, modern man, believes in "continuity and causality," he "unconsciously" resents them (IP 109); they are seen as afflictions that destroy "the magic of genuine earth time" (IP 110). Time is linear for modern man and it is measured carefully and in units. Eiseley finds "causality plays a significant role in our thinking because we have been stitched together from the bones and tissues of creatures which are now extinct" (IP 107). Humans are survivors of the ice age—a geological time of great extinctions. Once we become aware of that evolutionary history, causality governs our way of thinking. Our evolutionary road is erroneously seen as inevitable rather than the product of many unpredictable circumstances. He points out that "as our knowledge of the evolutionary past, has increased, we have unconsciously transferred the observed complexity of forms leading up through the geological strata to our cultural behavior" (IP 107). In building his cultural world man takes evolution as a process aiming toward perfection—his own perfection. Because of his secret weapon—the brain—with which he escaped the specialization that led to species extinction, man assumes that he has achieved the finality of evolutionary advancement. He allows the fossil record to confirm his sense that he is master of the world.

Even if man thinks that he knows his evolutionary past well, there is still mystery concerning it, especially as far as the human mind is concerned. We now know something about life's origins, but "[evolution] the idea, the structure itself, however, looms ever vaster and more impenetrable. It is linked with the mysteries within the atom as it is also linked with that intangible, immaterial world of consciousness which no one has quite succeeded in identifying with the soft dust that flies up from a summer road" (DC 325–26). In Eiseley's interpretation, our knowledge of our development, though accumulated for three centuries, still resembles a vast maze. The idea of evolution is researchable at the material level—through such things as fossils and carbon dating—however, there is something unsolvable in it and it has something to do with the immaterial. Science alone is not enough to explore this dimension of human existence and something beyond science is called for.

There are still puzzles beyond what man can conceive, even with his science, as Eiseley exemplifies, "Though science has enormously extended the cosmic calendar, it has never succeeded in eliminating that foreknowledge of the non-existence of life and of individual genera and species which the Christian creation introduced" (IP 107). Man has not eliminated the mysteries about the world before life appeared. Even the questions about the varied species or sexes of humans or nonhumans that the creation myth of Genesis tries to explain cannot be fully answered. To Eiseley, man seems small and ineffectual in front of the world that his science has revealed: "This world of the prisons is the world of man; the vast maze offers no exit" (IP 107). He uses the image of the "prison" to indicate humanity's limited vision of the universe. Aware of the limits of knowledge, Eiseley worries that scientists are entrusted by modern society to answer "questions involving the destiny of man over prospective millions of years" (IP 105); and he declares that "the future may be guessed at, but only as a series of unknown alternatives" (IP 108). He urges his readers to see that the future is rather unpredictable. As an evolutionist and anthropologist, Eiseley wants us to regard earth time with awe and consequently to examine man's acts critically in the modern era: "'to know time is to fear it, and to know civilized time is to be terror-stricken'" (IP 102). To sense the power of time is to feel "terror" because of what is going wrong in the present.

Different Measures of Time

Eiseley compares modern and traditional cultures and shows a huge gap between how those two groups see their places in the web of life, in nature, and in time. Most cultures acknowledge their links to animals in some way, but their attitudes to it are widely different. Eiseley believes that "man knows he springs from nature and not nature from him. This is very old and primitive knowledge, a genuine scientific observation of the foretime" (LN 153). Time-conscious modern man has much knowledge concerning his evolutionary road; he knows that life began in the swamps and that he comes from nature. However, having been busy building his own cultural world, he ignores this older understanding. Modern man is alienated from his origins; he has forgotten how his ancestors revered nature as the divine mother (FT 131). Now that this ancient history has been laid aside in favor of "the rise of science and its dominating role in our society," modern man tries to shape and control nature (FT 131). The results of the two ways of thinking are different: in modern technological civilization the relations between man, science, and nature are unbalanced, as man tries to dominate his environment; on the contrary, "on a subsistence level of economic activity, the primitives[2] had actually arrived at an ecological balance with nature" (IP 114). What's more important, those other cultures had rituals and myths that "created another world of reentry into that nature upon a psychical level" (IP 114). Like many intellectuals of his time, Eiseley characterizes people from non-industrial cultures as primitives, but unlike many of his contemporaries, he does not use the term condescendingly, for he praises the primitives' mentality. In depending on the environment for subsistence, they needed to attune themselves psychically to nature. These peoples' respect for the material world means that they neither destroy their environment nor provoke ecological disasters; there is a balance between their living world and nature. In their spiritual world, the native inhabitants of their land attained something that modern men fail to acquire—the ability to reconnect with nature and reenter the green world from whence they came.

Modern science and technology help shape modern man into the world destroyer. Eiseley declares that "man is basically not a consciously malicious time effacer" (IP 113), and "is not by innate psychology a world eater"; however, "the rise of Western urbanism, accompanied by science, produced the world eaters" (IP 114). Eiseley holds out the hope that man by nature is not condemned to damage the earth and forget his past. He finds the contrary, positive example in looking at modern men's brothers—the indigenous peoples. In exploring their living environment, these traditionally minded peoples were curious about the unknown. They learned the harshness in nature and then chose to "mythologize and thereby make peace with it" (IP

114). Modern men can learn from this different attitude to nature, finding in it ways to avoid becoming the planet destroyer and the time effacer.

Fixed Custom and Illusion

Human beings' worldviews—their world of custom—can threaten the environment that they depend on. Eiseley believes that the moderns have lost their former place in the world, where they lived according to the laws of nature, establishing instead "a substitute for the lost instinctive world of nature." Culture took the place of nature: "Custom became fixed: order, the new order imposed by cultural discipline, became the 'nature' of human society. Custom directed the vagaries of the will. Among the fixed institutional bonds of society man found once more the security of the animal. . . . But the security in the end was to prove an illusion" (FT 124–25). While modern society finds its own world of custom secure and fixed, Eiseley feels this is an illusion because it ignores the power of nature.

Eiseley believes that "there is something wrong with our world view" as "we see ourselves as the culmination and the end" (IJ 57). Further he explains that "so far as the Christian world of the West was concerned. . . . The earth was the center of divine attention" (FT 125) and "it is this religion, par excellence, which took God out of nature and elevated man above nature" (FT 138). He blames Western Christianity for the split between man and nature, since it places man above other forms of life. In answer to a man who protests that to deny "we are the end" is "to deny God" (IJ 57), Eiseley takes a walk in a swamp and marvels at the potential for new forms of life that he sees.

Eiseley emphasizes that we are not the center of the universe. He looks into the past from which man evolved—"the old road through the marsh" (IJ 59) and helps us see more clearly man's smallness compared to the spectacle of life visible there. There is no essential form, for everything is in flux: "The eternal form eludes us—the shape we conceive as ours. . . . We are one of many appearances of the thing called Life; we are not its perfect image, for it has no image except Life, and life is multitudinous and emergent in the stream of time" (IJ 59). In this perception, man is one aspect of various forms of natural life, so a complete understanding of nature and time is still far beyond man's reach. Eiseley urges modern people to acknowledge man's limited, anthropocentric worldview and to realize that "among the many universes in which the world of living creatures existed, some were large, some were small, but that all, including man's, were in some way limited or finite. We were creatures of many different dimensions passing through each other's lives like ghosts through doors" (UU 51). Eiseley puts different forms of life—large or small—side by side, and puts man on the big stage of the universe, part of the vast spectacle of life, and he observes that each type of life is somehow finite and yet mysterious to other forms. Living in different time dimensions and experiencing their surroundings differently, humans and other-than-humans inhabit "many universes." All can coexist, even without encountering each other, haunting the same space, "passing . . . like ghosts through doors." Through metaphor and paradox Eiseley captures his wonder at the endless variety of the universe. In this way he links the material world with the abstract idea of time.

The writer's poetic imagination conceives of other ways that man's evolutionary past may possibly turn out, thus allowing readers to understand the relativity of time. Eiseley sees humans as "remote descendants of the Snout," one among many other possibilities that could have taken shape during man's transitional states; we could have been "mammalian insects" or "more likely we should never have existed at all" (IJ 52). Creating a shocking effect, he leads man to realize that the life forms that later changed into man had the potential to become many other things. Those who in the present think that as human beings they embody the eternal and perfect image of God might never have existed at all.

That we are the only species privileged with the prospect of eternity is man's own small dream, an illusion. He sees the world from the narrow perspective of human eyes, ignoring all the possibilities of the natural world and the universe. A perceptive naturalist and evolutionist, Eiseley reminds us that though we have abandoned the ignorant belief that the sun revolves around the earth, our view of the natural world and life is still restricted. He asks, "What if we are not playing on the center stage? What if the Great Spectacle has no terminus and no meaning?" (FT 118–19). These questions challenge the self-satisfaction of scientific society and humans' certainty about the oncoming future. Eiseley's writing denies man's role as the center of the drama of life or as the dominator of the world. The illusion that nature exists only for humans' benefit will be swept away in the constantly onrushing future, and the realization that nature benefits and includes all forms of life needs to be acknowledged with a gentle and tolerant heart.

The limitations in modern man's worldview are particularly evident in his vision of the future. Eiseley doubts the scientist's cheerful announcement that humans have "some ten billion years of future time remaining" (IJ 56–57). Modern man's certainty about his far-reaching and promising future seems illusive, for it stems only from the restricted human viewpoint, or worse, from a man-centered (or man-privileged) perspective. Eiseley declares that we have not only got the wrong worldview, but also we conceive of the relationship of the past, the present, and the future wrongly: "We teach the past, we see farther backward into time than any race before us, but we stop at the present, or at best, we project far into the future idealized versions of ourselves" (IJ 57). Modern scientific knowledge allows us to see the past more clearly than any previous generations; however, unfortunately we focus on only human interests and imagine humans' future to be static and endless. When twentieth-century man imagines the future, Eiseley says the descriptions "involve just one variety of mankind—our own—and they are always subtly flattering" (IJ 128). White men like to think of men of the future as white (IJ 129). Eiseley is upset that modern society's worldview is a narrow and arrogant one where all other possibilities of life are excluded (IJ 139).

Ironically, Eiseley's students' projections of how the future would look can be found in the fossil record from times past, in the bones found on a South African beach. When he shows his students the skull, they see the humans of the future, with a bigger ratio of brain to face, like "our children of today" (IJ 132). The students who habitually dismiss the past as irrelevant unknowingly take that prehistoric skull as the ideal model of the future man. Eiseley is disappointed that modern youth are comforted by the image of man of the future as "somebody with a lot of brains and will save humanity at the proper moment" (IJ 129). The lesson allows him to make an important point: "The need is not really for more brains, the need is now for a gentler, a more tolerant people than those who won for us against the ice, the tiger, and the bear. The hand that hefted the ax, out of some old blind allegiance to the past fondles the machine gun as lovingly. It is a habit man will have to break to survive, but the roots go very deep" (IJ 140). He puts aside what the common man imagines evolutionary advancement to be—the enlargement of the brain—and turns to emphasize the gentle heart. He declares that the violence that helped primeval men to fight against the tiger and the bear is no longer necessary for surviving now. It is the tolerant man that needs to survive for the future. Maybe modern man needs to drop the feeling of triumph about excluding other forms of life along his road of development; and as the descendant of the primeval world, the hard-hearted modern man needs to get rid of the belief in the individual's competitive struggle as the key to survival and to break the habit of destroying and killing others with his weapons.

Biodiversity

To show what is wrong with man's worldview and his self-image, Eiseley recounts the evolutionary history of planetary biodiversity. He wants to insist on its marvelous dimension. It is miraculous that "the evolution of a lifeless planet eventually culminates in green leaves" and "only after long observation does the sophisticated eye succeed in labeling these events as natural rather than miraculous" (UU 96–97). The transformation from lifelessness to liveliness is a miracle to him. In his essay "The Snout" in *The Immense Journey*, Eiseley's speaker expresses his attraction to the octopus and other odd creatures that people usually tend to find frightening. He sees the variety of life as "heartening," because "it gives one a feeling of confidence to see nature still busy with experiments, still dynamic, and not through nor satisfied because a Devonian fish managed to end as a two-legged character with a straw hat" (IJ 47–48). Humorously, Eiseley sketches a caricature of the Darwinian theory of evolution in which man is the perfection and end of the whole process; in contrast, he reminds us that nature is still busy creating all sorts of other-than-human life forms. He celebrates the dynamism of nature and life. Therefore, he cautions readers to "never make the mistake of thinking life is now adjusted for eternity" (IJ 48). Humans' certainty about their own centrality makes them ignorant about the continuously changing flow of life.

Human encounters with animals can lead readers to recognize the diversity of life. To awaken readers' interest in this subject, Eiseley uses narratives to approach the subject from an unusual angle. For example, he retells an episode from Homer's "Odyssey" in which the disguised Odysseus returns to his home and is recognized immediately and welcomed by his dying dog, Argos. Whereas humans fail to know the hero after his long absence, the dog loyally acknowledges him. For Eiseley, "the magic that gleams in an instant between Argos and Odysseus is both the recognition of diversity and the need for affection across the illusions of form" (UU 23). Man and dog have a bond that transcends the differences of species. More than that, the dog has a form of knowing that is unavailable to men.

Eiseley shows his appreciation of animal diversity elsewhere in his writings when he describes how people see (or ignore) the animals whose paths they cross. He tells a story in which a young lady charges her professor with anthropomorphism (UU 151) when he mentions "a tiny deer mouse, a wonderfully new and radiant little creature of white feet and investigative fervor whom I have seen come into a basement seminar upon the Byzantine Empire" (UU 150). In contrast to the young woman's skepticism, the professor wants to see the mouse's apparent interest in the seminar as a sign of some future evolutionary transformation: "who is to say what may happen when a mouse gets a taste for Byzantium rather beyond that of the average graduate student? It takes time, generations even, for this kind of event to mature" (UU 151). Eiseley's speaker has more confidence in the mouse's interest in the lecture on time and bygone history than in that of a human student. Fancifully, the professor describes the incident as "something like Alice in reverse" (UU 151). Rather than a child following a rabbit down a rabbit hole into a magical world, the mouse follows the lead of humans into the future. Enigmatically, he says that it takes generations "for this kind of event to mature," suggesting that in generations or millennia it may be mice or any other-than-human life forms instead of *Homo sapiens* that survive the test of time and nature.

Eiseley's narrator expresses his disappointment that his concept about time is misunderstood by the young woman who, although she represents the new generation, "'is evidently part of a conspiracy to keep things just as they are.... This is what biologically we may call the living screen, the net that keeps things firmly in place, a place called now'" (UU 152). He reveals the narrow view of twentieth-century youth about the possibilities of interactions between humans and animals. The young woman concentrates only on the human present and believes that species' places in nature are fixed. She fails to understand Eiseley's perception on life's diversity and species' evolution. In his notebook, Eiseley records his apprehensions about the dangers of misunderstanding time: "A society whose youth believe only in the Now is deceiving itself: A now that is truly Now has no future. It denies man's basic and oldest characteristic, that he is a creation of memory, a bridge into the future, a time binder. Without that recognition of continuity, love and understanding between the generations is impossible. A true Now standing all by itself is the face of Death" (LN 197). He urges his readers, especially the youthful ones, to keep the future in their eyes in order to live the present well, because man carries his history, and the past exists as a bridge to the future. He warns us that if man only pays attention to the present moment, he is facing a dead end.

In his essay "Big Eyes and Small Eyes," Eiseley tells another story about how a rat seems to be an intellectual messenger to man. During an eloquent speech in which an American writer eulogizes humans' power over the earth, Eiseley describes how he catches sight of a rat under the writer's chair. The rat "upreared himself and twitched his whiskers with a cynical contempt for all that white-gowned well-clothed company" (NC 34). Eiseley's efforts to personify the rat can not only be sensed by the personal pronouns "himself" and "his," and the humanizing expression "cynical contempt," but also, his expression of the feeling that "for an uneasy moment that the creature might ironically applaud" (NC 35). Through this anecdote Eiseley criticizes anthropocentric attitudes that take nature to be merely the raw materials for human endeavors. He tries to reduce the difference between human and animal. He claims that the rat holds a message for humanity.

In these two incidents in which intelligent rodents listen to either a historian's speech on the perished Roman civilization or a novelist's boastful lecture about man's power in shaping and altering the earth, Eiseley shows his awareness of the possibility of new evolutions and of the need for biodiversity on "the living screen known as the biosphere" (UU 157).

Eiseley's conception of biodiversity is supported by Edward O. Wilson, who devotes his writing to questions of environmental conservation. In his book *Biophilia*, Wilson says "the urge to affiliate with other forms of life is to some degree innate, hence deserves to be called biophilia."[3] Like Eiseley,

Wilson emphasizes the importance of interaction between humans and other creatures. How much have humans influenced nonhumans? And what responsibilities should humans take for the problems in the natural world, including a big issue like species extinction? Wilson's essay, "The Conservation Ethic," gives a very clear answer to those questions. He explains why men should care for the environment and why too much pessimism is counterproductive. The assumption that we can solve the problem once and for all is unrealistic; the important thing is to begin to care more and to change behaviors. However, he regrets that "in our own brief lifetime humanity will suffer an incomparable loss in aesthetic value, practical benefits from biological research, and worldwide biological stability."[4] In many historical periods humans lived in harmony with nature, so "human destructiveness is something new under the sun."[5] Why do the moderns think that they can control and conquer the world? Industrial progress may be to blame, but Wilson suggests that "little can be gained by throwing sand in the gears of industrialized society, even less by perpetuating the belief that we can solve any problem created by earlier spasms of human ingenuity."[6] Like Eiseley, he focuses attention on the importance of developing humanity's contact with nature even within an urbanized environment. He suggests we inquire: "why people care about one thing but not another—why, say, they prefer a city with a park to a city alone. The goal is to join emotion with the rational analysis of emotion in order to create a deeper and more enduring conservation ethic."[7]

To build a conservation ethic is very complex, however. People tend to inquire about the purposes of almost everything. Our judgment of the value of the nonhuman, both animate and inanimate entities, is often based on their functions. Wilson explains that people fail to think of the very distant future and are unwilling to sacrifice personal interests for remote descendants. "The difficulty created for the conservation ethic is that natural selection has programmed people to think mostly in physiological time."[8] Like Eiseley he feels that people have difficulty conceiving of a span of time beyond the immediate present. He suggests that "only through an unusual amount of education and reflective thought do people come to respond emotionally to far-off events and hence place a high premium on posterity."[9] Therefore, moral reasoning is the practice humans must develop to assume their responsibilities.

Wilson bases his argument for conservation on the importance it represents for human beings. He appeals to our instinct for self-preservation, warning readers that "the destruction of the natural world in which the brain was assembled over millions of years is a risky step."[10] Hence ecologically sound practices are for our own good; preserving the natural environment sustains our species and personal genes. Yet to do this, we need to pay attention to preserving all that is other-than-human, something that will take a great effort: "the one process now going on that will take millions of years to correct is the loss of genetic and species diversity by the destruction of natural habitats."[11] Humans cannot afford to lose the natural world's diversity and to bear the results of species extinction.

Great Man? Greater Nature

Foreseeing the disaster of species extinction, Eiseley urges modern men to be in awe of something bigger than themselves—the earth. He compares the earth to a living being and uses the pronoun "she" to describe it, embracing the rather unscientific view handed down from antiquity of seeing nature as a mother or a goddess. At the same time, he anticipates the Gaia thesis, developed in the late twentieth century by James Lovelock and Lynn Margulis and promulgated in our own century by Bruno Latour. In Eiseley's eyes, the earth is capable of producing life as a female does. He emphasizes the earth's potential for creation, particularly her biodiversity: "Earth is the mightiest of the creatures. . . . She is the wariest and most complete of animals, for she lends herself to no particular form and in the end she soundlessly forsakes them all. . . . The rest, including man, are in some degree fragmented and illusory" (UU 148). In his interpretation, earth tolerates all forms of life, and man is only a fragment of a greater whole; thus man's appearance seems transient in the coming and going of life in earth's time.

Eiseley senses the potentiality of violence in modern man that would lead *Homo sapiens* down the road of self-destruction and points out that "our acts may ensure the disappearance of our species from the earth or, on the contrary, that we, like these small-brained, massive-jawed forerunners of ours, may be the bridge to a higher form of life than has yet appeared. 'Mother Nature . . . lets things make themselves.' There is a great deal in that remark for the human species to ponder" (DC 292). Rather than seeing man as Nature's final accomplishment, Eiseley is certain that in the future humans will either become extinct or they will develop into another form of life. Mother Nature deals with man as she does all the other life forms—"lets things make themselves"—the problem is how humans—the changelings who have strayed outside of nature—respond to her.

Prophetically, the twentieth-century naturalist warns his readers to be wary of the messages coming from nature because "nature sends no messages to man when all is well. . . . When man becomes greater than nature, nature, which gave him birth, will respond. She has dealt with the locust swarm and she has led the lemmings down to the sea. Even the world eaters will not be beyond her capacities" (IP 115). Eiseley foresees that nature will respond to the world eaters' incursions upon the planet Earth; he gives the examples of locusts and lemmings to indicate what may equally happen to modern men. The locust swarm causes great damage to agriculture and the green world in their mass migration; the lemmings are known for the strange habit of "suicide" by blindly jumping into the rivers or seas when in migration. Through the two examples, Eiseley says that the world eaters (interestingly the locust and the lemming are known for their quick consumption of plants too) cannot escape nature's retribution. In his words, nature takes an active role in dealing with the locust swarm or the lemmings; however, it is they themselves that rush to their own deaths or periods of extinction. Here Eiseley warns that with the increasing human population and mass migration to urban areas, in which "process" the green world is rapidly and destructively consumed, nature or rather man himself will lead the species to a dead end.

In traditional cultures, Eiseley says, a "shaman might have found a raven to carry" the message from nature to man (IP 115). A raven, especially in the cultures of the Native Americans, is usually spoken of as a creature of knowing. Showing his respect for this literary and cultural tradition, Eiseley emphasizes the importance of communicating a warning to his contemporaries. Native Americans would receive this message either from the wise man (shaman) who foresees the future and who is aided by the knowing animal (raven) as the messenger. For modern man, the naturalists—Leopold, Eiseley, Wilson, or their followers—have to take on the shaman's role.

To conclude, regarding the short scale of human life in the vast span of geological time, Eiseley observes the brief era of his own technological civilization and reveals that "the rise of a scientific society means a society of constant expectations directed toward the oncoming future" (IP 104). He condemns the attitude of modern American men about time and is upset that his society focuses on only the immediate present or the future that seems right before their eyes and dismisses the past. In Eiseley's eyes, though modern men and the native peoples are brothers in nature, the gap is widening between "degraded remnants of the hunting folk" and "the world eaters" (IP 114) because of their different worldviews. Eiseley urges modern men to reenter nature as the indigenous peoples would do and retain awe for the unknown in life and time. Maybe by achieving this perspective, modern men can gain a new and different attitude toward their environment and their past and thus their future. While practicing science and technology in his modern era, man should keep his eyes on the future not only in the sense of technological time but also that of planetary time. Eiseley reminds readers that man is neither the beginning nor the end of life, of nature, or of universe. The green world holds the keys to the biodiversity of life within it, and as only one element of the biosphere, man should respect nature's power.

5.2. THINKING BEYOND THE MODERN SPLIT

Questions about Mortality

In the course of his writings, the naturalist-philosopher inevitably turns to questions about mortality. Eiseley goes to childhood for a moment that "must have raised a first question in my mind about mortality" (LN 239): "I can still remember with astonishment a boy in my backyard telling me triumphantly, 'If anything hits your heart, you will be dead.' Dead? I did not understand the word. . . . Death did not come so easily. I knew because, being early of an experimental cast of mind, I had promptly struck myself. . . . I am sure that my failure to die, whatever that meant, did not convince me that I was immune to natural law" (LN 239). He didn't die in this childish experiment but he learned that he was not "immune to natural law," for the conversation intimates that man cannot escape death's inevitability.

Another childhood memory that stimulates Eiseley to think about mortality is the toy that accompanied him when he was little. In his poem "The Face of the Lion," Eiseley's speaker refuses to accept that his lion is only a child's toy. It has a face, reminding us of the importance Donna Haraway gives to face-to-face relationships with animals in *The Companion Species Manifesto*. As the speaker gets older it accompanies him still; it becomes a reminder of his mortality. Addressing the lion toy as "he," Eiseley's speaker shows his thoughts about the significance that one can give to a cherished object and thus the power the object in turn offers to man. Eiseley's speaker is not afraid of his own final hour and sees death as an uninterrupted sleep into which "no light ever came" (NA 24). This echoes Hamlet's famous soliloquy in which he compares death to a sleep. It also resonates with Momaday's dialogue between a bear and God called "Dreams" in which the bear reverses those terms: "what sort of concept is sleep anyway? It is a bit like death if you ask me."[12] In "The Face of the Lion," death comes in the guise of his lion, an animate messenger who helps him understand and accept his mortality. In this poem, the beginning and end of a human life converge as Eiseley brings together a childhood memory about clutching the mane of the lion when he was frightened by his mother's violence and the apprehension about dying felt by an aged man clutching the remnants of childhood memories. The "greater dark" (NA 25) refers not only to the dark room in which the child huddled up with his lion toy but also, in an abstract way, to death, or further, to the void in the universe. If death is darkness, with the kindness that something or someone provides even only in memory, an aging man can get comfort when he has to face his own dying hour. The toy lion symbolizes that kindness—the kinship can be found with animals as well as humanity. "To . . . the watcher I will trust my sleep" (NA 25) suggests both that the lion toy is the watcher and also that the "watcher" can be an abstract image—the end of man in earthly time. The earth's deep geological time will witness the end of one man's life, and to it man can trust his eternal sleep.

The man-made lion toy is not the only object that Eiseley links with the image of death; there are things in nature that serve as carriers of Eiseley's meditations on death too. The imaginative linking of facts and symbols to fathom the meaning of death is never lacking in Eiseley's prose and poems. For example, Eiseley compares man's death to that of autumn leaves: "If men could only disintegrate like autumn leaves, fret away, dropping their substance like chlorophyll, would not our attitude toward death be different? Suppose we saw ourselves burning like maples in a golden autumn" (LN 115). Would our fear change if we imagined ourselves as "burning . . . maples in a golden autumn"? The images make human death seem more beautiful and more acceptable by being linked to the natural processes of plant life.

The poem entitled "A tropical swamp at midnight" also compares life and death in nature to human existence. The speaker describes several images of life hovering above the seemingly dead tropical swamp in an eerily tranquil scene:

> A green uncertain glow wavers eternally
> Green phosphor flames
> Nod prettily and blossom wide
> On sucking, bloated mud . . .
> Green phantom flowers of light
> Drift on the black water
> And fade . . .
> Fade . . .
> Far back
> In the endless caverns
> Of cypress . . .
> And darkness . . .
> And death.
> So, on the trembling morass of consciousness
> Float the pale
> Flowers of remembrance
> Until the brilliance fades to green . . .
> The green to blue . . .
> And they sputter . . .
> And go
> Out. . . . (LN 23–24)

The poem begins with a description of the swamp strangely lit up at midnight by the exhalations of gas; then it turns to make an analogy of how human life begins and passes away. The words "uncertain" and "eternally" indicate the metaphysical thought about the meaning of life that the tropical swamp represents. The seemingly macabre scene of the swamp may be unpleasant to common people, since the words "sucking, bloated mud" evoke something dead and decomposing. Nevertheless, the poem makes the swamp come alive, and its emanations appear pretty and flourishing as the initially "uncertain green" transforms into "flowers of light." Then, as the lights fade far back in the endless cavern of cypress, readers are taken back to the era of the primeval world—before men. The dark and dead water resembles the darkness and death man's ancestors struggled against in order to survive. The poem's last few lines turn to a meditation on the brain, memory, and death. Human memories are "the pale / Flowers of remembrance," like the ephemeral images cast up by the swamp, for when a man ages and faces his dying hours, forgetfulness conquers remembrance and the bright memories fade. Still, as they disappear they change color: the pale flowers turn to green like the swamp and then to blue. The blue that comes just before extinction recalls the blue worm that will take everything in the end, evoked in the essay "The Blue Worm," where Eiseley mentions his mother's death. He expresses the natural procedure of a man's life, from growth to death in the change of color here. In his writing, Eiseley does not express fear of ghosts or death as common people do, maybe because he sees the human species in the broad sweep of time and places mortality among the constantly evolving expressions of nature.

The Material World and the Dreamtime World

As an American of settler stock, Eiseley is greatly interested in the life and history of the American Indians; it seems there is an inevitable connection between the two peoples. First, Eiseley speaks of the link with his personal history: "a gene or two from the Indian, is underwritten by the final German of my own name" (LN 238). Tracing his inheritance, Eiseley identifies with the American Indians, believing that somewhere in the past he has an Indian ancestor or two. Nonetheless, he believes their civilization has faded in the twentieth century, for he claims that he was born into a silence left when "the bison had perished, the Sioux no longer rode" (LN 239). Literally "born into that silence" reminds us that he was born in the house of his deaf mother, but there is also the suggestion that the civilization of the American Indians had been suppressed into silence.[13] The settlers' westward movement changed the homeland of the North American Indians.

Eiseley relays a vision of the American territory in which the indigenous peoples' way of life and the natural life forms that corresponded to it have diminished or disappeared. He contemplates a rather desolate scene: "Only the yellow dust of the cyclonic twisters still marched across the landscape. Of that dust my body had been made. . . . I knew its anger in the days of the dust bowl" (LN 239). Eiseley's speaker declares in a poetic phrase that the dust of the Midwest made him. He refers to his real geographical origin, but he also echoes the Bible story of how God formed man from the dust of the ground. However, Eiseley's phrase also has a scientific origin, for he knows that bodies are formed from the elements available in the landscape. If the land usually sustains living things, it can also become destructive. He mentions the famous dust bowl that occurred in the 1930s to remind modern man of the destructiveness of the drought, which can be seen as a sign of nature's anger and power in responding to man's reckless abuse of the environment. The dust can destroy man as well as make him. Putting the two facets of nature's power together, Eiseley warns that nature will react with force to what men have done to the earth and her inhabitants.

Eiseley has an anthropologist's interest in the civilization of the Native Americans and studies the possessions that scientists have garnered from them for clues about their owners' lives and their beliefs. He muses that "'where is magic there is no death'" (IP 110), suggesting not only that magical beliefs have the power to sustain life, but also that the magical objects themselves have a form of immortality. Eiseley gives the example of a small Pawnee medicine bundle that he examines. The medicine bundle is a precious possession used by American Indians for prayers and other ritual activities; it is a necessary component of their spiritual lives. When the modern anthropologist touches the bundle, he meditates that "the bundle held in my hand had been a sacred object among a people who believed implicitly in its powers and who understood the prayers and fastings through which the owner had been instructed. I was an outsider to whom the nail could never denote more than a nail, or the flaked weapon stand for more than a bygone historical moment" (IP 110). Eiseley's speaker understands that the objects inside the bundle offer different meanings to him and to its original owners. If to the modern observer the bundle includes an ordinary nail and a piece of flaked agate, to its previous owner, the things are not inert objects but powerful things endowed with magical capacities. The twentieth-century anthropologist regrets that he has no access to those mysterious forces. In his hands they have become demystified and relegated to the past: "no way of telling from this cracked receptacle what powers had been given its possessor or what had been his dreams" (IP 110). More than regret for the lost meaning of the rediscovered objects, Eiseley's anthropologist feels sorry that the magic the objects carried and the spiritual life its owner had are forever inaccessible to modern man's eyes. They can be examined as museum objects, things that tell the story of antiquity, but something escapes the observer's physical eyes and cannot be fully grasped—the meaning behind the object. Through this anecdote, Eiseley shows his dissatisfaction with modernity's objectifying and mortifying gaze. Hence, in Eiseley's writings we sometimes find expressions of weariness with his profession. The scientist's gestures are like the undertaker's or the mortician's: "I, . . . who had been in my time a burrower among tombs, as well as a wielder of the dissecting knife in anatomical laboratories, had had enough" (ASH 230). Even when he describes modern man's skill in burrowing and dissecting in the pursuit of knowledge, we can sense a degree of weariness: "the time dimension, by the use of other sensory extensions and the close calculations made possible by our improved knowledge of the elements, has been plumbed as never before, and even its dead, forgotten life has been made to yield remarkable secrets" (FT 118). Through the tone of speech, it seems Eiseley is less proud than the average twentieth-century scientists about the ability to eliminate the mysteries of the "dead, forgotten life." The sensory extensions and calculations can reveal secrets, but they cannot bring anything back from the dead.

Thus, Eiseley shows the limits of scientific knowledge and mechanical experiments in approaching time past: "they would tell me, at best, only how living phantoms can be anatomically compared with those of the past. They would tell nothing of that season of the falling leaves or how I learned under the night sky of the utter homelessness of man" (ST 148). Modern science can help the present man see the material aspects of the past, for example, the similarities between the DNA of modern humans and that of the Neanderthals; however, it cannot regain the vitality that existed but has now disappeared from the living world. Man's mental reactions toward the world cannot be regained by the scientific method. A poetic imagination and a humanistic view of the past are also needed.

Ideally, scientific observation would be combined with humanistic speculation as a method of approaching the past, since the material world and the mental world are interrelated in human experience. The Australian aborigines' thoughts about the living present and the future impresses Eiseley; in the cosmic vision of these peoples there are two kinds of time that coexist: "the time of human beings and the time of the supernaturals" (IP 111). He explains, "man, in his human time, subsists also in a kind of surviving dreamtime which is eternal and unchanging" (IP 112). The belief in dreamtime is the religion of Australian aborigines, and it is very specific to them. In their totemic society, "both men and animals come and go through the generations a little like actors slipping behind the curtain, in order to reappear later, drawn through the totemic center to precisely similar renewed roles in society" (IP 112). In this thought, time is cyclic and one's life does not end because it will return again in a similar or different form of life. This aboriginal belief inspires Eiseley's own thought that time is cyclic and natural.

Eiseley admires how the two different scales of time can coexist at the same time, so that quotidian life is permeated with intimations of eternity: "the common day of ordinary existence" is coterminous with "the period of 'dream time' or dawn beings which precedes the workaday world." To conjure up this shimmering, "elusive, . . . immaterial" form of time, he speaks of the Australian aborigines' dreamtime as "an autumnal light" (IP 112) that suffuses the everyday world. Since the dreamtime is sacred time, "it is, in reality, timeless; past and future are contained within it" (IP 113). Though living the visible present, the aborigines also live in a timeless dimension. The "timelessness, the happy land of no change," Eiseley says, is the world beyond reality that Plato searched for in his theory of forms, and in his contemporary Margaret Mead's words from her poem "Absolute Benison," this ideal world is the "'world of the first rose, and the first lark song'" (IP 113). Eiseley finds an echo of his idea of the eternal world—the world above the material world, the natural world—in Mead's poetic words.

Thanks to the beliefs of the native peoples of Australia in the two scales of time, Eiseley learns how to imagine how a mortal living being can also exist in eternity. Through totemic rituals, the aborigine "has remolded nature in mytho-poetic terms. . . . As closely as mortal can manage, he exists in eternity" (IP 113). To achieve this, he has to seek out the company of animals that bring counsel from divine powers appearing in his dreamtime. This is an approach to the environment that the future-oriented modern man has dismissed and should learn from. The aborigines hold their land sacred because of their belief that "the divine beings still exist, even though they may have shifted form or altered their abodes. Man survives by their aid and sufferance" (IP 112). They have knowledge that modern science has swept aside, although in doing so it has narrowed man's vision of the world. Eiseley asserts that "the acceptance of the supernatural is a widening of our grasp of the universe, its own numinous quality, which the man who sticks to daylight fails to grasp, for the universe itself is as supernatural as the great white whale" (LN 234). With these words, Eiseley explains why he introduces the topic of the indigenous Australians and their belief in dreamtime—to make modern people aware of another way to see the universe, one that widens their vision of nature and time. The universe, as Eiseley interprets it, is like the white whale in *Moby-Dick*, which can be seen as a symbol for the power and the unknown in nature that man should hold in awe and carefully watch instead of recklessly working to capture and destroy it.

Memory and Forgetting

In his poem "The Face of the Lion" the speaker meditates on the wisdom of investigating the personal past. The metaphors he uses to describe such acts of interiority are drawn from his profession as an anthropologist. The speaker looks back on his life as one immersed in the relics of the past and asks what remains of that lost time. He has spent his time with "ash heaps," "broken skulls and shards," (NA 23) images that are easily connected to death; and he creeps in "sepulchral chambers" (NA 23), places where the long-departed lie. In the manner of someone repenting of a crime or a mistake, he says he rescinds those activities. It seems his digging is paradoxical: he is looking for "living hours" (NA 23), but while he searches among the dead, he wants the past to remain undisturbed. The investigation into his own past life—"the terrible archaeology of the brain" the search for "one simple childhood thought"—inspires terror (NA 23). Thus, the ability to forget is as important as the ability to remember.

Momentary glimpses of things or scenes can stimulate Eiseley's personal memories of the past and provide the impetus for him to work out his thoughts on time. He narrates an incident of one such momentary perception in the chapter "The Last Neanderthal" from *The Star Thrower*. He describes a scene glimpsed from a window as an adolescent: "Before me passed a broken old horse plodding before a cart laden with bags of cast-off clothing, discarded furniture, and abandoned metal. . . . The wagon had been passing the intersection between R and Fourteenth streets when I had leaned from a high-school window a block away, absorbed as only a sixteen-year-old may sometimes be with the sudden discovery of time" (ST 141). To the young Eiseley, the worn-out old horse and the things men have abandoned—clothes, furniture, and machines—all give him "a deep nostalgia for the passing and unrecoverable moment."[14] As he declares in the essay, "the junk man is the symbol of all that is going or is gone" and the youth regrets that "no one can hold us. Each and all, we are riding into the dark" (ST 141–42). One meaning of this sentence is that the wagon is riding out of the schoolboy's sight, and he will never see it again; the deeper symbolic meaning is that each individual's life is helplessly passing away into oblivion. "Riding into the dark" evokes the end that all living beings will ride to—death. Though the darkness is connected with death, it could also be the future—both are unknown to the observer in the present.

In desperation, Eiseley's narrator decides not to forget this scene of the junkman departing before his eyes. If he keeps it in mind, then it will never be gone. Indeed, this scene can still replay in his memory, though the young boy becomes the old professor, and the man on the wagon and the old horse are long dead. Eiseley is thus content about his belief in "the powers latent in the brain" (ST 142). The brain preserves memories. This incident stimulates his wonder about the brain: "a starving man's brain will be protected to the last while his body is steadily consumed. It is a part of unexpected nature" (ST 143). Obviously, time consumes a man's body by imposing physical changes, yet his brain can recover and preserve memories and let time past live again; in other words, it seems the old man's brain can keep the youth alive. Eiseley attributes this marvel of the way the human mind can preserve or hold the things or scenes that are gone to the unexpectedness of nature and the universe. However, he also condemns the fact that this unexpected quality of life fails to get deserved attention from "the rational universe of the physical laboratory" (ST 143). They take too much for granted the everyday marvels of things such as energy provision or the organization of animal, plant, and human life.

Eiseley reveals man's dilemma in the face of time: "There are two diametrically opposed forces forever at war in the heart of man: one is memory; the other is forgetfulness" (IP 97). The past relates to what happens in the material world, though the human brain holds memories about it in the mental world. Eiseley classifies the first world as "the life of the world we call natural," and he contrasts it to "the second visionary world evoked in the brain of man" (ST 150). This speculation can be attributed to his interpretation of Bacon's "second world" that "could be drawn out of the natural by the sheer power of the human mind" (ST 150). The sense of time happens in man's visionary second world where the experience of the natural world can be stored or can be reworked by the brain into a new image.

Eiseley insists on the importance of making a distinction between the first world and the second world even though they are related and convergent: "The secret was to travel always in the first world, not the second; or, at least, to know at each crossroad which world was which" (ST 152). Knowledge of vast geological time teaches him this secret. His emphasis on traveling in the first world is, I think, to make man appreciate the flow of time in the natural world and to realize that man's second world can be illusory and individual. To differentiate one from the other helps to balance the relation between the past and the future, and between the material world and the mental world. Eiseley urges modern man to live within the natural world so that when he tries to draw out his own second world, he will know what natural order was, or is, or in what sense it can restored (ST 150).

Eiseley claims that for modern people "science, as it leads men further and further from the first world they inhabited, the world we call natural, into a new and unguessed domain, is beguiling them" (IP 106). He argues that the twentieth-century scientific society should not fix its regard only on the present but needs to pay attention to the past, and even the scientific method demands an understanding of history. The cultural contexts of scientific research need to be taken into account. Bacon, the forefather of modern science, "was dreaming of the new world of invention, of toleration, of escape from irrational custom" (ST 150) not of the world of artless, dehumanized men that Eiseley fears in his own time. While modern science seeks to exhaust the knowledge about the natural world and become future-oriented, modern man is engaged in the process of inhabiting "the second visionary world" (ST 150), and the conflict between the two worlds is becoming increasingly serious and dangerous.

Seeing the Past and the Future

Eiseley encourages modern man to see deeply into time and pay attention to the continuity between the past, the present, and the future. However, the concept of geological time is difficult, and it is not easy to understand the past while living in the present. Eiseley is aware that "when the past intrudes into a modern setting . . . it is less apt to be visible, because to see it demands knowledge of the past, and the past is always camouflaged when it wears the clothes of the present" (ST 145). He illustrates this idea in his essay "The Last Neanderthal" with an anecdote about meeting a young girl whose face carries the features of an ancient people. The encounter happens when Eiseley's speaker is a young man, and his team of young researchers goes bone hunting in a region where "the country people were reserved and kept mostly to themselves" and a young girl with strange features delivers them food (ST 144). In Eiseley's words, the young girl is a throwback to the last Neanderthal—"she herself and her ulnar-bowed and golden-haired forearms were a part of a long reach backward into time" (ST 146). He sees the girl's physical appearance as a bridge to a distant era of the past. So a modern youth encounters an ancient ancestor—a resurgence of the past in the present.

Eiseley's narrator has personal sympathy for the girl after gently though briefly talking with her. He worries about the future marriage of the "last Neanderthal girl" and her descendants: "It would be her fate to marry eventually one of the illiterate hard-eyed uplanders of my own kind. Whatever the subtle genes had resurrected in her body would be buried once more and hidden in the creature called *sapiens*. Perhaps in the end his last woman would stand unwanted before some fiercer, brighter version of himself. It would be no more than justice" (ST 146–47). Through Eiseley's description that "by modern standards she [the young girl] was not pretty" (ST 145); and though the girl possesses "powerful thighs, the yearning fertility" (ST 145), he knows that "hard-eyed" modern man would not appreciate her and the fate of the gentle girl is to marry the unmatched "illiterate" modern man. What's more, he is disappointed that the girl's "subtle genes . . . would be buried" in a child of *Homo sapiens*, through which we can sense Eiseley's regrets for the extinct Neanderthals. He contrasts them favorably with the men that superseded them. Ours, in Eiseley's eyes, is a fiercer species. He mourns over this imaginary tragic fate of the girl—"more than an injustice." He speaks apologetically of the injustice modern man imposes in condemning the girl and her kind to a fading existence. It is we "who eliminated her long ago" (ST 145). Is it the inevitable course of time that creates this injustice or it is the hard-hearted modern man who makes the fate of the girl so sad? The incident stands for more than just the destiny of a single girl. It has to do with "some agonizing, lifelong nostalgia, both personal and, in another sense, transcending the personal. It was—how shall I say it?—the endurance in a single mind of two stages of man's climb up the energy ladder that may be both his triumph and his doom" (ST 147). Something hurts his gentle heart; it is something "personal" stemming from his sympathy for the girl, but also something "transcending the personal" arising from his meditation about the fate of the whole of humankind. Evolution means climbing up "the energy ladder" so that when a form of life reaches the peak (and this is how modern man thinks of himself), then the bottom inevitably waits for it, and the bottom presages disaster, maybe species extinction. Is this a hint for modern man who is so boastful about the certainty of his existence, his conviction that he has attained the highest order of creation with his technological civilization? Is Eiseley suggesting that a fall awaits him?

Though Eiseley may have made up this incident (ST 143),[15] he presents readers with a compelling image of the last Neanderthal girl, and also he creates a live conversation with her that allows the modern youth to access her thoughts and also to lay careful and gentle eyes on her physical appearance. Eiseley asks us to see the girl through both scientific and humanistic eyes so as to realize the fate of our own species—*Homo sapiens*.

Eiseley foresees the fading of *Homo sapiens* in this meditation by identifying with one of the last Neanderthals. His genotype is destined to disappear just like theirs: "the code changes by subtle degrees through the statistical altering of individuals; until I, as the fading Neanderthals must once have done, have looked with still-living eyes upon the creature whose genotype was quite possibly to replace me" (UU 59). He imagines that some day, *Homo sapiens* will face the same fate as the last Neanderthals—to see new human species eliminate them. Nature and the genetic code play a game of chance with *Homo sapiens*. Why does Eiseley hold up the possibility for humans living or flourishing now to see with their own eyes the disappearance of their species, or to see a new type of living being to replace them? It is difficult to imagine that long centuries after his own century, human genes will have altered so much that future creatures would be radically different from modern humans. Will humans still be called "humans" on that day? Will contemporary humans become "obsolescent" in those new creatures' eyes? Eiseley's imagination and his portentousness force readers to think deeply. If they devote time and energy to that thought, the world eaters who focus on the present and project themselves confidently into the unknown future may become more attuned to the tenuousness of their putative domination of the planet.

Ice and Indians

The feeling of nostalgia for ancient life, especially for the ones whose characteristics modern humans continuously carry within themselves is expressed not only in the above tale about the last Neanderthal girl but also in a poem Eiseley writes about his own physical relation to his remote ancestors. "Men Have Chosen the Ice" illustrates the idea that men carry the marks of time within them. The speaker offers his personal family tree, claiming that his grandparents carry physical characteristics of the ice-age men and Indians. The speaker himself carries neither of those physical marks and speaks of himself as a "compromise" (NA 29). The literal interpretation of "compromise" is that he blends the genetic mixture of his grandparents so that it is no longer visible; the further meaning is that he is the newcomer born from a compromise that the native "buffalo people" (NA 29) made between themselves and the colonizers, a kind of truce between the "pale fighting blue" and the "fierce black" (NA 29). The speaker recounts the history of the contact between peoples whose dwelling on the land can be traced far back and the newcomers—the white settlers. Whereas the speaker respects that history, telling "tales / in the Medicine Lodge" and carrying on the ways of the first peoples by "offer[ing] the pipe," (NA 30) the descendants of the newcomers reject history, coldly turning away from their responsibilities to the land and its first people.

Moving beyond the personal meditation on his ancestors, Eiseley ponders the fate of the whole of humankind. When the speaker "see[s] the beginning and the end" (NA 30), he may refer to his awareness of the way contemporary American society came into existence and came to dominate the land, possibly moving toward its destruction. This may refer to the settler myth of the "vanishing Indian." On the other hand, he may also refer to the prospective end of settler culture—the ice blue of the colonists' eyes may presage the return of a natural phenomenon like the ice age that will alter the face of the land and make them disappear. The ups and downs of one family's history make Eiseley see the beginning as well as the end of humanity. He knows few will take the proffered peace pipe, and his discussions about the forgotten history and the lost traditional human values will not get much of their deserved attention. The "red pipe from the sacred quarries / miles away in Minnesota" (NA 29) is a holy thing, very important to prayers and ceremonies for the American Indians, who regard the pipestone and the grounds where they can be found as sacred. Nevertheless, "few will take it" (NA 30) now, perhaps because in Eiseley's time fewer natives lived in their traditional way after the settlers' interventions and so fewer descendants will take the pipe, or perhaps it refers to the fact that the knowledge of the sacred ceremony has been effaced by modern men, so that fewer understand the pipe's meaning than before. In violently effacing the past, "Men have chosen the ice / before its return" (NA 30). The poem thus hints that men have chosen to be as cold and unfeeling as the ice, for elsewhere Eiseley mentions that man "himself has retained a modicum of that violence and unpredictability that lie sleeping in the heart of nature" (UU 98). The violence man has done to the earth as well as the inhabitants living on it may finally lead to another violent result in the oncoming future; the ice will come back and modern man may become extinct just as mammoths and others had done in the past ice age.

Learning from Former Civilizations

As an archeologist, Eiseley's work concerned the study of former civilizations. He hopes that modern society can learn lessons from them. In his note titled "Autumn—A Memory,"[16] Eiseley records a visit to Aztec ruins: "Red and somber, with many lights on purple stone the afternoon was fading" (LN 22). Here, the speaker experiences the actual afternoon fading, but as he stands before the ruined monument, his description evokes the fading of the ancient civilization. "Red and somber" refers to the color of the sunset on the purple stones, but also conjures images of the blood, death, and darkness that accompanied a defeated civilization. Eiseley is therefore looking for the reason for the disappearance of the Aztec culture and finds that it may have gone because "prayers and the gay-colored prayer stones . . . lost power" (LN 22). The Aztecs' purple stones for prayers correspond to the pipestone in Minnesota and the pipe that the North American Indians used for ceremonies. Though geographically Minnesota and Mexico are different places, the similar imagery in the two texts suggests Eiseley believed that the Native Americans inhabiting those two places might have practiced similar ceremonies in their spiritual lives. His meditation fits into a tradition of meditations in American literature on the discovery of the remnants of former cultures discussed by Gesa Mackenthun. Eiseley's speaker suggests that the holy and magic power failed the native peoples who prayed, and whatever their dreams were, when the power failed, their dreams and their existence came to an end. Although it seems curious for a modern scientist like Eiseley to give an explanation that draws on the indigenous peoples' mythology, I think he intends to make modern readers wonder what will happen when the power of science that they regard as magic also fails the future-oriented men. Will the fading and then disappearance of technological civilization follow that of the Aztecs?

Standing before the Aztec ruins, Eiseley feels lonely, maybe because he is the only visitor before the ruins or because he senses the isolation of the people that departed while their monuments remain before the modern man's eyes. He says, "It is a lonely thing to look on men's broken handiwork and muse wide-eyed over their disappearance . . . Still, perhaps it was their dust that floated in a slight breeze over the ruined wall" (LN 21–22). There may be real dust floating above the ruins, and this happening in the material world stimulates Eiseley to see it as the ghostly remains of the men who lived and worshipped there. Their "floating" dust suggests their spirits remaining after death. Eiseley mourns the disappearance of the ancient peoples and is inclined to believe that the atmosphere of the past still persists. Then he draws an end to this visit, "A star burned with a steady silver flame. I was a shadow among shadows brooding over the fate of other shadows that I alone strove to summon up out of the all-pervading dusk" (LN 22). He takes no comfort in his status as an archeologist, an anthropologist, a scientist, and a modern man. With his understanding of time, he knows that he will face "the fate of other shadows"; in other words, as an individual or as the member of a culture, he will follow the faded (or fading) ancient (or still living) civilizations and peoples. Ancient men and modern men are brought together here, and we all were or are shadows. Thus the writer places the ancient civilizations and the modern civilization together for readers to compare, which also allows us to measure time. He teaches the lesson that modern civilization can decline just like other once-flourishing civilizations.

The monuments with words or engravings on them carry human thoughts; in other words, they are objects with meaning, bearing the stories of perished civilizations. Eiseley observes that "monumental structures known as civilizations" "are transmitted from one generation to another on invisible puffs of air known as words—words that can also be symbolically incised on clay. As the delicate printing on the mud at the water's edge retraces a visit of autumn birds long since departed, so the little scrabbled tablets in perished cities carry the seeds of human thought across the deserts of millennia. In this instance the teacher is the social brain but it, too, must be compressed into minute hieroglyphs, and the minds that wrought the miracle efface themselves amidst the jostling torrent of messages" (UU 59–60). Words are "the abstract inventions of the mind."[17] Though the human minds may "efface themselves" going through the turbulence of different epochs, these abandoned objects that encode the products of men's minds travel the "deserts of millennia" like seeds waiting to find a suitable time to blossom once again. Eiseley thus retains hopes for the survival of the wisdom of these forgotten cultures and civilizations, saying "Like a mutation, an idea may be recorded in the wrong time, to lie latent like a recessive gene and spring once more life in an auspicious era" (UU 60). In his eyes, the remains of perished civilizations can be transmitted like genes and can become productive and live once again in the new era. He connects the transmutation of the biological genes and the transmission of civilizations; while the former carry the secret of life, the latter tell of the ingenuity of thought. Both are products of the unexpectedness of nature—the hidden teacher for humans.

Natural history prompts a meditation on human civilization. In his poem "Men Have Their Times," Eiseley expresses a critique of modern technological civilization because he sees a conflict between modern science and the natural world. He reflects on our "talk of atoms and the terrors men have gained / from lasers and great clever new machines" while "look[ing] out upon the nodding jungle flower" (AKA 33) in the ruins. Eiseley declares that unlike human civilization that can be carried by words and hieroglyphs, the natural history of the jungle flower has a message to be deciphered. In fact, the syntax of the poem is fluid, so that the "unread hieroglyph" (AKA 33) can be the "jungle flower" or the inscription on a man-made brick. He imagines that the man who made the brick—or touched the jungle flowers—is gone and has become sand and flower, demonstrating the natural process of life. As a form of natural life, the jungle flower continues to exist. The jungle flower may have appeared in front of the human species that existed before *Homo sapiens* and now stands before modern men's eyes, and will appear before the future human species if they exist at all. In Eiseley's eyes, time in nature is cyclical. The individual's brain can only grasp a fragmentary period of the flower's duration, for he lives in a short period of geological earth time. Beauty in nature has accumulated over the millennia, whereas a human encounters the flower, has his human thought about it, and disappears. Similarly the objects humans "conceived" are "smashed into shards" (AKA 33) in time. These objects may refer both to the ruins of former human civilizations and to the "clever new machines" they have learned to manufacture. In this poem, Eiseley makes a strong contrast between nature and human civilization, so that modern men can wonder at the power of natural life and understand the slightness of human achievement in comparison. Still, the poem enfolds humanity back into the natural cycle by suggesting that we become sand or flowers in the course of time.

In one of his notes, Eiseley ponders the meaning of ancient objects in modern society; he talks about his profession as an anthropologist who uses an ancient fossil for teaching purpose: "I am only a professor and an academic, but the stone ax on my desk that is worn with handling I sometimes realize is not there for classroom purposes, nor is the dirk in the desk drawer. They wait their moment, the falling moment of the great structure I pretend to serve" (LN 238). He admits that he is only an academic member of the society that he "pretend[s] to serve." "The stone ax" belonged to the ancient man who had turned an object in nature into a human's tool. There exist two possible interpretations of "they wait their moment": first, the modern man and his technological civilization will disappear to be replaced by the new kind of man, so "they" may refer to that new species in the future; second, after humanity's extinction the world will finally be reclaimed by nature—returning to the world before human's appearance—so "they" may refer to life excluding *Homo sapiens*; third, the "they" may refer to the objects themselves that wait to be put to use again, either as weapons or as something not yet imagined. The ancient man created the stone ax or dagger to depend upon it for living; however, in modern society where there are new, more deadly machines, such weapons are no use anymore but serve only as objects "for classroom purposes." Eiseley shows his different view of such objects, for he sees in stone ax and "the dirk in the desk drawer" the power of time and the huge potentiality for changes it promises.

In conclusion, Eiseley senses darkness and death even in his youth and he preserves the strong feeling of them in his works. Though he believes that the end of the individual's life is oblivion, he sees it as a unique journey. The concepts of time and nature are of eternal value to humanity. He ponders on time and is sensitive to the past, meditating on things like the fossils of extinct animals or the ruins of perished civilizations to discover the meanings of past, present, and future life. He shows concern about the decline of human values in the modern era and speaks in apologetic tones about his contemporaries' silence about the life and culture of the native peoples like the American Indians, just as he is moved by the fate of the last Neanderthal girl with her ancient genes in the modern era. Eiseley believes there are lessons to learn from neglected or forgotten human cultures because their beliefs may contain the wisdom to face nature and time and to show kindness to other forms of life. As a modern man, he hopes that the lessons of the past can be rediscovered and transferred to the modern world just like genes that can be carried, inherited, and transformed by future generations.

Eiseley's essays and poems look like personal narrations; however, his texts are actually hybrids combining scientific information and discussions about humanity and history. To study him, one has to consider a span of time that reaches beyond the few hundred years of his nation's short history. Many things contribute to Eiseley's ability to travel back and forth in time. First, it is his profession as an anthropologist and archeologist who studies the long-departed past. His field experience of bone hunting cultivates his sense of time since the landscapes and the environments he moves in bear the marks of the ages.[18] What's more, his searches are not restricted to the material bones and stones of his profession (ST 55); he digs for more than tangible things. Observing skeletons in caves or natural scenes that tell him the story of evolution, he travels through time. Finally, Eiseley's sensitivity can be attributed to the poet's gift of imagination and feeling of sympathy. Without his attentive feelings and romantic wonderings, readers would not be so moved by his descriptions of the ancient past and the bone hunting incidents that illustrate his abstract meditations and philosophy.

Eiseley's essays and poems look like personal narrations; however, his texts are actually hybrids combining scientific information and discussions about humanity and history. To study him, one has to consider a span of time that reaches beyond the few hundred years of his nation's short history. Many things contribute to Eiseley's ability to travel back and forth in time. First, it is his profession as an anthropologist and archeologist who studies the long-departed past. His field experience of bone hunting cultivates his sense of time since the landscapes and the environments he moves in bear the marks of the ages.[18] What's more, his searches are not restricted to the material bones and stones of his profession (ST 55); he digs for more than tangible things. Observing skeletons in caves or natural scenes that tell him the story of evolution, he travels through time. Finally, Eiseley's sensitivity can be attributed to the poet's gift of imagination and feeling of sympathy. Without his attentive feelings and romantic wonderings, readers would not be so moved by his descriptions of the ancient past and the bone hunting incidents that illustrate his abstract meditations and philosophy.

Eiseley criticizes the narrow worldview of twentieth-century society, especially modern man's certainty about the durability of current forms of life and the superiority of the technological civilization. The nature writer condemns the unbalance between science and nature and reveals a bigger picture of life to remind his readers that man is only one fragment among others in the natural world. Eiseley admires the complexity in nature and life and the mysterious balance that it maintains for living beings. He praises the web of life, "the net, the living film that at any given moment of earth time seems to hold all the verdant world in an everlasting balance, [and] is secretly woven anew from age to age" (UU 158). Looking at the earth's geological time, he marvels at the vitality and biodiversity in the web of life.

For Eiseley, something is wrong with modern man's conception of the past, the present, and the oncoming future. Modern society has become future-oriented and event-oriented; while at the same time, it dismisses the past. Eiseley sees this modern split as a war inside modern men's hearts: "'When evil comes it is because two gods have disagreed,' runs the proverb of an elder people. Perhaps it is another way of saying that the past and the future are at war in the heart of man" (IP 69). Eiseley searches for solutions to the conflict and turns to human antiquity for lessons. He introduces other-than-modern-man's thoughts about how to exist in eternity. He discusses the proper way to balance man's material world and mental world in order to make the world of human time and the world of dreamtime coexist.

As Eiseley says, "The door to the past is a strange door" (IJ 54). He opens this door to modern readers and shows the past—the past of Native Americans, of the Aztecs, of the ice age, or of the Neanderthals. The mystery and unexpectedness of past times attract him. He criticizes the injustice in the modern world eaters' effacement of "defeated men and broken cultures" (IP 111). He sees their discredited knowledge as important to the present, convinced that "all of primitive man's meaningful relationship to his world is thus not history" (IP 113). The past is not only the past; it can foretell humanity's future or actually help build a sustainable future.

Humanity began when man became the fire-maker and tool-user, which justified us in calling ourselves "*Homo sapiens*, the wise" (IP 54). Man's fire-making enabled him to banish the darkness. Eiseley suggests that the solution to avoid man's extinction in the near future is ironically to believe that "again, the dark may bring him wisdom" (IP 55). Imagining modern man facing darkness and coldness again as their ancestors did may help us rethink our place in the natural world and measure the achievement of modern technological civilization on the vast scale of earth time. After all, pictures of imagined future disasters may be more remote and less convincing for modern men to realize the seriousness of their situation than the more easily imaginable harsh situations in prehistoric times. Leading readers to see the future in the past, Eiseley urges all, especially the youngest readers, to learn from the past and think beyond the modern split between science and nature, between the first world and man's second world.

NOTES

1. This is exactly what Latour does in *We Have Never Been Modern*.
2. Eiseley uses this term to refer to peoples like Australian Aborigines and Native Americans, as well as to cultures from other epochs; therefore, I will retain it for my study, with the understanding that this usage is specific to his time.
3. Wilson, *Biophilia*, 85.
4. Wilson, *Biophilia*, 122.
5. Wilson, *Biophilia*, 122.
6. Wilson, *Biophilia*, 122–23.
7. Wilson, *Biophilia*, 119.
8. Wilson, *Biophilia*, 120.
9. Wilson, *Biophilia*, 120.
10. Wilson, *Biophilia*, 121.
11. Wilson, *Biophilia*, 121.
12. Momaday, "Spiritual Mountain," 56. Momaday chooses the name for God as Yahweh, and the name for the bear as Urset. Bear or Urset seems to be the symbol for man.

13. Eiseley's references to the trope of the vanishing Indian to reveal a prejudice shared by many Americans of his generation.

14. Angyal, *Loren Eiseley*, 7.

15. Obviously this incident contradicts our knowledge that the Neanderthals went extinct long before modern humans; however, the interbreeding of Neanderthal and *Homo sapiens* may have continued to exist since certain individuals carry more or less ancient genes and genes bear memories.

16. Angyal says this "prose sketch . . . probably originated as a class assignment, 'Autumn—A Memory,' later appeared in the October, 1927, issue of the *Prairie Schooner*" (Angyal, *Loren Eiseley*, 9).

17. Momaday, "Spiritual Mountain," 57.

18. "The brown needles and the fallen cones, the stiff, endless green forests were a mark that placed me in the Age of Dinosaurs" (FT 163).

18. "The brown needles and the fallen cones, the stiff, endless green forests were a mark that placed me in the Age of Dinosaurs" (FT 163).

PART III

Human and Animal Split

Chapter 6

Familiarity and Similarity

On occasion people speak of encountering animals that seem very familiar to them. This chapter focuses on three different settings for this kind of encounter: first, men habitually bring domestic animals like dogs or cats into their own houses; second, they may encounter wild animals just behind their own backyards or in rural neighborhoods; third, they may hunt and kill animals for food or as trophies, or they may trap them to place in zoos or museum collections. Eiseley's descriptions of different forms of contact with animals explore the paradox that although men may find animals familiar, there is a world to which animals have access but from which humans feel excluded. In particular, night is another realm, different from the sunlit world that men find familiar and welcoming, and perhaps because of this it is a privileged time for animals. That Eiseley is also a habitué of the night suggests his affinity for other species and his recognition of his own animal nature. This chapter focuses on the nighttime experiences in Eiseley's essays and poems in which he blurs the boundaries between humans and animals, the civilized and the wild.

From banal incidents in his stories, Eiseley offers philosophical thoughts about the origin of life and reveals the evolutionary road of animals and its continuity in human life. Though humans and animals were netted together in the ancient past, humans use their own standard for intelligence to separate themselves from animals, for example, in taking tool-using and language as humans' specialties. Eiseley suggests that with this kind of anthropocentric view of animal life and nature, man imprisons himself in a solitary world and the resulting loss of contact with nature is what causes man's ultimate loneliness. The twentieth-century nature writer urges us to think outside the rigid categories that we have put in place in order to define ourselves and others, thereby opening up new possibilities for existence. Eiseley admires the indigenous peoples' legends in which animals enrich human existence through mutual interaction. Thus, he suggests that there is a mutual need for companionship between humans and other animals and we can live all together, wild or tame, humans or wild animals.

6.1. STRANGE PROXIMITIES—ENCOUNTERS WITH ANIMALS

Becoming Wild at Night

Man turns to domestic life to survive, taming and mastering wild natural elements for his own ends and thereby following a road different from his animal brotherhood. Fire was man's means of distancing himself from the animal world. Eiseley reminds us that "man, long before he trained the first dog, had learned to domesticate fire" (UU 116). Possessing the skill of fire-making, humans create a man-made and man-friendly environment, while predatory animals are at home in darkness. Man is ill-adapted to thrive at night; he possesses "small day-born eyes, fears the ghosts of the dark above all things" (NC 32). Thus, in Eiseley's view, man fears the vast darkness in nature and takes steps to conquer it:

> Maybe that is the real reason why men string lamps far out into country lanes and try to run down everything with red eyes that happens to waddle across the road in front of their head-lights. It is cruel but revelatory: we are insecure, and this is our warfare with the dark. It began when man first lit a fire at a cave mouth and the eyes he feared—very big eyes they were then—began to blink and draw back. So he lights and lights in a passion for illumination that is insatiable—a poor day-born thing contending against one of the greatest powers in the universe. (NC 32)

The "red eyes" that men "try to run down" are those of animals. Do humans react in this way because they see the road as their exclusive property or because they fear that wild animals threaten their security? The speaker explains that "we are insecure" in confronting the dark like our human ancestors. He leads readers back to the time when man resided in caves and used fires to make wild animals withdraw. Making the link between those ancestors and his contemporaries, he regards the darkness in awe and speaks of it as "one of the greatest powers in the universe"; thus, man's desire to illuminate against it, though "insatiable," seems doomed.

Humans encounter the experience of becoming wild when an everyday domestic environment is penetrated by wildness, especially when it is in the dark. There is always an other-than-human agent in these meetings. Eiseley acknowledges that rats "are the real agents of the night and there is a sort of malign intelligence about them that is frightening" (NC 33). He hints that man fears darkness because he risks meeting the eyes of these "malign" agents of night.

Domestic space is defined by the exclusion of the wild, so when wildness intrudes into a man-made environment, the response can be one of shock and fear. In *The Night Country*, Eiseley gives one example of his friend who was startled by a sewer rat the size of a house cat sitting on his legs when he was sleeping in a hotel room. The man is terrified to find that he shares his hotel room with "a demoniac-eyed rat" crouching on the hotel bed. Before he lights a match to get a better look at the nocturnal visitor, he takes the creature to be a friendly tomcat from the fire escape. He then has an eye-to-eye confrontation with the rat by the light of a match flame: "That one match flare, so my friend told me afterward, seemed to last the lifetime of the human race. Then the match went out and he simultaneously hurtled from the bed. From his incoherent account of what happened afterward I suspect that both rat and man left by the window but fortunately, perhaps, not at the same instant" (NC 33). This confrontation oddly recalls Eiseley's confrontation with his childhood friend the Rat by the light of a candle. It seems to break down the divisions between human and animal, the civilized and the wild.

People are more comfortable with domestic animals like cats and dogs sharing an inhabited environment with them. These animals are permitted to enter man-built space because they are tamed and familiar. It is for this reason that Deleuze distains them. Beaulieu argues that Deleuze "is sensitive to something in animals and cannot stand them when they become too familiar. He candidly admits to not liking 'rubbers' (*frotteurs*) or the canine barking he considers 'the shame of the animal kingdom.' He claims to better tolerate the wolf howling at the moon."[1] Rats, though they share our domestic space, are dangerously alien and independent of us. Yet Eiseley is aware that even familiar animals can become strange to us and allow us to encounter wildness: "Even man's own domestic animals, the creatures he has chosen to bring in to the fire besides him, grow suspect in the evening. His cat hunts alone through the weeds and his dog whines and snuffles at the door. They all have that allegiance to the dark. They are never wholly his" (NC 32–33). At another, earlier time, men and dogs (as the descendants of wolves) were not friends; indeed, domestic animals can demonstrate untamed behaviors that exclude human beings.

Eiseley tells a personal anecdote to show "how domestic animals get out of hand at night."[2] One winter night he works alone on some fossils among which there is the leg bone of a fossil bison, and his dog "Wolf" accompanies him. The name given to the dog is interesting. Perhaps Eiseley sees the wolf as a distant relative of his dog. Perhaps he is drawn to the wildness that remains in the dog's nature.[3] A strange thing happens when the hour passes midnight, the sleeping man is awakened by the growling noise of the dog, who holds the bison bone in its mouth. With a threatening gesture Wolf snarls at his beloved owner, refusing to yield the bone. To explain this uncharacteristic hostility, Eiseley says, "There was nothing in that bone to taste, but ancient shapes were moving in his mind and determining his utterance. Only fools gave up bones. He was warning me" (UU 94). In speaking of the dog's "utterance," a word usually employed to describe man's speech, Eiseley might seem to be drawing an anthropomorphic picture of Wolf. In fact, he is doing the opposite; he is imagining how the world looks to a dog. Using "he" to refer to the dog already puts Wolf on an equal footing with man. Then he uses free indirect discourse ("Only fools gave up bones.") to enunciate his dog's thoughts. He imagines Wolf to be attracted to the ancient bone because the shapes of long-extinct prey move in his mind, like some ancestral memory. The bone sprang from the natural world where the ancient animals also lived. For Eiseley it provides a link to both canine and human origins. Neither dog nor man wants to give up the fossil bone, and we could see this as a way to underline the importance of remembering the ancient past, that of humanity and of the other animals. The episode has all the elements that allow Eiseley to project the two of them back into that prehistoric time: "'It is midnight. We are in another time, in the snow'" (UU 94). Eiseley imagines them inhabiting the ice age when primitive man struggled against the cold and darkness, and wolves and men were enemies and lived separately and differently.

Wild Animals Nearby

It is not necessary to travel very far to encounter wild animals. Some of them are right there in our backyards. In recounting instances of contact with animals, Eiseley shows that although we may live close to them, they live very differently to human beings. As the speaker states in his poem "The Cardinals": "The ways of the wild are queer / by human standards" (NA 93). In this poem, Eiseley describes two cardinals (a male and a female). They "suddenly exchange seeds" in what may be some kind of mating behavior, which he calls "an ancient ritual / welcoming spring" (NA 93). The speaker observes that the wild birds are not dependent on humans for food; however, they come to his window ledge, so he wants to join in their ritual by offering them seeds. A feeling of awe is raised in the man's heart and he admires the two wild birds because they are "grave and dignified"; therefore he wonders whether he can, with correspondingly "proper manners" (NA 93), feed them. This incident offers a complex thought of Eiseley: on the one hand, he stresses that wild animals have their own ways that distance men from them; on the other hand, he expresses the desire to make contact with these animals in "proper" ways, as if he could find a common language or mode of behavior. However, the poem remains ambiguous, because it could be read as a love poem, addressed to the speaker's lover. In that case, the speaker would be imitating the birds' behavior and instigating his own mating ritual.

Interestingly, Eiseley mentions the cardinals again in another poem, "Magic," which develops the anecdote into a series. In "Magic," the speaker feeds the wild cardinal family that come to his window ledge, but he is particularly fond of the first cardinal that comes to him. The connection between him and bird is much more intimate. Eiseley uses "he" for the cardinal and describes the bird's sound as "telegraphing in quick clicks" (NA 68) the verb that is used when man uses mechanical clicks to transfer information. The bird seems to communicate with the speaker when it tries to "fly back and forth"—the movement attracts the man; and he understands the bird's "morning song" (NA 67). It seems that the two parties are developing a common language or cross-species communication.

The speaker never forgets his first meeting with the redbird, perhaps because he knows that it is rare for a wild bird to come to a man naturally. The speaker regards the bird as having a particular personality and says it is special. It raises a reflection on how we humans can become much more engaged with an individual than with the more abstract concept of a species. So the poet uses the idea of avian individuality to make us care for birds. There is a kind of zooming in and zooming out—moving from many to one. The poem begins with a generalization about animals ("I have lived much among animals") and then moves to "our cardinal family" (NA 65) that visits his home over generations, to finally remember his special friend, the first redbird that comes to his house.

The bird in the man's eyes is "very different" (NA 67), maybe because it not only comes to him but also because it gives a performance to get the human to feed him. The speaker speaks highly of the bird as "the most brilliant," "the most responsive" (NA 68). Meanwhile in the poem the speaker describes himself as "the strange / giving animal" (NA 66); he tries to see the man who offers the seeds from the bird's view. In doing so, he undoes the boundary between humans and animals. Eiseley stresses that the bird understands and exchanges information with the human. In the poem, the speaker "performed the ritual" (NA 67) in giving seeds to the bird. He admits plainly that he is happy about participating in this "ritual" because the bird convinced him "we were on the same path" (NA 68). The speaker shows his willingness to align with wildlife and the natural world. "The same path" suggests that humans and animals have the same origins and are on the same course in cherishing life.

Unfortunately and unexpectedly, the special redbird later disappeared—"the nest was deserted" (NA 68). This indicates the uncertainties in nature or it may hint it is because of humans' interference. In the poem, the speaker continues to feed other birds that come to his window though they are more doubtful about the "ritual" of feeding. The speaker's memory of the first cardinal remains, and he perhaps waits in hope that another bird will come, one like the "most responsive" one—another "friendly magician" (NA 68). He seems to feel embarrassed to share the happiness that the bird brought to him with his fellow humans, which indicates the ideological power of human-defined categories about the wild. How can a bird communicate with a man? Repeatedly, the speaker says the bird performs "magic" and is a "friendly magician," and feels glad to be "enchanted" (NA 69) by him. It shows his respect for the mystery in nature and his affection for the unexpected.

Fragile Wildlife

In her book *When Species Meet* Haraway tells a story where she feeds regularly four feral cats in an old barn in the country. At first she wants help in the form of "predator control" over the mice that damage her car; later she finds that "our cats seem more into ranching than predator control."[4] She emphasizes that these cats are wild, however, "their lives are palpably fragile. They are not pets; they do not get the care of a middle-class pet."[5] She calls for more care and attention from people for the animals whose existence is very different from that of domestic animals but who still share companion relationships with men.

Haraway values the daily contact between her and the cats just like Eiseley's speaker with his first cardinal, and both call their meetings with these animals *rituals*, applying to their interaction, a term normally reserved to human cultures. Haraway says "They and we have rituals of expectation and affectionate touch enacted on a daily basis."[6] Choosing the word *ritual*, she makes the encounter with the cats important and solemn. She is happy to touch the cats, while the feral animals keep "lookouts" as their nature teaches them to. In a 1988 interview with Claire Parnet, Deleuze mentions that an animal is "a being on the lookout," and he says "An animal never keeps still. While eating, it has to watch out if anything is happening in its back, on its sides, etc. Such an existence on the lookout is terrible."[7] Though Haraway's cats stay on "terrible" lookout, they still "wait" to meet their people, through which Haraway indicates that mutual confidence and reliance between humans and animals can and must be constructed. The story interests me because Haraway does not simply adopt the cats as pets. However, the cats are not totally wild either because they receive food from her. Their interaction rather takes place in a middle zone where humans and animals benefit from each other's existence and respect each other.

In the above incident, Haraway helps the animals for a few years, and she finds that feral cats need more care than domestic animals; in comparison, among many cat incidents in Eiseley's stories, there is also a hungry stray cat comes to him "out of a bush" (NA 99) and calls for his help. In his poem "Confrontation," the speaker emphasizes the role man plays in interacting with animals, especially the ones that come easily to man, allowing the possibility for them to be domesticated by him. In the poem, the speaker claims that the cat "is my follower" (NA 99), which indicates the companionship between the cat and the man. In the last lines of the poem the speaker asserts "We need no followers, / ours is the night" (NA 99). The syntax is ambiguous: in claiming that that night is their follower, he suggests that darkness comes at the end of the day, or in a further meaning, the end of one's life; at the same time, in saying that the night is "ours" he claims the night as their time, their territory, and in so doing, he aligns himself with wild creatures. In evoking the cycle of life and death, as well as asserting his affinity with the darkness, perhaps he reminds readers of their animal past and warns them to value the natural world.

Hunters of the Wild

Hunting is one of the ways modern men come into contact with wild animals. In so doing they reenact ancient behaviors. The ice-age men used fire to draw "red eyes" away from the mouths of their caves at night, and in order to survive they worked in packs to hunt the wild animals. In his book *The Night Country*, Eiseley tells a story of humans trapping wildlife, thereby showing the human as a hunter. It is an anecdote relating one of his experiences with hunting. Three men in a stripped car are chasing a running antelope. Among them, Eiseley's speaker is a false hunter. "I did not want to kill him. I looked for a barrier, a fence, an obstacle to wheels, something to stop this game while it was still fun. I wanted to see that unscathed animal go over a hedge and vanish, leaving maybe a little wisp of fur on a thorn to let us know he had passed unharmed out of our reach" (NC 11). Eiseley's complex emotion and contradictory desire finally seem to be resolved when the antelope steps across a ravine that stops the hunting men and sends their car into a ditch. The ravine is visible to the hunted animal, but to the hunters it is an invisible barrier, a line that they could not see. This is the invisible line that separates the civilized and the wild, one that the older Eiseley crosses in playing the role of hunter but from which he holds back in not wanting the prey to be killed. He has to join the world of men and disguise himself as a hunter. But he learns that the lines are there between man and the wild.

Not all the hunting experiences in Eiseley's writings end with the wild animal escaping the hunter's capture. In another story Eiseley regrets that one life ended with a shot from a hunter's gun: "the collecting man that I once tried to prevent from killing an endangered falcon, who raised his rifle, fired, and laughed as the bird tumbled at my feet. I suppose Freud might have argued that this was a man of normal ego, but I, extending my childlike mind into the composite life of the world, bled accordingly" (ST 193). The speaker bleeds as the falcon does, though it is a metaphor to express his empathy for the dying bird. Eiseley identifies not with the hunters but with their prey—the wild animals, which illustrates his becoming wild.

The "collecting man" who "laughed" at his trophy might be seen as going "wild" too. His feeling of triumph may come from that his satisfaction with his shooting skill or his capacity to locate the wild animal. The latter would suggest that he has an animal relationship with wildlife. In Deleuze's view, the real hunter has a more natural relationship with animals than the homeowner with his pets. In his interview with Claire Parnet, Deleuze says that an animal relationship with the animals is quite beautiful and he gives the example of the hunter. He blurs the distinctions between nature and culture, arguing that both man and animals inhabit domains of signs. He says: "animals ceaselessly emit signs; they produce as well as react to the signs. Take a wolf sign, a wolf track, for example, I admire enormously people who know how to recognize tracks, like the real hunters who can recognize the animal that has passed by; and at that point, they are animals, they have an animal relationship with animals." For him animals' "constituting a territory is nearly the birth of art."[8] Deleuze admires that the real hunter can track animals and recognize the territory marked by animals.

On the contrary, Eiseley, who identifies himself with animals, holds a quite different point of view of hunters from Deleuze. Eiseley's poem "Flight 857" even holds a warning for hunters. The speaker observes that fossils of "the Ice Age long-horned bison" (NA 45) are found, while of men from that time are never found but "only their flints" (NA 46)—the weapons they made for hunting. Through this comparison of the vastness of time and short scale of human existence, Eiseley warns hunters in the modern world of the danger that lies in their present course of hunting and killing. Even ice-age hunters "had the grace to tiptoe / away with the last mammoth" (NA 46); why then have modern hunters become so arrogant and obsessed in their existence and mastery?

In comparison to the role of human hunters, Eiseley admires what animals achieve as hunters. His poem "Snow Leopard" illustrates this idea, and more important, it holds some clues as to what Eiseley's "becoming wild" is. In this poem, the speaker expresses his sympathy for the leopard imprisoned in the zoo. He regrets that the wild animal behind the barriers distains to meet the speaker's eyes. Leopards are great hunters in the wild; however, this particular leopard is imprisoned in a zoo because humans "trapped" him (NA 34). The wild creature does not meet the visitor's eyes; instead, "he" extends his gaze beyond the horizon to the freedom in the wilderness. Interestingly, in another poem, "The Bats," Eiseley mentions again the "unbearable blank stares" (NA 87) of Himalayan leopards in the zoo, which gives the readers the impression he is remembering the same leopard. In a Mexican church, the speaker thinks of the wild animal's "blank stares" and feels uncomfortable, maybe because these "blank stares" show its complete indifference to human beings. The look is "unbearable" because frustrating for him to understand nothing in the wild animal's gaze, not only because it is uninterested in the human world, but also because the eye contact is "a queer event" (NA 87) that shows the strangeness of God's created world.

Maybe because the man feels desperate about the insurmountable distance between him and the wild leopard, he expresses his desire to become this wild hunter through imagining that he possesses his eyes for seeing at night and his "long-tailed supple body" (NA 34) for hunting. Sharing the physical characteristics of the wild animal, the human may think, is a way to see through its eyes and to know how it understands the world. Again, he identifies with the wild animals. He loves the idea of hunting, not as a day-born human hunter, but as a nocturnal wild animal. The great animal hunter that Eiseley admires belongs to a different world from human hunters.

In summary, animals have a stronger bond with night and darkness than day-born men. Eiseley recounts the stories where animals, whether wild or domestic, "are back in a secret world from which man has been shut out, and they want no truck with him after nightfall" (NC 37). This secret world is "the night country" where man draws the line and chooses to live rather in his safe, human world of lights. The wild (even domestic) animals "want no truck" with man at night and this is again Eiseley's effort to see from the angle of the animals. He imagines that the wild animals are afraid of men: "man and his lights must truly hold a demonic menace" (NC 44). In the same way, humans feel unsafe in the dark without "machines with lights and great noise" (NC 37) in other words, their trucks or guns, etc. Ironically, the demon in the dark is man himself with lights instead of the "red eyes" he fears. Eiseley says his encounters with these nocturnal animals "may be among the last to be reported from that night world" (NC 37), which shows his sorrow for our loss of the bond between humans and animals as well as his own claim to a special relationship with wildness.

Man fears darkness, maybe because he fears meeting eyes that can see in the dark. Man draws a boundary line between light and darkness, and between himself, the civilized, and animals, the wild. Even domestic animals have secret lives, and through anecdotes of encounters with different animals Eiseley explores what we know and what we don't know about them, which stimulates people to realize the physical and mental inheritance of these animals from their wild kin in nature. Unlike other animals living within nature, humans have always sought to gain mastery—the authority, power and control over their environment (as I've discussed in the previous chapter about Eiseley's critiques of science). The idea of mastery is affirmed here again: humans are not in control of other forms of life though they may think they domesticate or dominate or possess animals. Through declaring this idea, Eiseley tries to show how irrational it is that "rational" man regards himself as a privileged player on the stage of life in which nonhumans are ignored. He advocates attempting to communicate with animals in encountering them. Eiseley's discussion of the relationship between animals and humans is complex. On the one hand, animals have their own world that excludes humans even when humans try to tame or capture them. On the other hand, all are enmeshed in nature and life; thus Eiseley suggests that we should reconnect to animals and to the animal in ourselves.

6.2. CONTINUITY AND CONTRAST— HUMANS ARE ANIMALS

Men Were Toads

In the essay "Toads and Men," Eiseley recounts an episode where the young speaker "had a horned toad" in his sack (ASH 55). The "horned toad" is not really a toad but a type of lizard who gets this name because of its resemblance to the amphibian. Interestingly, Eiseley uses the word *toad* (not horny toad or lizard) thereafter in the whole text. At the beginning of the account, the speaker records the casual talks among the hobo camp he joins. A prisoner who is heading home says about men: "People can make railroads, people can build all them buidin's . . . but they can't figure *themselves*" (ASH 56). Through the plain words of the ex-convict, Eiseley tries to show that though men are powerful and skillful in tool-using—building railroads or skyscrapers—there are things they cannot understand even about themselves. Coincidentally, after this thoughtful statement and the complaints from other men about their hard life, the speaker's horned toad "began to rustle" (ASH 57); maybe the timing suggests that the creature shows its agreement (or disagreement) as if it understands these men's concerns. The lizard then evokes the surrounding men's interest, and in their eyes, it might be food, "poison," "medicine," a lucky charm like a "four-leaf clover," or a companion to travel with. The boy simply likes the lizard, especially since when he rubs it, it puffs up. Nevertheless, when related by the naturalist philosopher this banal incident becomes an occasion for a reflection on the relationship between man and other life forms.

After this informal chat about the speaker's lizard, the conversation goes deeper to discuss whether humans and lizards or toads share a similar origin of life. A man wonders "where all them toads come from," and someone follows up, "Men or toads—they all had to come from somewhere. . . . Calling 'em toads or calling 'em men don't answer that. Mark my words, something had to have a hand in making us." And another agrees, "if you ask me, we're all out of the same mold" (ASH 58). In this dialogue Eiseley shows different views about where men and animals are from, yet he may quietly show his own concerns about the evolutionary road of animals and its continuity in human life by recording the voices of others. The speaker reflects on the philosophical questions raised in the exchange:

> We would throw stones and break what we could not understand, as before. It was part of us, that restless, manual cruelty from some dark tree in a vanished forest. It was our glory and it was, at the same time, our ending. I felt, though young, the long shadow of the coming night, and a great loneliness gathered in me. I spoke to the toad in my shirt, but of course he made no answer. He could only puff and tilt in a fatuous friendliness, not realizing there was no more desert and that he was engaged in a dangerous journey among monsters. . . . There was an outside world this toad was not equipped for—and men were toads—what had the old man said? Men were like toads in a desert of their own. Perhaps we were too limited to understand it. Like the toad in my shirt we were in the hands of God, but we could not feel him; he was beyond us, totally and terribly beyond our limited senses. (ASH 58–60)

In relating this anecdote, Eiseley meaningfully describes the men that gather around the railway tracks waiting for the departing trains in ways that underline the resemblance between themselves and the toad: "they sat or squatted" and "crouched . . . in the shade" (ASH 55–56). The men and the toad share physical similarities in their posture. However, the humans are distinct from the toad in their predilection for violence. They "would throw stones" at other creatures, a trait that refers back to the ancient time when man uses stones as a tool or a weapon to kill or defend himself. The point the speaker makes here is that we break things we don't understand both in ancient and modern times. In poetic words, Eiseley expresses that the force that helped our ancestors survive may lead to an impasse—an ending of humanity. He sees irony in the violent traits that once aided humanity, but now seem to lead to a dead end. He predicts a doomed future for men, because they cannot move beyond the impulse to destroy the unknown. The speaker in the essay may be a new type of human being, however, for he cannot bear the loneliness and tries to communicate to the friendly lizard even if he receives no reply.

The description of the lizard's situation suggests an allegorical reading. In leaving its desert home the creature attracts the attention of the greedy eyes of the men, ("monsters") who are interested in eating or dissecting it. We can take those words as a reference to the harsh situation for all wildlife.

The natural living environments like the lizard's desert are disappearing as rapacious humans make use of them for food or other materials. The speaker refers to the possibility of a higher power in whose hands men are as helpless as the lizard in the boy's shirt. This argument is not so much an attempt to convince readers of the existence of God as an effort to persuade them to show mercy to the fellow creatures whose lives they threaten. The young man sets an example the following morning in that he leaves the lizard "in some sand along the right-of-way" (ASH 60) and sincerely hopes the small thing can survive. However, as an older man writing this episode, he knows that the horned toad couldn't make it out. That's why he mourns that "let men beat men, if they will, but why do they have to beat and starve small things," and he confesses, "that's why I am a wanderer forever in the streets of men, a wanderer in mind, and in these matters, a creature of desperate impulse" (ASH 63). It seems the speaker understands man's violence to man, but feels disgusted by his eagerness to hurt other, smaller animals. Eiseley's revelation makes people consider: our evolutionary road lies close to that of lizards or toads, they are even our ancestors somehow; however, man's cruelty breaks this bond and calls into question the goodness of humanity.

This horny toad anecdote concludes several important points that Eiseley makes about the human-animal relationship: first, there is an evolutionary continuity between human life and animal life—we come from the same origin—we are netted together; second, the violence in the nature of man leads man to see nonhumans from a utilitarian perspective; third, feeling the loneliness that comes from this broken relation, some people seek communication with nonhumans; however, it is difficult. Therefore, there is a need to examine how we divide ourselves from our brothers, the animals, through the violence directed toward other life forms.

Tool-Using and Language

Eiseley is aware that the "chasm between ourselves and the rest of life" (UU 116) has widened since man became the fire-user. The human brain made a great leap of development thanks to man's harnessing of fire. Though humans and animals were netted together in the ancient past, humans use their own standard for intelligence to separate themselves from animals. Humans describe their own activities as culture, while they classify those of other animals as belonging to nature. In particular, the marks of culture are taken to be humans' monopoly on tool-using and language.

Eiseley reveals the role of man in changing the natural world through his tool-using. He argues that unlike "animals [that] are molded by natural forces they do not comprehend" (ST 37), "man is particularly a creature who has turned the tables on his environment so that he is now engrossed in shaping it, rather than being shaped by it. Man expresses himself upon his environment through the use of tools. We therefore tend to equate the use of tools in a one-to-one relationship with intelligence" (ST 39). The idea that man has higher intelligence than other creatures because he is a better tool-user is obvious to some people but not to Eiseley, for he goes on to suggest that this standard is unconsciously anthropocentric. He urges us to think outside the rigid categories that we have put in place in order to define ourselves and others, thereby opening up new possibilities for existence. For Eiseley, man's overconfidence in human intelligence blocks him from seeing equivalent or more complex intellectual capacities in other life forms. He encourages readers to wonder whether "man is so locked in his own type of intelligence—an intelligence that is linked to a prehensile, grasping hand giving him power over his environment—that he is unable to comprehend the intellectual life of a highly endowed creature from another domain such as the sea" (ST 38). Since man is a land animal, he tends to ignore other forms of intelligence in the world of waters—where all life begins and also where the development of the brain begins.

Concerning language in humans and animals, the very first point Eiseley makes is to admit animal intelligence, even if he does not believe that they have linguistic systems:

> All animals which man has reason to believe are more than usually intelligent—our relatives the great apes, the elephant, the raccoon, the wolverine, among others—are problem solvers, and in at least a small way manipulators of their environment. Save for the instinctive calls of their species, however, they cannot communicate except by direct imitation. They cannot invent words for new situations nor get their fellows to use such words. No matter how high the individual intelligence, its private world remains a private possession locked forever within a single, perishable brain. It is this fact that finally balks our hunger to communicate even with the sensitive dog who shares our fireside. (ST 42)

Without the ability to communicate new ideas, Eiseley believes that individual members of other species are enclosed in their own consciousness. In unfamiliar situations, they can communicate neither with each other nor with individuals of other species. In this way, Eiseley does not go beyond the anthropocentric thinking that Matthew Calarco discusses in his book *Zoographies*. In a discussion of Derrida's *The Animal That Therefore I Am*, he argues that the French philosopher "*is* interested in arguing that the 'lack' of human language among animals is not in fact a 'lack' or privation. To think difference privatively, which is the dominant way of thinking found in Heidegger's and Levinas's discourse on animals, is the dogmatic and anthropocentric prejudice that Derrida's work on the question of the animal is aimed at overcoming."[9] Given that philosophy has traditionally defined the human in opposition to other animals, it is not surprising that Eiseley maintains this difference; however, he is open to proof to the contrary. Actually, how man gains his language in the first place remains mysterious. Eiseley explains how "the potentiality of language is dependent upon the germ plasm. Its nature, not its cultural expression, is written into the motor centers of the brain, into high auditory discrimination and equally rapid neuromuscular response in tongue, lips, and palate. We are biologically adapted for the symbols of speech. We have determined its forms, but its potential is not of our conscious creation. Its mechanisms are written in our brain, a simple gift from the dark powers behind nature. Speech has made us, but it is a human endowment not entirely of our conscious devising" (UU 114–15). Here Eiseley clarifies that language is a natural feature, made possible by biological features; but at the same time, the capacity for speech makes men become human. He questions whether it is a uniquely human cultural specialty. He then brings up the "ascertaining" question of whether the whistles and clicks made by porpoises "represent true language—in the sense of symbolic meanings, additive, learned elements—or whether they are simply the instinctive signals of a pack animal. To this there is as yet no clear answer, but the eagerness with which laboratory sounds and voices were copied by captive porpoises suggests a vocalizing ability extending perhaps to or beyond the threshold of speech" (ST 42). Eiseley suggests here that the sounds of the dolphins may equate with what we set as standards for true language.

In this discussion of language we can see that Eiseley regrets the fact that humans and animals cannot communicate directly with each other. It seems this fact makes him see more clearly the loneliness of humans. If language has made man fall out of nature, Eiseley regrets its acquisition, even as he uses it to communicate with readers. He imagines that man, like the porpoise, should live in silence. On the one hand, "this role would now be a deserved penitence for man." On the other, he thinks that this penitence might be salutary: "Perhaps such a transformation would bring him once more into that mood of childhood innocence in which he talked successfully to all things living but had no power and no urge to harm. It is worth at least a wistful thought that someday the porpoise may talk to us and we to him. It would break, perhaps, the long loneliness that has made man a frequent terror and abomination even to himself" (ST 43–44). Silence may be necessary to release man from his solitary human world and permit a less destructive mode of existence with other creatures.

Certainly Eiseley is interested in the interactions between men and animals, and he hints that there may be ways to communicate between them other than through language—"beyond the threshold of speech" (ST 42), given that the parties involved are intelligent living beings. Similarly, in her book

When Species Meet, Haraway points to the way in which men and animals sometimes communicate. She introduces the sport[10] in which she and her dog work together and particularly emphasizes the importance of mutual communication in this game: "Cayenne and I must communicate throughout our being, and language in the orthodox linguist's sense is mostly in the way."[11] She clarifies that she and her dog manage to communicate in a way that is beyond the level of traditionally defined language. Without words, mutual regard becomes all the more significant; dog and woman work together in "not a wild dash, but trained regard."[12] Her dog is intelligent enough to be trained and gives her human companion a necessary regard. In describing her dog as a partner, Haraway wants to show how we can all be linked. Moreover, she feels happy about the mutual communication (language and regard) between them and speaks of her dog very sweetly: "Am I happy? Is Cayenne a Klingon warrior princess? Oh yes. How do I know? Because the sun is still shining."[13] The use of "Klingon warrior princess"—a reference to intelligent extraterrestrials from the *Star Trek* series—points to the likeness between the dog and the woman and to the possibility of finding interspecies modes of understanding. This view sounds similar to the one expressed in Eiseley's story about Mickey (discussed in a subsequent chapter) a dog who is prone to become a human being.

Talking Animals and Woodland Wisdom

Eiseley maintains that "the distinctions between animals and men that have been established by biological science do not obtain in the primitive mind" (IP 111). Although the word *established* suggests that he takes the distinctions to be scientific facts, he is sympathetic to the other cultures' interpretations. He mentions, taking the Australian aborigines for example, that though a mortal being, man can actually be eternal; however, to find that higher power, he needs animal companions that talk to him and give him counsel. In dreams such divine powers appear and nature has a different meaning: "In his own fashion, he has remolded nature in mytho-poetic terms. He lives his life amidst talking animals and the marks of the going and coming of the dream divinities who are both his creators and the guardians of his days. As closely as mortal can manage, he exists in eternity" (IP 113). In this belief, man gains help from the natural world and takes guidance from animals he encounters.

N. Scott Momaday tells a story about a talking dog who saved a man abandoned by his kind in a dangerous land.

> [The man] was prepared to die, when a dog came up to him and said: "Oh you are in deep trouble. I wouldn't want to be in your moccasins. Enemies all around. You are completely surrounded. Oh it looks bad." And the man, given

that news, said: "Well, you don't say something I don't know, what can I do about that?" And the dog said: "Well do you know I could save you." And the man said: "Well if you can save me, please, do." And the dog said: "Wait a minute"—you know how dogs are—"wait a minute, I have puppies, they are little, they are hungry, they are cold. If you will take care of my puppies I will save you." The man agreed of course, the bargain was struck. And the story ends: the dog led the man round and round and they came to safety.[14]

In this story, the dog not only talks but also saves the man with its intelligence about surviving in a mountain, at least better than the man does. In requesting that the man take care of the puppies, the dog also makes a bargain with the man that ensures the survival of his own species. This story offers a legendary explanation for the special relationship between humans and dogs.

In contrast to the sense of isolation that Eiseley finds in modern man whose knowledge separates him from the rest of the world, Momaday's story is part of a tradition in which animals enrich human existence through mutual interaction. There is also an allusion to animals speaking to men in David Abram's *Spell of the Sensuous*: "According to Nillungiaq, an Inuit woman interviewed by ethnologist Knud Rasmussen early in the twentieth century":

> . . . a person could become an animal if he wanted to
> and an animal could become a human being.
> . . . All spoke the same language.[15]

In these indigenous people's tales, there is something magical about the talking dog that saves the outcast's life and the animals that speak the same language as man does and that shift between man and animal.

Eiseley points out that so long as "man was still existing in close interdependence" with the natural world (IP 143) he could project "a friendly image upon animals: animals talked among themselves and thought rationally like men; they had souls. Men might even have been fathered by totemic animals" (IP 143). He suggests that more respect should be given to the indigenous people's belief in talking animals that help man out of trouble. That form of wisdom could offset modern man's pride in his domination of nature.

Man's Loneliness in a Limited World

Children may have access to that lost communion with the natural world, especially with animals, but later on adulthood prevents this possibility: "When we were children we wanted to talk to animals and struggled to understand why this was impossible. Slowly we gave up the attempt as we grew into the solitary world of human adulthood; the rabbit was left on the lawn, the dog was relegated to his kennel. Only in acts of inarticulate compassion, in rare and hidden moments of communion with nature, does man briefly escape his solitary destiny. Frequently in science fiction he dreams of worlds with creatures whose communicative power is the equivalent of his own" (ST 37). The imagination and pleasure in talking with animals diminish along with man's development from innocent childhood into adulthood. Adults think they can share information with others only if the other party possesses the equivalent communicative power to their own as human language, which is a narrow man-centered point of view. Nevertheless, the longing for interspecies communication persists in modern man and appears in science fiction's fantasies of contact with extraterrestrials.

A more illustrative example of man being locked into an anthropocentric point of view has to do with humans naming animals. In his poem "The Bats," Eiseley, through the voice of the speaker, perceives that bats and men may be "fragments of the original creation that was done / upon the seventh day" (NA 86). In his opinion, animals and humans are fragments or in other words, elements of life. In his eyes, our human world is a "fallen" one with a fall from animal to human, from nature to culture. This alienation from other elements of creation causes our fragmentation. We have separated ourselves from our animal past and we have lost the kinship with our creaturely brotherhood. Maybe that's why later in this poem, Eiseley talks about returning to the very beginning of creation—before the naming of animals. The speaker wants us to return to where animals, plants, and humans regard themselves not as "solitary occupants of night" (NA 88) but as coinhabitants of the same garden. The reference to humans' nighttime loneliness refers to the way men domesticated fire in order to take possession of the night;[16] however, they are "solitary" because the fire sends away other animals.[17] Animals and plants are capable of living with the darkness, since they have not fallen out of nature. The speaker hopes that bats, leaves, or men can present themselves as "the tenants of a Garden" (NA 88): looking backward, the capitalized "Garden" refers to the biblical garden where "serpent and Eve and Adam and the creatures" (NA 89) lived; but it also refers to the whole biosphere. Here, on the one hand, the speaker acknowledges the differences between humans and the rest of life, especially when night comes; on the other hand, he seems to focus on what we share with each other. The speaker tries to bring men, animals, and plants back to the very beginning of life; he yearns for a return to a time before the fall—a time of harmony and innocence.

For Eiseley, human beings and other animals have some similar preferences concerning the necessities for existence. Taking his personal example, he reveals that like other animals he seeks a safe and tranquil place in nature: "My youthful isolation resulting in love of quiet and retreat as the animal in general seeks hideouts and silence because noise increasingly (in the human world) represents the first aspects of possible danger and violence.

Man with his voice began to change the natural world for animals long ago" (LN 187). The claim that the noise in the human world displeases both the animal and the writer gets further developed in his essay "How Natural is 'Natural'?" In the incident related there, Eiseley's speaker is unexpectedly approached by a muskrat that still lives in a lake that has already been taken over by human water activities and machines. He describes the animal as "an edge-of-the-world dweller" who is "in the wrong universe" (FT 156), showing sympathy for the animal in the face of man's usurpation of its dwelling place.

To warn the muskrat that man can be "a very terrible and cunning beast," the speaker throws a little pebble at his feet in order to show him that man throws stones (wields weapons) both in ancient and modern times. We see Eiseley's empathy for other creatures in his description of the muskrat's reaction: "he made almost as if to take the pebble up into his forepaws. Then a thought seemed to cross his mind—a thought perhaps telepathically received, as Freud once hinted, in the dark world below and before man, a whisper of ancient disaster heard in the depths of a burrow. Perhaps after all this was not Eden. His nose twitched carefully; he edged toward the water" (FT 156). Eiseley indicates Freud's theory about "the archaic heritage of human beings,"[18] the memories of our ancestors' experiences. In order to support his theory of the existence of ancestral memory, Freud tries to provide the evidence that the parallel can be drawn "between, on the one hand, the instinct of animals, which is simply the memory of what was experienced by their ancestors, and, on the other, the archaic heritage of human beings."[19] Eiseley does not make that distinction between animals and humans, for he imagines the muskrat suddenly recalling an ancestral experience; the "ancient disaster" suggesting some violence imposed on muskrats by humans in the distant past. Like a man coming to terms with a fallen world, the speaker's muskrat understands "this was not Eden." Humans and animals can no longer live together peacefully. Even though there is a half-joking tone to this passage that comes from the anthropomorphic projection of buried collective memories onto small rodents, the boundary lines between man and animal have been blurred.

Another similarity shared by men and animals that Eiseley's writing emphasizes is that all live in a universe bounded by the limitations of the knowledge relayed through their senses. This echoes Jakob von Uexküll's insights about the "umwelt." Uexküll says that each species lives in a world of its own perception, only paying attention to the things that are important to its own existence. In the incident of the muskrat, the scholar reveals that "the muskrat's world is naïve and limited, a fraction, a bare fraction, of the world of life: a view from a little pile of wet stones on a nameless shore" (FT 158). The muskrat's world is restricted and naïve, first of all because of its small size and its need to live close to the water, and second, because it lacks any knowledge of man. When the muskrat innocently approaches the speaker, the scholar is surprised and says that it "plainly had come with some poorly instructed memory about the lion and the lamb" (FT 156). On the one hand, the reference to "the lion and the lamb" refers to the danger the small creature incurs though contact with man. The reality is that lions eat lambs, man being like the lion and the muskrat like the lamb. On the other hand, "the lion and the lamb" refers to a popular idea that in some future age of peace, the two creatures will live without violence. This idea comes from a poorly remembered version of the verses from chapter 11 of Isiah's prophesies in the Bible ("The wolf also shall dwell with the lamb, and the leopard shall lie down with the kid; and the calf and the young lion and the fatling together; and a little child shall lead them. Isaiah II.6).[20] The small muskrat "with some poorly instructed memory" forgets the two aspects in man: good and evil, and is unaware that his capacity for violence is stronger than his potential for peace. The animal has no awareness that man intends to conquer animal life and sacrifice other species for the good of man.

At the same time, men seem just as ignorant as the muskrat in Eiseley's text—"The view of the motor speedsters in essence is similar and no less naïve" (FT 158)—perhaps because they are unaware that in destroying the muskrat's habitat, they also destroy their own. Eiseley critiques humans first because they lack adequate knowledge about themselves and others. Second, he shows that men fail to connect with the rest of life; they are incapable of communicating with others. These two privations in man's mind and body imprison him and cause his enduring loneliness. Eiseley observes that man's loneliness can be drawn from a very remote source:

> The story of Eden is a greater allegory than man has ever guessed. For it was truly man who, walking memoryless through bars of sunlight and shade in the morning of the world, sat down and passed a wondering hand across his heavy forehead. Time and darkness, knowledge of good and evil, have walked with him ever since. It is the destiny struck by the clock in the body in that brief space between the beginning of the first ice and that of the second. In just that interval a new world of terror and loneliness appears to have been created in the soul of man. (IJ 125)

Eiseley reads the story of the fall from paradise as an allegory about the time when early man had no recorded past and no sense of time. However, somewhere between the first and second ice age (perhaps eras when human mortality became quite evident?) man developed a sense of time, a fear of the cold and dark, and thereby a "knowledge of good and evil." With the development of memories and morals, humans became conscious of their own impending deaths, an awareness that isolates them from all other animals. By reconnecting with other species, he can lessen that alienation. By rethinking his own definition of intelligence as manifested by tool-using and language, he can revise his sense of his dominant position in relation to other life forms and thereby narrow the divide that cuts himself off from the other beings.

In summary, the personal stories Eiseley narrates in his essays work to turn the reader's attention to philosophical discussions about man's place among other life forms. He emphasizes that humans and animals share similar natures and origins in spite of apparent differences, and thus there is continuity between their lives, though they have taken different evolutionary roads. Taking the example of the porpoise, he says, "porpoises left the land when mammalian brains were still small and primitive." Through his imagination and his training as an anthropologist, Eiseley sees where we have been separated from the sea world and he declares that these "great sea mammals have yet taken a divergent road toward intelligence of a high order" (ST 43). He reveals that we are blocked by our anthropocentric view of intelligence, like equating tool-using (which privileges human hands) with intelligence, and therefore we are unaware that other life forms could also be as intelligent as we are. We give up communicating with animals like naïve children; when we reach adulthood we assume animals lack language (speech or words). In the anthropocentric view language is only connected to humans, for man names and defines animals, which in Eiseley's view, restricts the multiple possibilities of a live creature to what we think an "animal" is. He feels sorry for the friendly muskrat living in the quiet lake because the noisy machines and loud human voices intrude on its natural world. The small muskrat knows little about man and his intention to violate the environment; yet, Eiseley regrets more how humans lack understanding of the natural world and how they consequently threaten it. The muskrat's world is limited; it sees others from "a little pile of wet stones" (FT 158). However, Eiseley reveals that man's world is also limited; he sees others only from a human point of view, in other words, that of a land animal whose bodily features give him only a certain access to reality. Eiseley feels sympathy for the animal life that is disrupted by humans with their narrow views; however, he feels sympathy for man since he sees his loneliness. Nostalgic for a time before the great division between wildness and modern civilization, Eiseley regrets that humans and animals cannot respond to each other.

Eiseley argues that men lack understanding concerning the origins of life, as well as adequate knowledge about ourselves and others. He reveals that even domestic animals go wild at night, as his dog Wolf snarls at him because of his ancestral memory of the bones. Eiseley sees the origins of both man and canine, and though modern man or his dog now live together beside the hearth, the two creatures bear their own ancestral memories. Now we allow domesticated animals to share our safe space, while we fear wild animals, and we either expel them or escape from the spaces we share with them.

Eiseley admires what animals achieve as hunters and reveals that they belong to a different world from human hunters. Man sometimes shows too much obsession with mastery and violence in killing others. That's why Eiseley identifies with wild animals rather than the human hunters, which illustrates his becoming wild. He suggests that we should show mercy to the fellow creatures whose lives we threaten. Reconnection with nature may offer us the opportunity to find release from the self-imposed limitations of being human. Man's enduring loneliness comes from the broken relationship between himself and his brotherhood—the animals. Eiseley argues that the presumption that man has higher intelligence than other creatures because he is a better tool-user is unconsciously anthropocentric. He shows his confidence in the abilities of other animals, and this conviction leads him to admire the myths in indigenous people's cultures in which animals transmit knowledge to humans. He suggests that there are other kinds of knowledge beyond that demonstrated by modern science and technology. Thus Eiseley advocates exploring man's relation to other life forms by seeking communication and continuity beyond the threshold of language or even physical difference.

NOTES

1. Beaulieu, "Deleuze's Thought," 70.
2. Christianson, *Fox*, 414.
3. Eiseley had many notes including the start, the end, some chapters, and a rough outline prepared for his novel, which he titled *The Snow Wolf*, but which, never was completed. These notes are collected in *The Lost Notebooks of Loren Eiseley* (193–208). And in *Fox at the Wood's Edge*, Gale E. Christianson gives a brief summary of the unfinished story by Eiseley and offers his explanation of why this novel was never completed (419–421).
4. Haraway, *When Species Meet*, 280.
5. Haraway, *When Species Meet*, 279.
6. Haraway, *When Species Meet*, 279.
7. Hurth, "A Comme Animal."
8. Hurth, "A Comme Animal."
9. Calarco, *Zoographies*, 144–45.
10. "The sport is called agility, a game made up of twenty or so obstacles on a hundred-foot by hundred-foot course, in patterns set out by a diabolical judge, who evaluates the dog–human teams for speed and accuracy of performance" (Haraway, *When Species Meet*, 175).
11. Haraway, *When Species Meet*, 176.
12. Haraway, *When Species Meet*, 176.

13. Haraway, *When Species Meet*, 179.
14. Momaday, "Spiritual Mountain," 52.
15. Abram, *Spell of the Sensuous*, 87.
16. In his essay "The Angry Winter," Eiseley says, "the first fires flickering at a cave mouth are our own discovery, our own triumph, our grasp upon invisible chemical power. Fire contained, in that place of brutal darkness and leaping shadows, the crucible and the chemical retort, steam and industry. It contained the entire human future" (UU 115).
17. "There are, however, lingering legends that carry a pathetic symbolism: that it was fire that separated man from the animals" (UU 116).
18. Quinodoz, *Reading Freud*, 269.
19. Quinodoz, *Reading Freud*, 269.
20. A popular American image of this is Edward Hicks's painting *The Peaceable Kingdom* (1826).

Chapter 7

Animals as Mysterious Others

This chapter focuses on Eiseley's exploration of how far man can go into the unknown and mysterious animal world in encountering other animals in both natural and man-made settings. There are two main themes I will discuss here: how Eiseley elaborates the mysteries of animal life and how his discussions evoke readers' awe of other animals. By taking a look at Eiseley's observations on man's evolution, which he relates to that of the crustaceans, the amphibians, and mammalians, we can see why he wants to emphasize the whole picture of life and to insist that our "others" can be reflections of man himself. He is awed by the forces of nature and the evolutionary power that continue and multiply in individual lives. Eiseley draws an image of being that accords with the real properties of a human—he is "a many-visaged thing" (FT 168).

Eiseley's writings demonstrating the mysteries about animal life are often interwoven with supernatural stories and the purpose is of course to evoke eeriness and produce a feeling of awe in the readers. He understands that animals have their own ways of existing in the world, so he depicts their experience in ways that recall Jakob von Uexüll's "umwelt." He uses his imagination to think of how an animal sees the natural world. It is by adopting the other's angle of viewing that Eiseley makes us realize that we actually lack many forms of knowledge about the natural world and animal life. He tells his uncanny experiences of becoming-animal as he tries to fly and see with a group of pigeons, which, however, surprisingly make him realize the differences between man and other animals. Consequently, he chooses not to go too far into the unknown animal world. Maybe the instinctive fear of the unknown in nature either from his human ancestors or his animal past still flames in him. Nature inevitably shows a cold, cruel side to its inhabitants. Eiseley draws the analogy between the unresponsiveness of both humans and nature to small beings. Each living being has to face its mortality in confronting the indifferent human world as well as the violence and death in nature. Imagining the end of life as a pile of autumn leaves burning, Eiseley offers his philosophical thought that humanity's purpose in the life-burning process is to show empathy to others, humans or nonhumans.

7.1. THE POETICS OF ALTERITY—
AWE AND THE UNKNOWN

The Sea and the Mind: "The Versatility of Life"

Eiseley sees animals, including man, as a part of a vast ecological complex: "the interlinked web of life" (FT 75). He holds the point of view that humans and nonhumans share a common heritage, and with his imagination he brings us back to the sources of all life forms—the sea. The evidence of this origin is detectable in our very bodies: "The lime in our bones, the salt in our blood were not from the direct hand of the Craftsman. They were, instead, part of our heritage from an ancient and forgotten sea" (FT 82). In declaring that the minerals that sustain the human body come from "an ancient and forgotten sea," Eiseley makes it easier for readers to imagine the kinship between our life and other categories of life found on earth and in the sea.

In his essay "The Long Loneliness" in the book *The Star Thrower*, Eiseley tries to link the image of the land animal, man, and the sea animal, the porpoise: "both man and porpoise were each part of some great eye which yearned to look both outward on eternity and inward to the sea's heart—that fertile entity so like the mind in its swarming and grotesque life" (ST 43). He emphasizes the significance of organs of perception in both man and porpoise, and imagines that "some great eye" exists—some questing intelligence or higher power that looks at all life forms and explores all environments. He draws a relation between the sea and the mind; both are a "fertile entity" that produces "swarming and grotesque life." The fantastic creation of animal life in the sea world mirrors the mind's capacity to imagine strange forms. This drive to find analogies between the microcosm and the macrocosm suggests how Eiseley's imagination is shaped by transcendentalist philosophy.

Moreover, as a serious archeologist, Eiseley insists on the fact that man and porpoise share an essential structure; he is convinced that the development of the species has not necessarily stopped at its present stage. The porpoise is capable of learning from man and developing new capacities. Eiseley's reflections on Dr. Lilly's work with dolphins show his willingness to marvel at those new possibilities:

> We both bear in our bodies the remnants of a common skeleton torn asunder for divergent purposes far back in the dim dawn of mammalian life. The porpoise has been superficially stream-lined like a fish. His are not, however, the

cold-blooded ways of the true fishes. Far higher on the tree of life than fishes, the dolphin's paddles are made-over paws, rather than fins. He is an ever-constant reminder of the versatility of life and its willingness to pass through strange dimensions of experience. There are environmental worlds on earth every bit as weird as what we may imagine to revolve by far-off suns. It is our superficial familiarity with this planet that inhibits our appreciation of the unknown until a porpoise, rearing from a tank to say Three-Two-Three, re-creates for us the utter wonder of childhood. (ST 39)

Eiseley admires how nature is bold in its experiments and is constantly creating interesting yet "weird" forms of life like a porpoise that looks like a fish but is a mammal. Through the incident he reports of the dolphin making language-like "verbalizations" in imitation of the sounds heard in the laboratory, Eiseley reaffirms to modern people what his scientific influence, Darwin stated: "no environment is completely static, and that selection therefore is constantly at work in the production of new organisms as time and slowly changing geological conditions alter the existing world" (FT 80–81). Eiseley reminds his readers that the unknown and unpredictable can be found on our own planet, as nature constantly and creatively invents life forms, as testified not only by the beings that existed before us, but also by those that coinhabit the same time and space yet remain mysterious to men.

Alterity as Oneself: "The Several Might Be One"

We divide ourselves from animal life whose existence we separate from our own, making animals our "others" in order to define humanity. However, Eiseley believes that animals are "many versions of oneself" (FT 82). In *The Firmament of Time*, Eiseley describes being "by accident, locked in a museum," confined within "a lengthy hall containing nothing but Crustacea of all varieties" (FT 82–83). Being impressed by the variety of crab specimen that look alive behind the display windows of the natural history museum, Eiseley, through the voice of the speaker, declares his thoughts on the relation of the myriad forms of life to the essence of life: "they [the crabs] were one, one great plan that flamed there on its pedestal in the sinister evening light, but they were also many and the touch of Maya, of illusion, lay upon them" (FT 83–84). Eiseley uses the past tense "were" here, on the one hand, because he saw these samples years ago; on the other hand, he points to the past in the geological time that these crabs lived through, descending from the same origin and dividing into a seemingly infinite variety of forms. The reference to Maya needs to be unpacked. Maya is the name of the Buddha's mother, but it is also a term standing for illusion in Hindu thought. In these Eastern philosophies, the natural world is "appearance (maya, 'illusion') spun over emptiness (sunyata)."[1] The speaker, awed by the variety of crustacean forms on display, experiences a crisis of doubt and detachment. The crabs seem to shake his connection to the material world.

Moreover, they cause him to question not only human centrality, but also the primacy of the individual (a foundational American tenet): "Around us in the museum cases was an old pattern, out of the remote sea depths. It was alien to man. I would never underestimate it again. It is not the individual that matters; it is the Plan and the incredible potentialities within it. The forms with the Form are endless and their emergence into time is endless" (FT 84). Here Eiseley measures the distance between humans, who he believes came from the ocean, and the marine creatures that inhabit it. Even if we think that we are familiar with certain forms of crabs, there are whole Crustacean families that we don't know or can't know. They are made on an "old pattern"—a phrase that emphasizes their long-term existence in geological time. The capitalized "Plan" and "Form" make a link to the capitalized "He" in Christianity—evoking different creation stories. However, "the Plan" and "the Form" are eternal while the Christian time scale that measures the world's duration is short.[2] "The Plan" may refer to the systematic arrangement of various life forms as elements in the biosphere.

If the strangeness of the crabs is unsettling, the belief that there is some order to the dizzying display of difference is reassuring: "The species alter, one might say, but the *Form*, that greater animal which stretches across the millennia, survives. There is a curious comfort in the discovery. In some parts of the worlds, if one were to go out into the woods, one would find many versions of oneself, with fur and grimaces, surveying one's activities from behind leaves and thickets. It is almost as though somewhere outside, somewhere beyond the illusions, the several might be one" (FT 82). Eiseley feels the power of life in nature. He regards "the *Form*" as a "greater animal" that unifies the mass of life in nature and allows different forms of the life force to survive in time. This recalls his literary inspiration Thoreau, for whom "the world was no mere system of mechanical order but a flux of energy capable of welding all things into an animated *kosmos*."[3] Belief in this continuity can efface the borderlines between different species, namely, the forms of individual lives including that of man. The creatures with "fur and grimaces" can then be seen as reflections of man. Maybe that's the reason he warns that modern man has to be careful about the "surveying" eyes behind him in the darkness. We are not the only life form born from the "greater animal," and we are among many strange others. Those others have the power and agency to look back at us and to judge our behavior. Eiseley confirms this idea by admitting that his speaker in this anecdote learns a lesson from these crabs:

> They reminded me that an order of life is like a diamond of many reflecting surfaces, each with its own pin-point of light contributing to the total effect. It is a troubling thought, contend some, to be a man and a God-created creature, and at the same time to see animals which mimic our faces in the forest. It is not a good thing to take the center of the stage and to feel at one's back the amused little eyes from the bush. (FT 85)

Eiseley doubts that the thought that only humans are "God-created" holds water. The fact that other animals are reflections of us disturbs our privileged place in the universe. To see the whole picture of life—the Plan—is to realize that our place remains within the natural world where multiple forms of life coexist. We are not above nature or outside it. Our form of life is just one "reflecting surface" of the diamond of the whole biosphere and we'd better not assume that we "take the center of stage" because "the many-faced animal of which we are one flashing and evanescent facet" (FT 86) will outlive us.

This "many-faced" being is one among many keywords in Eiseley's philosophical thoughts about animal life. He relates one anecdote in which, as a university professor, he is questioned by a youth: "Do you believe there is a direction to evolution?" (FT 167). In response, he sees with his imagination the evolutionary road from the swamp to the young student, and this prompts the following reflection:

> And who among us, under the cold persuasion of the archaeological eye, can perceive which of his many shapes is real, or if, perhaps, the entire shape in time is not a greater and more curious animal than its single appearance? . . . I too am a many-visaged thing that has climbed upward out of the dark of endless leaf falls, and has slunk, furred, through the glitter of blue glacial nights. I, . . . am the single philosophical animal. I am the unfolding worm, and mudfish, the weird tree of Igdrasil shaping itself endlessly out of darkness toward the light. I have said this is not an illusion. It is when one sees in this manner. (FT 168)[4]

The "cold" archaeological observation sees the sweep of evolutionary history, but it takes the imaginative eyes of the poet to see the possibilities that this implies. The continuity in the various forms suggests to the "philosophical animal" that he is more than his singular appearance. The speaker, the human professor, is just one of the "many-visaged" aspects of the "Form" of "Life" that Eiseley discusses in the crab story. The speaker is human but also a worm, a mudfish. . . . Returning to the notion of Maya evoked earlier, Eiseley clarifies that the natural world is not an illusion. Seen from the archeologist/poet's point of view, all these differences are branches of "the weird tree of Igdrasil," an image of the immense possibilities of life. This realization builds a basis for feelings of sympathy for other forms of life.

Man's Ignorance of Strangeness in Nature

Eiseley's refection on differences within species raises a difficult philosophical problem. From a humanist perspective, an individual can hardly be representative of all his own kind, not to mention of all animals. Eiseley's paradoxical assertion that "the several can be one" seems a solution for this problem. He enters into the philosophical debate about humans and animals—the difficult question of the relationship between humans and other-than-humans—through talking about an individual animal.

In his essay "The Ghostly Guardian," Eiseley talks about "an animal that is followed everywhere by a ghost. The ghost floats uncannily a little above and just back of the animal's head." The following paragraphs reveal the mystery: the animal is the spider monkey and the ghost that follows it everywhere is its "tremendously lengthy" tail. The reason Eiseley speaks of the tail as "in very truth, a guardian ghost" of the spider monkeys as well as other creatures who possess "tails of this general type" in the Amazon basin is that he sees the tail's "almost preternatural grasping power," as the thing that makes its owner's survival in the rain forest canopy possible. The tail that keeps the monkey from falling earns the "guardian" title; and it is named a "ghost" because it has "an independent life of its own" thanks to its sensitive "muscles and nerves" (ST 76–77). The words like "uncannily" or "preternatural" that Eiseley chooses to describe the tail show his curiosity about nature's creative hand in making different life forms.

There are good reasons that Eiseley is impressed by the strangeness of the monkey's tail; however, he is developing a more important idea: "the tail itself is not nearly so mysterious as the way in which numerous diverse creatures in one particular area of forest have acquired these hovering appendages" (ST 77). Eiseley's speaker is not satisfied that the biologists and "present-day experimentation" explain away this existence only as "the result of chance adaptations" (ST 79). He then goes back to Darwin and finds that he had doubt over why "apt variations were all conveniently at hand in this one place." Darwin could not explain everything with his theory of evolution and he "used to speak of the mysterious and unknown laws governing these matters" (ST 81). He reveals that Darwin was more humble than his followers and felt awe about the surprising features of the animals he studied.

Eiseley explains that Darwin had some doubt about "chance mutations": "Once he expressed himself to the effect that the independent duplication of a single animal form, if proven for two separate areas of the world, might force him to entertain the possibility of some other explanation for evolution than that offered by chance mutations acted upon by natural selection" (ST 81). This twentieth-century scientist therefore offers his explanation for the "hypothetical case proposed by Darwin" and reveals that though the two groups were separated long time ago, the monkeys of South America are very similar to "those of the Old World" (ST 81). Eiseley then meditates: "creatures of very similar brain, face, habits, and general appearance would have come into being in separate parts of the world from ancestors far below the monkey level. Such a development might suggest latent evolutionary powers not entirely the simple product of what we, in our ignorance of a better word, call chance. We are not in a position as yet to verify absolutely this interpretation of the separate origins of the Old and New World monkeys, but it is the most reasonable theory that we possess" (ST 82). Through his consideration of the mysteries related to these monkeys, Eiseley tries to make his point that life is governed by an evolutionary power that is running continuously and inscrutably. The "chance mutations" that the science world tells us about do not seem adequate to explain away the evolution in animal life.

In pointing out Darwin's wonderment in the face of an inexplicable coincidence, Eiseley highlights our ignorance of the strangeness in nature. Confronted with "the inscrutable way of tails in nature," (ST 77) we either ignore the question or we simply explain it away by saying that "it's the way of monkeys." He reveals that "the 'way of things' is a cover-up for our ignorance" (ST 78). To emphasize further his point of view that man is limited in explaining things and should have respect for the mysteries in nature, Eiseley reminds us of the scale of the Amazon forest and the comparative insignificance of man: "the real life of the rain forest lives among the rafters of a thousand-mile attic more than one hundred feet above the ground," while man "is still a puny shadow who, a few feet from the protecting river, may vanish without a trace" (ST 78–79). Through his tone, it sounds clear that in the vast but threatened world of the forest, man possesses much weaker capacities to live or survive than these monkeys, even though "harried by the fires and axes of man, forests are everywhere in the process of disappearance" (ST 78). Interestingly, Eiseley draws a parallel between the rain forest and the sea, regarding that "this world *is* a sea, a sea over whose swaying green billows pass the wind and the birds. Below the depths are still" (ST 79). This image links up the meditation on the crabs and that on the monkeys' tails. The two "sea" worlds are alien to man, and their unfathomed depths can surely evoke man's awe and humility.

The Angle of Vision of Manhattan Pigeons

In asking us to see the rain forest as the sea and in revealing that these realms possess vastness and depth beyond human reach, Eiseley attempts to change people's angle of viewing the natural world. Eiseley uses his knowledge and experiences with nonhumans to expand people's views about the natural world.

There is one anecdote in which Eiseley's speaker in his midnight reading catches sight of a beetle in his very clean living room and examines the creature from an unusual angle: "I pulled my feet up in the chair and leaned down until I was practically standing on my head. It was no illusion. A huge black bug—not a roach, but a fat-bodied and particularly odious beetle of dubious affinities—was marching right across the carpet under my nose" (NC 36). It seems the beetle comes from nowhere and its disappearance also holds mystery. The man witnesses the beetle entering from under the chest in the living room; however, he never sees it again, even after removing the furniture to verify. The description of how the man sees the beetle may recall Thoreau's words in his journal: "I look between my legs up the river across Fair Haven. Subverting the head, we refer things to the heavens; the sky becomes the ground the picture."[5] The transcendentalist says in his journal of August 5, 1851, "It's not what you look at that matters, it's what you see." In Eiseley's story the speaker also sees with an upside-down view and he learns that there are "manifestations of the night country" (NC 36) like the beetle that we don't see in daylight and from a usual angle. In contrast to his wife, who would get the bug out of door with "an exterminating broom," the speaker must "stand in awe" (NC 36) of the dark world where the black creature he encounters comes from.

Eiseley is a discoverer of the miracles in nature. There are two kinds of encounters in Eiseley's stories: encounters in natural settings and encounters in man-made settings. He offers encounters with animals in familiar human environments to bring back nature and the wild to modern city dwellers, encouraging readers to be aware and think over their relationship with other creatures. By telling people about his meetings and exchanges with animals, Eiseley tries to show another dimension of the world. For example, watching a dozen pigeons soar high up over the lofts of a modern city at dawn, Eiseley regrets not having wings and being "only a man" (IJ 167). Looking down at the birds from the inverted angle of his hotel room in a skyscraper, he shows that even a midtown like Manhattan is not fully man's. It is shared with other creatures. Here it seems that Eiseley emphasizes that animals and humans are more like "coinhabitants" even though they are not always aware of one another's presence.

However, though possessing great passion in his quest to discover nature, Eiseley reveals the moments he draws back and realizes the difference between animals and humans. In the anecdote of the pigeons in Manhattan for example, the speaker is so enchanted by these white-winged birds flying in silence that he imagines he is one of them: "Perhaps I, myself, was one of these birds dreaming unpleasantly a moment of old dangers far below as I teetered on a window ledge" (IJ 166). Here the speaker becomes the bird and imagines that he remembers the threat that he felt from land dwellers—humans—perhaps in the form of a gunshot from below. The speaker almost joins these birds: "the muscles of my hands were already making little premonitory lunges" (IJ 166); however, his coat on the chair in the hotel room reminds him that "there was a way down through the floors, that I was, after all, only a man. I dressed then and went back to my own kind" (IJ 167). The dream of flying with the pigeons as one of them is broken when he realizes his way to get down is to descend the stairs on foot, not to leap out of windows. The speaker's reaction of getting dressed with his coat may remind readers what Derrida does after he finds his cat stares at him when he is naked—"dress myself, even a little."[6] Both feel awkward when meeting other animals' challenge, as if they are afraid of going too far into the unknown animal world.

Despite the recognition that he cannot fly, Eiseley's speaker still imagines the possibility of something other than the seemly, rational decision of not flying with these pigeons. In great detail he describes his idea that "I should have to launch out into that great bottomless void with the simple confidence of young birds reared high up there among the familiar chimney pots and interposed horrors of the abyss" (IJ 166). He imagines what the city looks and feels like to a flying pigeon. Through Eiseley's tone and choice of words, one point is clear: when the material things that man finds familiar (the skyscrapers and even the chimney pots he builds) are seen from another angle (a birds' eye view), the city is suddenly made strange. A hotel room gives way to a "bottomless void" or "the abyss."[7] Eiseley draws the image of space beyond the space that humans can see and touch, conjuring it out of its invisible status as a transparent, unconsidered background. Through his act of imagination, Eiseley tries to reveal that the void is not a figurative expression but also a realistic existence, if one sees from the perspective of other-than-humans.

To some degree, Eiseley thinks, animals can also manage to see from an inverted angle, adopting the perspective of humans. In his essay "The Judgment of the Birds," Eiseley tells an incident in which a crow, a bird that normally "takes good care to stay up in the very highest trees and, in general, to avoid humanity," deviates from its usual behavior. One morning of thick fog it almost knocks into the speaker's face and apparently looks "lost and startled" (IJ 168). The bird seems to think that the man walks in the air, which, in Eiseley's opinion, eventually changes the crow's normal knowledge about man. Eiseley imagines the crow "had thought he [as usual Eiseley uses 'he' for an animal; here it's a crow] was high up, and when he encountered me looming gigantically through the fog, he had perceived a ghastly and, to the crow mind, unnatural sight" (IJ 169). Wendy Harding and Jacky Martin comment on this: "By imagining himself in the crow's mental world, Eiseley tries to ensure that readers do not revert to the normal binaries and hierarchies of human knowledge. He insists that birds and other animals have their own certainties."[8] Coming to the conclusion that the human world and animal world are interpenetrated by each other, Eiseley continues to reverse man's ideas about animals by confirming that the animals are miracles in the universe.

Departing or Staying: A Journey with Pennsylvania Frogs

Another illustration of Eiseley's complex feelings about how far man can go in encountering animals is found in the description of one man's night journey with a number of toads that Eiseley narrates in "Big eyes and small eyes." The speaker is delighted to find "along a section of damp sand," "several large toads" are also traveling at night as he does. In observing them, he notes: "there was something so attractive about their little bursts of energy that, tired as I was, I began to skip with them. I was delighted now to have even lowly company" (NC 41). However, this feeling of delight does not last long. Though the man is happy (almost jumping automatically with the toads), he realizes they are heading on different paths, and that although he wants to share their journey, their ways must eventually part. He admits to a complex feeling, mixed with fear and maybe hope: "I do not know where they might have eventually led me, though I had a feeling that if I stayed and hopped with them long enough I might acquire this knowledge in some primordial manner. With this thought I parted from them at a turn in the stream bed and made my way again over open rolling foothills in the dark" (NC 41). The speaker seems to be afraid of going too far with these toads, and though "this knowledge" may be gained "in some primordial manner," he departs from these amphibians.

Interestingly, in his essay "The Dance of the Frog" in *The Star Thrower*, Eiseley tells a story about his old colleague jumping with the toads that are leading him to a river. The anecdote begins with the young narrator giving a lecture about the "'shaking tent rite'" in the religious beliefs of the Indians of the northern forest, in which gigantic leaders of animal species, the so called "'game lords,'" are summoned in this ritual as "'their voices ... emerge from the shaking tent'" (ST 107). "'The Indians believe it, but do *you* believe it?'" is the question his old colleague, an amphibian expert, poses to him, and the young man gives a hurried answer that "'I am a scientist'" (ST 108) to avoid this troublesome question. Here, in italicizing "you," Eiseley implicitly turns the question to his readers, inviting us to accept what native peoples believe—the existence of "the game lords" that "'partake of human qualities, will and intelligence, but they are of animal shape'" (ST 107). He questions whether modern men can suspend their scientific skepticism and accept the animal voices emerging from the tent as credible manifestations.

The young speaker meets the old zoologist later in a bar, and the young scientist pleads with Dr. Dreyer to tell what he knows about the woods and frogs, admitting that "'I'm too young to be saying what I believe or don't believe in at all'" (ST 109). Again, this suspension of disbelief sounds like the response Eiseley solicits from his readers, for he writes as the renowned professor looking back at his youthful self. After the young man shows his respect to the old zoologist, Dreyer begins telling his personal experience relating to "the game lords." It happened in "'a road that came out finally in a marsh along the Schuykill River'" (ST 110)—an area long inhabited by the indigenous people of Delaware who later got pushed out—a place meaningful to Eiseley as it includes both wilderness and city, in other words, a city where men can encounter the wilderness.

The old man takes a midnight walk and encounters thousands of frogs skipping to "'the water for mating and egg laying.'" As he recalls, "'it was late, and the creatures seemed to know it. You could feel the forces of mighty and archaic life welling up from the very ground. The water was pulling them—not water as we know it, but the mother, the ancient life force, the thing that made us in the days of creation, and that lurks around us still, unnoticed in our sterile cities'" (ST 112). Through the voice of the old man, Eiseley lists several contrasts in the natural world: mighty and ancient forces working at night even in urban settings. "Sterile" may refer to the privation of wildlife in a fully man-made environment, or it may indicate the minds of the city dwellers who lack the capacity to imagine other worlds. Since the old man is "'more aware of the creatures'" (ST 112) and when he sees various frogs hopping along the "'roadway leading to the river'" (ST 112), he begins to skip pleasantly with them. As he himself explains, "'you will skip because something within you knows the time—frog time'" (ST 111). In his narration, the old man emphasizes the vitality in wild things and shows his awe and respect for the force of life.

The mystery or, more exactly, terror comes when the old man "'began to grow conscious that I was not alone'" and "'it was only as we passed under a street lamp that I noticed, beside my own bobbing shadow, another great, leaping grotesquerie that had an uncanny suggestion of the frog world about it'" (ST 112–13). It seems that the mysterious game lord—the supernatural, giant frog—is jumping behind him. The man does not turn around, though he acknowledges that his listener might think "'it would be the scientific thing to do'" (ST 113). In putting this protest in the old zoologist's mouth, Eiseley anticipates the readers' potential objection. The old scientist explains that he fears what he might see there "'on an empty road at midnight'" (ST 113). Unlike the conventional scientist who seeks to eliminate the unknown, the old man fears its power, which is precisely the counterpart of the familiar world: "'You do not look—you cannot look—because to do so is to destroy the universe in which we move and exist and have our transient being'" (ST 113). In evoking the danger inherent in a mortal being like man catching sight of the immortal, Eiseley is suggesting that there is a need to approach alterity with respect. The old man's terror continues because he has encountered a force that threatens to transform him: "'Even as I leaped, I was changing. It was this, I think, that stirred the last remnants of human fear and human caution that I still possessed. My will was in abeyance; I could not stop. Furthermore, certain sensations, hypnotic or otherwise, suggested to me that my own physical shape was modifying, or about to change. I was leaping with a growing ease. I was—'" (ST 114). In the course of the telling, the atmosphere becomes more mysterious; not only does the man get a glimpse of a supernatural being, but he himself begins to undergo a physical shifting—maybe into a frog because he seems to jump more easily than he leaps with his human body. His terror reaches a climax when he sees the wharf at the end of the road—where the frogs are heading, and he realizes that "'man is a land animal'" and jumping into the river together with his wild company is not an end of this seemingly pleasant journey but an end of his human life. Thus the desperate man cries for help from God though he is not religious man; moreover, he stops as if "'release[d] from demoniac possession'" (ST 114). At the end of his narration, the old zoologist removes the glove that he always wore on one of his hands, and shows the young man what it covers—"a webbed batrachian hand," which shocks the young man, who then chooses to flee away from the bar. Maybe the young scientist is escaping from this account of supernatural forces that contradicts his scientific training, or perhaps the question his elder colleague poses to him—whether he should have jumped into the wharf with the frogs—strikes him as more or less like madness. The zoologist's tale is open to interpretation—it can be dismissed as an old man's rambling or taken as a testimony to the existence of alien spiritual forces.

Several elements make the story mysterious and meaningful. First, the story takes place in a realistic setting—a riverbank of Pennsylvania, that Eiseley's readers may actually find familiar. Second, in this normal setting the teller witnesses a supernatural thing, in that the game lord of frogs jumps after him as he skips happily with the frogs at midnight, and he is becoming a frog (he even has a frog's webbed palm as a proof). Third, the story relates to native belief as well as Christian belief: out of fear of ending up jumping into the wharf with the frogs and their game lords, the old man cries out "'*Help! In the name of God, help me! In the name of Jesus, stop!*'" and he does stop and finds no more game lord following him but just "'some tiny froglets'" (ST 114–15) jumping at his feet. It seems a dream or an illusion has been broken. It is a story that mixes realistic and fantastic scenes and thereby offers readers room to imagine or even to believe. There comes also a meaningful warning from Eiseley that humans have the potentiality to become animals and are subject to the control of mysterious life forces.

There are many other stories that Eiseley narrates in which people experience terrors similar to that experienced by the old zoologist. The resulting discomfort in the face of mystery is well explained by Rudolf Otto in his book *The Idea of Holy: An Inquiry into the Non-Rational Idea of the Divine and Its Relation to the Rational*:

> It first begins to stir in the feeling of "something uncanny," "eerie," or "weird." It is this feeling which, emerging in the mind of primeval man, forms the starting point for the entire religious development in history. . . . It implies that the mysterious is already beginning to loom before the mind, to touch the feelings. It implies the first application of a category of valuation which has no place in the everyday natural world of ordinary experience, and is only possible to a being in whom has been awakened a mental predisposition, unique in kind and different in a definite way from any "natural" faculty. And this newly-revealed capacity, even in the crude and violent manifestations which are all it at first evinces, bears witness to a completely new function of experience and standard of valuation, only belonging to the spirit of man.[9]

In recounting these inexplicable, perhaps supernatural, happenings and exploring the protagonist's inner feeling toward these experiences, Eiseley seeks to renew in his modern readers the instinctive awe felt by our primeval ancestors, for the mysteries of the world that is neither made by humans nor familiar to them.

Concerning what is strange about life and what is ordinary about life, Eiseley has his distinctive point of view. He always insists that one's way of viewing depends on the human mind, which he assures can be improved and changed. One way to go outside the boundaries of the everyday in order to encounter miracles is to cross the boundaries of species. Another way is to cross the boundaries of time, relating the present to the remote past and to the future. And miracles, as perceived by Eiseley, are "particularly concerned with life, with the animal aspect of things" (ST 57). Contrary to the modern prejudice, Eiseley argues that miracles are not the superstitions of simple, uneducated people: "The common man thinks a miracle can just be 'seen' to be reported. Quite the contrary. One has to be, I was discovering, reasonably sophisticated even to perceive the miraculous. It takes experience; otherwise, more miracles would be encountered" (ST 57–58). Eiseley shows that man may need to see beyond what his physical eyes show him to experience other images of nature.

To conclude, in order to see and allow others to see the world with a fuller and newer view, Eiseley relates a number of anecdotes concerning his personal experiences. Through Eiseley's mental eyes, readers can reexamine what we know about animals. Rather than being defined by humans as the alterity that clarifies what it means to be human, animals are proof of the world's limitless variety. The vastness and versatility of life inspire and impress Eiseley and he reminds modern man of his evolutionary road and warns us that we are still under the control of a higher power, the mysterious force of evolution. Entering the philosophical debate about the mystery of life through individual examples, Eiseley expounds his theory that "the several might be one" (FT 82), in which he sees the divisions of life belonging to a greater animal that possesses endless possibilities of Form and Life. To change people's limited worldview, Eiseley proposes that men see the natural world as animals do. The result of his experience of seeing the busy city as pigeons do is surprising, as he says "I had seen, just once, man's greatest creation from a strange inverted angle, and it was not really his at all" (IJ 167). The inverted angle of animals seems to help man see more correctly his human world, or more importantly to see his place among other life forms.

Eiseley wants to convey to his readers his feeling of awe in the face of the inexplicable variety of the natural world. Through stories associated with native beliefs and supernatural happenings, he shows how humans' encounters with the wild, even in cities, offer the potentiality of man's transformation. Paradoxically, it is through man's experience of becoming-animal that Eiseley emphasizes the unknown in animal life that gives humans the feeling of the uncanny. James Goebel, in his essay "Uncanny Meat," explains that it's the suppressed knowledge of our own animality that gives us the feeling of uncanniness. He says: "for Freud, the corporeal dimension of the uncanny is marked by the recurrence of a repressed scene of loss or potential loss, that is, the castration complex. In my argument, 'uncanny meat' refers to the repressed site of indistinction or indiscernibility that I have been exploring thus far; a productive disavowal which, in the case of human-animal relations, lies at the heart and is constitutive of dominant narratives of human exceptionalism, based as they are on a rigid distinction between human and animal life."[10] This uncanny feeling is what Eiseley allows his readers to experience and thus to ponder the arbitrariness of the human-animal distinction and the evidence of human-animal relations.

In the stories that Eiseley tells, it may be the feeling of eeriness that prompts the protagonists who encounter wild animals as companions in their journeys, at last to decide to depart from them. When Eiseley's speaker gets dressed to come back to being "only a man," an important point seems to have been reached. We can wonder whether his decision to stop before going further (to respond to the invitation of the flying birds) is caused by fear of entering into the unknown world of animal life. The violence and death in animal life are aspects of the natural world that modern people may want to turn away from. Through exploring this domain in the next section, we can understand more about Eiseley's philosophical thoughts on man's relation with other animals.

7.2 VIOLENCE AND DEATH IN ANIMALS

"Cruelty of the Natural World"

Eiseley shows the threatening aspect of the natural world mostly through recording violence and death in animals. For example, he recounts an incident when he sees a dead dog on a seashore. The abandoned corpse demands a response from the speaker: "I stepped back a little hesitantly from the smell of death, but still I paused reluctantly. Why, in this cove littered with tin cans, bottles, and cast-off garments, did I find it difficult, if not a sacrilege, to turn away? Because, the thought finally came to me, this particular tattered garment had once lived" (ST 140). The speaker feels the dog cannot be thrown away like inanimate garments, even though the indifferent sea tides treat both in a similar way, throwing the remains of the dog to the shore like the other detritus. Eiseley shows a similar respect for the dead dog to that one would accord to a human body; to ignore it would be close to "sacrilege" because it had once lived a life. He sees the burlap bag that wrapped the dog's body is broken, and "vast natural forces had intervened to clothe him with a pathetic dignity." The warm-hearted scholar finds that the sea does not allow a proper burial for the dog (human standards demand that the body should be properly wrapped). Thus, he wants to bury the long-dead dog by digging a grave; however, "the stones would have prevented his burial" (ST 140). He feels the helplessness of a small being—whether man or dog—before the power of the vast sea.

Deleuze once argued that "it is not humans but animals who know how to die. This is because animals seek solitude to live out their last moments with dignity away from the group, on the edge of the territory, and with no expectation of posthumous celebration."[11] To choose to depart one's life in "the way wild things die" (NC 173) is a form of wisdom. Eiseley records such a death in his poem "The Blizzard." It tells of a lonely old professor who is "inept in human relations" (NA 62) whom the speaker sees in a snowstorm. The speaker is "out in it by chance" (NA 63) and sees that the old man makes his way with great difficulty. Though the old teacher glances at the speaker, he chooses to avoid contact, obviously "he wanted no one, / no speech, no arm, no elbow, no assistance" (NA 63). This is the last time the speaker sees the old man and clearly he respects the dying man's choice of walking into death by being covered in snowfalls. Because he respects the old scholar's choice, he refuses to treat him like a domesticated animal that he would lead to its "shelter" (NA 63). The speaker's poetic words give the man's solitary figure a romantic though cruel way of ending. He shows his respect for "the way wild things die"; however, he also shows that "the world is pitiless" (NA 62) to outcasts in human society.

Autumn Fire and Its Smoke

In an anecdote that challenges the modern pride in man's superiority Eiseley represents human beings as confined in bodies composed of sticks and pulleys. He tells how he once spends the whole night waiting in the empty corridor of the airport for a flight the next morning. A man approaches him clumsily, and the speaker is surprised, for "with an anatomist's eye I saw this amazing conglomeration of sticks and broken, misshapen pulleys which make up the body of man" (NC 177).[12] The sight of the man struggling with his disability evokes the scientist's desperate insight about the human body and its relation to humanity:

> How, oh God, I entreated, did we become trapped within this substance out of which we stare so hopelessly upon our own eventual dissolution? How for a single minute could we dream or imagine that thought would save us, children deliver us, from the body to this death? Not in time, my mind rang with my despair; not in mortal time, not in this place, not anywhere in the world would blood be staunched, or the dark wrong be forever righted, or the parted be rejoined. Not in this time, not mortal time. The substance was too gross, our utopias bought with too much pain. (NC 177)

On the one hand, the passage suggests that humanity is fallen and that the wrongs committed cannot be corrected or the separations rejoined. On the other hand, the very fact of man's physical vulnerability could be taken as a catastrophe. Our human world and our mortal time seem to be too restrained for restoration to be possible. Here Eiseley mourns the fact that we are trapped in the human body—"this mechanical thing of joints and sliding wires" (NC 177). He severely doubts that our "second world" drawn by our mind can save us from mortality, and suspects our hope to be futile that "children deliver us." We need something more to transcend our mortality. Curiously, the essay ends with an echo of an earlier passage in which he relates how a firefly lights up a passage from St. Paul: "Beareth all things, believeth all things, hopeth all things, endureth all things" (NC 176). He repeats the words: "'Beareth all things,' believe, believe. It is thus that one day and the next are welded together, that one night's dying becomes tomorrow's birth" (NC 178). Though this conclusion could be read as a conventional recourse to Christian theology, his literary corpus suggests a different interpretation. However, the struggle with despair is palpable in his work.

In what direction is Eiseley pointing in meditating upon man's mortality? His essay "The Last Neanderthal," in which he discusses life and energy transformation through the image of fire and smoke, contains some clues toward an answer to this question. Lynch and Maher refer to Jacqueline Carson's suggestion that this essay, "with the imagery of blue plums and smoke, serves as an emblematic representation of the interplay between organization and entropy and the capacity for human memory to store, transmit, and preserve energy as complex wholes, in spite of individual mortality and inevitable dissolution."[13] Nevertheless, the image of the plums and smoke can have more than one interpretation, for Eiseley links it to another memory that complexifies it. He takes his remembrance of the wild-plum thicket in an autumn fire he visited earlier and says, "the smoke from the autumn fields seemed to be penetrating my mind. I wanted to drop them at last, these carefully hoarded memories. I wanted to strew them like the blue plums in some gesture of love toward the universe all outward on a mat of leaves. Rich, rich and not to be hoarded, only to be laid down for someone, anyone, no longer to be carried and remembered in pain like the delicate paw lying forever on the beach at Curaçao" (ST 151–52). The "delicate paw" refers to the earlier episode in which a dog's body gets washed up to the shore by the sea tide. The speaker gives a detailed description: "The dog was little more than a skeleton but still articulated, one delicate bony paw laid gracefully—as though its owner merely slept, and would presently awaken—across a stone at the water's edge" (ST 140). On the one hand, the discovery of the poor dog may be a painful memory for him, one that he would be glad to relinquish; on the other hand, this memory together with others is, to him, like the "delicate paw" to the dead dog. The dog is gone, yet its paw still lies there to reflect its life; similarly, to Eiseley the past is gone, but the "hoarded memories" persist to reflect not only his life but also, perhaps, the history of humanity. Here he shows not only his sympathy for the dead dog, but also his nostalgia for the time past. It seems he finally decides to earn a personal relief and let go his "hoarded memories." Eiseley no longer wants to carry the painful emotions he has in recalling these past events.

The following paragraph records a romantic scene—Eiseley's becoming a pile of burning autumn leaves. He "leaned farther back, relaxing in the leaves" and feels that he "was no longer *Homo sapiens*.... Perhaps all I was, really, was a pile of autumn leaves seeing smoke wraiths through the haze of my own burning." There are many images referring to the dying process of the man: "I dropped my head finally.... It was all going, I felt, memories dropping away in that high indifferent blaze that tolerated no other light" (ST 152). I've mentioned in a previous chapter that Eiseley suggests that if we imagined ourselves as burning "maples in a golden autumn," (LN 115) human death would seem more beautiful and more acceptable by being linked to the natural processes of plant life.[14]

Why does Eiseley imagine his ending as burning leaves? What's the meaning of the fire and its smoke here? We can find the correspondence to this scene in the previous page in a strange comparison between the speaker and fire. Though the latter is "a nonliving force," it "can even locomote itself."

The mobility of fire, what Jane Bennet might call its vibrant materiality,[15] allows him to imagine his body as a burning house: "What if now—and I half closed my eyes against the blue plums and the smoke drifting along the draw—what if now it is only concealed and grown slyly conscious of its own burning in this little house of sticks and clay that I inhabit? What if I am, in some way, only a sophisticated fire that has acquired an ability to regulate its rate of combustion and to hoard its fuel in order to see and walk?" (ST 151). Eiseley speaks of himself "a sophisticated fire," which recalls another essay where he speaks of himself "the single philosophical animal" (FT 168). The adjectives *sophisticated* and *philosophical* reveal his acknowledgment of man's living as an intellectual being. But the terms *animal, fire,* and *house of sticks and clay* suggest that humanity is not so exceptional after all. The "sticks and clay" recalls the image of the human body composed of sticks and pulleys in the previous anecdote. All these images underline human beings' materiality and mortality.

The fire reveals the vulnerability of human flesh. He holds on to a more durable substance to give him the confidence to make his way through it: "I went on, clutching for stability the flint knife in my pocket. A blue smoke like some final conflagration swept out of the draw and preceded me. I could feel its heat. I coughed, and my eyes watered. I tried as best I could to keep pace with it as it swirled on. There was a crackling behind me as though I myself were burning, but the smoke was what I followed. I held the sharp flint like a dowser's twig, cold and steady in my hand" (ST 152). Eiseley's "eyes watered" from the burning smoke, but there is also the suggestion that he feels sad and there is something that the fire and smoke stand for he cries over. Eiseley says, "I have spoken figuratively of fire as an animal, as being perhaps the very *essence* of animal. Oxidation, I mean, as it enters into life and consciousness" (ST 151). Here, his eyes water perhaps for the way animal life hoards and burns off energy. Without energy, the life process cannot be sustained; however, a new life points to a new death. So, the involuntary tears express the speaker's sadness for his mortality.

Robert Franke suggests that the flint knife that Eiseley fingers in this episode can be seen as a "symbol of mankind's past."[16] According to his interpretation, Eiseley clutches onto the past; however, isn't it what all mankind clutch onto? The archaic object can be seen as a sign of the stability in mankind's history. Eiseley reveals that Neanderthal man had "his own small dreams and kindnesses" with the evidence that "he had buried his dead with offerings." He acknowledges that "beyond the chipped flints and the fires in the cavern darkness his mind had not involved itself with what was to come upon him with our kind—the first bowmen, the great artists, the terrible creatures of his blood who were never still" (ST 149). The Neanderthal made tools (chipped flints) and made fires against darkness as our ancestors did; however, in Eiseley's view, the flame of violence that our kind manifests seems not to be kindled in the mind of the Neanderthal man. Eiseley says that *Homo sapiens* is "a changeling cuckoo brood," and "the conquerors," and in our history "bronze replaced flint, iron replaced bronze, while the killing never ceased" (ST 149).

This melancholy reflection on *Homo sapiens* continues in the poem "The Deer," where mankind is said to carry the smell of death. Here again we find the image of the burning thicket and its smoke. The speaker in the poem meets and scares off a deer along the highway "but deep enough in the glade" (AKA 76). Eiseley uses "pine smoke" and "forest burning" (AKA 77) that echo the earlier episode about the plum thicket in fire and its smoke. In this poem the "fire" and "smoke" refer to the threat of death brought by humans. The speaker says that it's himself (a man) that brings the "never till then defined" word—death (AKA 77). Eiseley tries to emphasize that this kind of death is different from the natural death in the biosphere. He draws the analogy between an element in nature—smoke from a burning forest (though there is no hint about whether it's caused by humans or not)—and the intrusion of humans into the animal's world. Both indicate violence, damage, and death. Here Eiseley indicates that animals that are acute in identifying beings by their scent may understand that humans smell of death. In the poem, Eiseley regards himself as "the messenger" who sends the wildlife the message that man kills. He says, "Perhaps he [the deer] has not seen me as a man, I thought, / but as an emanation, a creature of warning" (AKA 77). Eiseley imagines what the deer sees about him and hopes that in the animal's eyes, it sees the danger of man. In Eiseley's eyes, the deer is "too innocent to savor fear / or the terror that followed him" (AKA 76), but man follows and kills animals. In spite of the sense of longing in the line "This is the nearest I have ever stood to the wild" (AKA 77), it seems that the speaker prefers that animals keep away from humans, maybe because he has no confidence in humans when they encounter animals. That's why he hopes the place where the deer comes from "lies there still just beyond the high road" (AKA 77), in other words in proximity to himself—available to his memory and imagination—but out of reach of his own kind.

To sum up the meanings of the fire and smoke that collect in the above essays and poem and to further substantiate the idea that his watery eyes are a sign of sorrow, I want to reiterate, first of all, that fire and smoke refer to the process of life consuming itself. The end of life calls for sorrow, though Eiseley accepts the fact of human mortality. Second, fire points to the violence in humanity. This is perhaps what Eiseley is suggesting when he speaks of how life forms struggle to resist entropy by storing up energy and how: "At the hands of man that hoarded energy takes strange forms, both in the methods of its accumulation and in the diverse ways of its expenditure" (ST

148–49). With their "strange forms" of power, humans bring violence and death to animals. Eiseley feels sympathy for the wildlife that is destroyed by human hands. Third, humanity somehow begins with man's fire-making; however, Eiseley foresees that fire also ends humanity if man smells of death to other animals. His tears thus are for the tragedy of his own kind. In Eiseley's writing then, fire and smoke point to death. Through his efforts to make this natural element define human beings' role in regard to the rest of life, Eiseley makes people see the potential for violence and death in man and leaves room for them to think beyond their own mortality. In saying that "the smoke was what I followed" (ST 152), he suggests the process by which he arrives at these conclusions, and perhaps, at the same time, he also imagines there is something nebulous that man can follow at the end of life.

Humanity's Object

What worries this warm-hearted anthropologist most is that man intensifies the likeness between the heart of man and the heart of nature—displaying violence and indifference to suffering. During his morning walk, Eiseley witnesses "a sick pigeon huddled at an uncomfortable slant against a building wall on a street corner"; however, "no one hesitated at that corner" (NC 175). This scene reminds him of the violent sea tides that treat the dog's body as a lifeless garment. The people of the city show less compassion than the inhuman sea: "New York also has a beach of broken things more merciless than the reefs and rollers of the ocean shore" (NC 174–75). He draws the analogy between the indifference of humans to the sick pigeon and the indifference of the sea to the dead dog. The hurrying steps of the city dwellers resemble the violent sea wave:

> I watched this human ocean, of which I was an unwilling droplet, rolling past, its individual faces like whitecaps passing on a night of storm, fixed, merciless, indifferent; man in the mass marching like the machinery of which he is already a replaceable part, toward desks, computers, missiles, and machines, marching like the waves toward his own death with a conscious ruthlessness no watery shore could ever duplicate. (NC 175–76)

Besides the descriptions of the cold sea and the unresponsive human world, another comparison stands out—man and machine. For Eiseley, in the busy cities where men ignore small life forms like the sick bird while participating in the fully man-made business world, men are losing the emotions that make them human. The suffering of one small animal leads Eiseley to reflect on the necessity for compassion in a world that seems increasingly "indifferent." Maybe that is the purpose that he finally finds for humanity; the capacity for empathy means that they will not be replaced by an inanimate being like a machine.

In his poem "The Horse in College Hall," Eiseley expresses his feeling of sadness and loss when he witnesses the replacement of an old horse by a modern machine. The horse lived in "a small stable once / in the vault" "diagonally" beneath his "cell," and was occasionally "led up" to draw an ancient lawnmower (NA 100). Seeing the familiar creature become obsolete leads him to reflect that this unnatural new world made by men will finally have no place for humanity, since machines may finally replace us. Eiseley's speaker feels "a little afraid to ask" (NA 102) what happened thereafter to the old horse, maybe because he well knows what fate waits for an old horse in the cruel human world. The speaker holds a different view from those who prefer machines since they see the horse only from utilitarian point of view. He argues there are things that machines cannot do, but man can. Man has the capacity to feel and to remember. Eiseley's speaker likes what he sees about the horse before: "his pauses and head tossings / and his little banquets / of green grass" (NA 101). However, he worries that in the future, maybe no one to record this activity of smelling grass as the old scholar does in noting this scene from his office window and adding it to the memories of his life. Kindness is something that gives men their humanity. Humans mourn their own kind when they are gone. The machines that replace the horse cannot remember the endearing activities of the animal, nor can they show sympathy for other animals, including humans. The poem shows that only if we are not cruel to other animals will we be kind to our own species. It is a kind of monument to the departed horse and also a meditation on the necessity for sympathy for all living things. It is Eiseley's philosophy to accept all forms of life and here he exhorts his readers to strive for this object.

This chapter has explored some of the ways in which Eiseley reveals the variety of life and the essence of life as well as the relationship between the two. Taking the variety of the Crustaceans for example, Eiseley talks about strange mutations that are possible in just this one species; he also talks about how humans and other animals share a common heritage—the water world—where he believes life begins. Eiseley introduces his notion of the "Plan" and "Form" of "Life." The "Plan" refers to the systematic arrangement of various life forms as elements in the biosphere. He wants to emphasize the whole picture of life and to insist that our "others" can be reflections of man himself. Based on this perception, Eiseley continues to reduce the split between the human world and nonhuman world. He also helps us see the strangeness in nature and animal life. Whether it is the black beetle that the man catches sight of through an upside-down view in the night, the pigeon that silently challenges the speaker's desire to fly with him, or the crow that inspires the scholar's imagination in viewing the natural world from an inverted angle, each changes man's conventional knowledge about animal life. Though it seems that a man may gain the knowledge about flying in the air, or knowledge about frog time, he hesitates before going too deep into the animal world because the risk he takes would sacrifice his existence as a human being. Man's transformative potentialities allow him to disconnect from the material universe for a while and provoke his meditation upon the fragility of the human body and the irreversibility of time. Eiseley is aware that we can learn about mortality by meditating on violence and death in animals. Animals seem to know better than humans how to confront death. Eiseley sees the wisdom in "the way wild things die" (NC 173); however, he sees also how man can accept his end of life with dignity too. He finds a purpose for humanity in the suggestion that man needs to accept all the forms of life and show sympathy with them. To make "one night's dying [become] tomorrow's birth" (NC 178), humanity can become better in showing empathy to others.

NOTES

1. Gottlieb, *Oxford Handbook*, 386.
2. Cf. "Bruckner, however, is still obsessed with the short Christian time scale" (FT 74).
3. Worster, *Nature's Economy*, 81.
4. The mirrored tree on the cover of the 1999 edition of *The Firmament of Time* could be an image of the tree of Igdrasil.
5. Thoreau, *Early Spring*, 58.
6. Derrida, "Therefore I Am," 379.
7. In their 2012 essay "Oscar, Derrida's Cat, and Other Knowing Animals," Wendy Harding and Jacky Martin also mention this scene and comment that "New York is turned upside down, so that the terra firma of the city streets becomes a 'bottomless void' and the sky becomes a familiar element" (Harding and Martin, "Other Knowing Animals," 11).
8. Harding and Martin, "Other Knowing Animals," 11.
9. Otto, *Idea of Holy*, 14–15.
10. Goebel, "Uncanny Meat," 183.
11. Beaulieu, "Deleuze's Thought," 71.
12. Eiseley tells a story in which his colleague "could see a body, even a walking body, as a three-dimensional collection of pipes, pumps, and pulleys" (ASH 151).
13. Lynch and Maher, *Artifacts and Illuminations*, 9.
14. See my discussion "Questions about Mortality" in 5.2. Thinking beyond the Modern Split.
15. Bennett, *Vibrant Matter*, viii.
16. Franke, "Blue Plums," 147.

Chapter 8

Reconciliation of the Split

This chapter will consider Eiseley's efforts to reconcile the split between humans and other-than-humans. The split implies the construction of boundaries between the different categories, while reconciliation expresses the intention to accept difference and to establish closer relationships with beings that are different from oneself. To investigate Eiseley's efforts in this direction, I will begin with a discussion of Eiseley's becoming-animal. Becoming-animal is an important notion developed in philosophers Deleuze and Guattari's book *A Thousand Plateaus*. Without exhausting all the aspects of becoming-animal in their philosophical theory, I observe Eiseley's becoming-animal in light of their explanation of "deterritorialization." Becoming-animal is a form of deterritorialization, and it is realized through crossing the boundaries that usually separate two different groups. This is what Eiseley does in his writings. He extends man's view of animal life beyond the threshold of language and physical differences; what's more, he disturbs the anthropocentric point of view of animal life or the whole biosphere. We'll see how several anecdotes featuring animals in Eiseley's essays and poems illustrate the ways he finds to exit the world of men and enter the world of becoming-animal. I will argue that Eiseley's becomings should be taken seriously because they imply an ethical attitude to other animals. He aligns himself with animal life. We can say that he writes in the place of other-than-humans, which inevitably projects a predicament for him: is this anthropomorphism, a variant of the anthropocentrism that he is trying to escape? To resolve this question, I'll explore Eiseley's conviction that man has the potential to project himself into other states.

Eiseley urges modern people to establish civilizations in which people cultivate the correspondence of the outer and inner worlds. He encourages his readers to realize the responsibility and nobility of human beings in encountering other animals. Donna Haraway develops the ethical position that Eiseley elaborates more pragmatically through her discussions of becoming with "companion species." Both writers emphasize man's empathy for and love of other-than-humans.

8.1. BECOMING WITH ANIMALS AND CROSSING THE BOUNDARIES

The Sorcerer and Becoming-Animal

I would like to link Deleuze and Guattari's thought about writers as sorcerers to Eiseley's role as a sorcerer concerning the topic of becoming-animal. The word *sorcerer* has synonyms like *magician* or *shaman* with reference to someone who possesses magical power. The word *magical* refers to something removed from daily life or to a power that defies conventional expectations or what are thought to be the laws of nature. Deleuze and Guattari say that "becoming-animal is an affair of sorcery";[1] and "if the writer is a sorcerer, it is because writing is a becoming, writing is traversed by strange becomings that are not becomings-writer, but becomings-rat, becomings-insect, becomings-wolf, etc."[2] Eiseley's writing fits into this model. First, let's see in more detail what Deleuze and Guattari imply when talking about a writer and what exactly his becoming-animal means:

> When Hofmannsthal contemplates the death throes of a rat, it is in him that the animal "bares his teeth at monstrous fate." This is not a feeling of pity, as he makes clear; still less an identification. It is a composition of speeds and affects involving entirely different individuals, a symbiosis; it makes the rat become a thought, a feverish thought in the man, at the same time as the man becomes a rat gnashing its teeth in its death throes. The rat and the man are in no way the same thing, but Being expresses them both in a single meaning in a language that is no longer that of words, in a matter that is no longer that of forms, in an affectability that is no longer that of subjects. Unnatural participation. But the plane of composition, the plane of Nature, is precisely for participations of this kind, and continually makes and unmakes their assemblages, employing every artifice.[3]

Deleuze and Guattari emphasize that Hofmannsthal's becoming-rat involves a "symbiosis" that connects both the writer and the rat. What's more, the rat becomes a thought in the mind of the writer; and the writer's language ("no longer that of words") expresses this thought; thus a writer writes like a rat or becoming-rat.[4] A fuller understanding of Hofmannsthal's becoming-rat can be gained if one has a look at Deleuze's interview with Claire Parnet, where he reveals that "writing means necessarily pushing the language, and pushing the syntax toward a particular limit":

If the writer is the one who pushes the language into a limit, limit that separates the language of the animality, the language of the cry, that separates the language of the singing; then, the writer is responsible for the animals that die. Responsible because he replies to the animals that die. He does not write for them, I will not write for my cat or my dog, but I will write in the place of the animals that die. It is pushing the language towards that limit. And there is no literature that separates the language and the syntax from the human being and the animal. One has to be sure of that limit. . . . One should always be on the border that separates oneself from the animality in such manner that one is not separated anymore. There is an inhumanity peculiar to the human body, and the human spirit.

Hofmannsthal's becoming-rat pushes the language to the limit. His language is no longer that of words because it is no longer clear whether it is human speech or the rats' cry. The distinction between human and animal language becomes blurred. This is the aspect of a writer's becoming-animal that I want to apply to Eiseley. I'll talk about responsibility for and "replies to the animals that die" in Eiseley's writings later. First, let's see how Deleuze's claim about writers pushing language to the limit can be connected to Eiseley's becoming-animal.

Eiseley encourages his readers to escape the prison of the cultural world built on man's invention of words. He reveals that even man's self-knowledge is limited by his worldview. He warns that "the terror that confronts our age is our own conception of ourselves" (NC 54–55). Taking man's vision about his future evolutionary path for example, Eiseley challenges men who presume to have understood everything about the past: "As our knowledge of the genetic mechanism increases, our ears are bombarded with ingenious accounts of how we are to control, henceforth, our own evolution. We who have recourse only to a past which we misread and which has made us cynics would now venture to produce our own future" (NC 53). Foretelling the future is another magical power attributed to the sorcerer. However, Eiseley is skeptical about the abilities of his fellow scientists to predict the evolutionary course: "The corpse-lifting divinations of the Elizabethan sorcerers have given away, in our time, to other and, at first sight, more scientific interpretations of the future" (NC 49). Indeed, Eiseley doubts whether modern science and technology can predict the future if it has already misread the past. He depends on his poetic imagination in order to see differently from most of the scientists of his time about man's evolution—either in the past or the future.

For Eiseley, nature has an opacity that comes precisely from the fact that it is never stable but is always moving into the future, into a zone of darkness that is both inspiring and terrifying.[5] He therefore suggests that humans should seek the guidance of animals and seek the divine animality within themselves: "'Trust the divine animal who carries us through the world,' writes Ralph Waldo Emerson. Like the horse who finds the way by instinct when the traveler is lost in the forest, so the divine within us, he contends, may find new passages opening into nature; human metamorphosis may be possible" (NC 52–53). To expand on this cryptic passage, Eiseley quotes Shakespeare's words in the tragedy play "Antony and Cleopatra" (Act 1, Scene 4), "'That he which is was wished until he were'" and comments on them. The Elizabethan poet "says, in essence, one thing only: that what we wish will come." This insight holds shamanic wisdom for Eiseley: "Shakespeare's is the eternal, the true voice of the divine animal" (NC 55). The voice of the divine animal refers to the thoughts of great writers like Shakespeare or Emerson; and Emerson's "divine within us" refers either to that poetic quality within ourselves or to the insight gained from seeing the genius's worldview. "What we wish will come" contains hints of both hope and terror, and there is a suggestion that man contains the potential of transformation within himself. In other words, man is what he'll become or wish to become.

I would suggest that "the divine animal" that Emerson talks about and Eiseley comments on may also refer not only to the "animal intuition and wisdom" (NC 53) of man, but also to that of other animals. In an anecdote Eiseley recounts in his poem "Magic," the speaker feeds a cardinal as a ritual response when it knocks on his window. The two parties are developing a common language or cross-species communication.[6] Commenting on the "special relationship" between the man and the first red cardinal, Diana Reiss claims that the poet "thought of the bird as a 'sorcerer,' and he was its 'apprentice.'" Moreover, "in Eiseley's eyes, being a sorcerer's apprentice meant he was in a position to learn some of the magic the sorcerer wielded."[7] The "magic" the red bird displays may refer to its brilliance and responsiveness in setting up the relation with Eiseley's speaker; what's more, the bird is a teacher that "convinced me / we were on the same path" (NA 68). "The same path" suggests that humans and animals have the same origins and are on the same course in cherishing life.[8] This awareness allows Eiseley to align himself with the wild animals, which is the manner of his becoming-animal.

However, not all scientists or modern men recognize the relationship to more-than-humans that Eiseley sees and feels. A scientist may dissect a still-living dog kept in the laboratory's animal house in front of a careless group of medical students just to illustrate a notion; a man may shoot an endangered bird with his hunting rifle and laugh at his triumph struggling and dying at his feet. . . . [9] Not all men are like Eiseley (or as he expects), seeking and respecting kinship with other animals or making efforts to connect to the natural world. Though the voices of wise men revealing the relationship between man and nature keep whispering, they seem to be ignored by such careless and reckless modern men. Eiseley's scientific forefathers and literary inspirations, as well as many eminent nature writers that Eiseley was contemporary with, provide a fund of wisdom that can accomplish as well as scientific knowledge what the dark side of man's inner world and his machines and weapons can destroy. So, if Eiseley foresees the future of his kind as a sorcerer does, it is because the magical power to see it is open to a perceptive learner.

As "the sorcerer's apprentice" either to the wildlife in the biosphere like the red bird or to human mentors like Thoreau or to teachers,[10] Eiseley manages to voice his prediction, warning readers of the disaster for his century: "man has become a spreading blight which threatens to efface the green world that created him" (IP 137).[11] The important thing is what to do to avoid this disaster, and Eiseley analyzes "the human predicament" in which the solution lies: "how nature is to be reentered, how man, the relatively unthinking and proud creator of the second world—the world of culture—may revivify and restore the first world which cherished and brought him into being" (IP 137). For Eiseley, man's object is to reenter nature and "revivify and restore" the first world to his cultural world. Therefore, as John Nizalowski argues, "Angyal is right to name Eiseley both alchemist and shaman, for like the alchemist he has united a knowledge of the material world with spiritual wisdom, and like the shaman he has journeyed far to bring back a message of great importance to his tribe, the human race."[12] Through his writings, Eiseley wants to reconcile the split between the natural world and the cultural world and thereby to earn the status of a sorcerer. However, to effect that reconciliation he needs the capacity to cross various boundaries.

Crossing Boundaries: Deterritorialization

Let's go back to Deleuze and Guattari's theory of becoming. Both Eiseley and Deleuze and Guattari discuss Melville's *Moby-Dick*. Eiseley believes that it "best expresses the clash between the man who has genuine perception and the one who pursues nature as ruthlessly as a hunted animal" (ST 198). For Eiseley, Melville's monomaniacal Captain Ahab represents modern science, ready to destroy the world in the pursuit of a narrow goal.[13] By contrast, Deleuze and Guattari feel that when "Ahab chooses Moby-Dick" he "enters into his . . . becoming-animal." In contrast to the scientific mind that classifies animals into species and the philosophical mind that treats man as an individual, Ahab enters an "anomalous" state that is "neither an individual nor a species; it has only affects, it has neither familiar or subjectified feelings, nor specific or significant characteristics. . . . It is a phenomenon, but a phenomenon of bordering."[14] For Deleuze and Guattari, Captain Ahab has "no personal history with Moby-Dick, no revenge to take, any more than [he has] a myth to play out; but [he does] have a becoming! Moby-Dick is neither an individual nor a genus; he is the borderline, and [he has] to strike him to get at the pack as a whole, to reach the pack as a whole and pass beyond it."[15] Here Ahab's journey (both sea voyage and mental transformation) shows his process of becoming-whale—the whale affects him. His example reveals a state when a man (or a writer) strives to pass a boundary so as to enter other dimensions beyond his own and thus reach his becoming-animal.

So, in one sense, becoming animal is a form of "deterritorialization," in which the human subject enters the territory of animals: the territory of living as well as death. In the 1988 interview with Claire Parnet, Deleuze says he is fascinated by the animal world, even when it is extraordinarily limited, like the world of the tick. Territory is important when animals constitute their world and for Deleuze, animals' "constituting a territory is nearly the birth of art." Deleuze is content with his invention (together with Félix Guattari) of the "barbaric" word—*deterritorialization*. He explains the notion of *deterritorialization* is exactly like Melville's *outlandish*.[16]

Displacement is an important element in leaving and entering territory in the process of becoming-animal. Deleuze and Guattari compare this to the nomad's movements: "One travels by intensity; displacements and spatial figures depend on intensive thresholds of nomadic deterritorialization (and thus on differential relations) that simultaneously define complementary, sedentary reterritorializations."[17] Here, it seems displacements have more to do with space and speed. However, man is capable of another kind of displacement implicit in Deleuze and Guattari's fascination with writers like Melville, Kafka, and Hofmannsthal. Eiseley speaks of man's invention of words as a form of displacement: "Linguists have a word for the power of language: displacement. . . . Displacement, in simple terms, is the ability to talk about what is absent, to make use of the imaginary in order to control reality. Man alone is able to manipulate time into past and future, transpose objects or abstract ideas in a similar fashion, and make a kind of reality which is not present, or which exists only as potential in the real world" (IP 144–45). Here the term *displacement* is used in the linguistic domain; Eiseley shows that with words, man's cultural world, man can imagine, control, or change the real material world. Eiseley talks about the past, present, and the future, which is a way to escape from the present and human condition, which accords with the "deterritorialization" theory. While this human capacity can help man to avoid awareness of his animality, it can also pave his way to becoming-animal.

Eiseley's most precious memories are about becoming. These becomings can express either his desires or fears; this is what gives them their intensity. In these confessions he narrates strange encounters with animals, and the changes of mind or behavior that they provoke. These transformations coincide with what Deleuze and Guattari say, "We can be thrown into a becoming by anything at all, by the most unexpected, most insignificant of things."[18] The liminal states that attract Eiseley have to do with changing from one form of being to another, in other words with becoming. An example of a seemingly magical metamorphosis is the old belief that mice are "generated spontaneously from bundles of old clothes," and Eiseley takes pleasure in something "so delightfully whimsical" (IJ 197). He relishes the unexpected and pleasant emergence of other-than-human life in the human world. Then he suggests "one could accept such accidents in a topsy-turvy universe without trying to decide what transformation of buckles into bones and shoe buttons into eyes had taken place" (IJ 197). In a normal man's view, the mice might seem to be an unexpected and unpleasant infestation—an unwanted incursion into human space; by contrast, Eiseley enjoys imagining the transformation of "buckles into bones and shoe buttons into eyes," which is, in a scientific/objective way, impossible. He emphasizes the mystery of the life of mice that generally goes on unknown to the people whose space they share, and he encourages readers to "take life as a kind of fantastic magic" (IJ 197).

Eiseley sympathizes with animals and finds in that cross-species emotion the basis of an ethical approach to life forms. For example, in the poem "Confrontation" the speaker claims an affiliation with the night that he shares with the wild cat he meets and helps. In saying that the night is theirs he claims the night as their time, their territory, and in so doing, he aligns himself with wild creatures.[19] Eiseley's empathy for the feral cat is real, his alliance with the animals of the nocturnal country is real; thus he succumbs to the magic of becoming-animal. This self-transcendence operates through his imagination and the alchemy of his writing. Though the stories in which the images of animals come up may be made up, their transformative power is real.

Becoming Human

The liminal state of becoming is not the prerogative of the human being alone. There are certain anecdotes in which Eiseley tries to blur the boundaries between species. There are times when the becoming-animal movement occurs in reverse and an animal seems to be on the verge of becoming human. In an example of an animal's becoming-human, Eiseley remembers a dog who intends to be human. In his essay, "Paw Marks and Buried Towns," speaking as an old professor, he recalls the "friendly" Mickey in the sight of the faint "dabbled paw mark" of the dog in the "cement sidewalks"—the result of mischievous childhood playmates (and little "me") (NC 79). The aging man admits his intimate feeling for this dog: "The mark of Mickey's paw is dearer to me than many more impressive monuments—perhaps because, in a sense, we both wanted to be something other than what we were. Mickey, I know, wanted very much to be a genuine human being" (NC 80). He says he knows the dog wants to become a real human and indicates he as a man wants to be something other than himself (an other-than-human animal). Eiseley describes the efforts of Mickey to be a human being: "If permitted, he would sit up to the table and put his paws together before his plate" and "would growl and lift his lip" because "he knew very well he was being mocked for not being human" (NC 80). His description of what the dog does is similar to humans' manner of sitting down and saying grace at the dinner table, and he insists that it is something that a dog can really achieve. The mention of the dog's facial expression of discontent discloses the sense of humor in Eiseley's writing. Eiseley speaks of Mickey as "a small boy" who participates in the adventures in the neighborhood with the children. He says, "Being of a philosophic cast of mind, [Mickey] knew that children were less severe in their classifications. . . . We children never let the fact that Mickey walked on four legs blind us to his other virtues" (NC 80). There is an amusing contrast here between the description of his childhood friendship with a dog and the vocabulary of a professor. He says Mickey owns "a philosophic cast of mind" which normally applies to human beings and it seems the children know better how to appreciate the "other virtues" of the dog than the adults who may be more serious about "classifications"—that is, making distinctions among species. In Eiseley's view, not only is Mickey a brave playmate who wants to become human, but also a teacher who gives him insight into humanity: "as I stood after the lapse of years and looked at the faint impression of his paw, it struck me that every ruined civilization is, in a sense, the mark of men trying to be human, trying to transcend themselves" (NC 80). Eiseley reveals that human civilizations are the impressions left on the earth to testify to their accomplishments as humans. As an anthropologist, he studies those marks just as he studies his dog's paw print left in the cement.

Not Anthropomorphism but the Voice of Many Things

In seeking kinship with the animals, in seeking to contain them in his imagination, Eiseley may be seeking his place in a pack. As Deleuze and Guattari say, "A becoming-animal always involves a pack, a band, a population, a peopling, in short, a multiplicity"; and "every animal is fundamentally a band, a pack. . . . It is at this point that the human being encounters the animal. We do not become animal without a fascination for the pack, for multiplicity" because we seem to be interested in "a multiplicity dwelling within us."[20] Eiseley's speaker claims, "I am born of these" (NA 22)—the foxes, the wolves, the coyotes—in other words, he claims to belong to a group and insists on the possibility for one individual man to become many other-than-humans. The idea that there is the "multiplicity" within the man is the key here.

Eiseley's becoming-animal, becoming-wild in the encounters with other-than-humans can be regarded as an effort to escape from anthropocentrism. Eiseley himself knows that there are centuries or worlds that are not his—either because he cannot enter or return to them even if he cannot resist trying to peer into them. In his poem "An Owl's Day," as a man Eiseley may learn from "the bird's wisdom," for the owl has "eyes that always / spelled wisdom in lost cultures" and an "ear that heard / every whisper on the night wind" (NA 115). He may try to see "as the owl saw" (NA 116), but a man's sight is inevitably limited by his human body and mind. Angyal comments on Eiseley's second volume of poetry *The Innocent Assassins* that: "As implied in the title poem, 'The Innocent Assassins,' and the dedication, this volume draws on experiences from his bone-hunting days, but is not limited to them."[21] Indeed, the title poem illustrates how Eiseley's capacity to travel imaginatively through time leads from a fossil discovery to a reflection on humanity. Angyal argues that Eiseley cannot escape anthropocentrism:

> Nature is a great charnel house of extinct forms that no sorcerer or magician can reanimate, so Eiseley evokes a personal myth of preexistence in order to probe life's origins. "I grasp all that went before," he announces in one poem, and "I have borne much to reach this thing, myself" in another. He dreams the ultimate atavistic dream: to revert to simpler, prehuman, preconscious forms of life. He hungers for the "innocence" of the world as it existed before man, but will as he might, he cannot cast thought in nonhuman shape. The very title of the volume betrays the anthropocentrism he wished to escape.[22]

Though Eiseley cannot "reanimate" any of these extinct animals whose fossils he finds and admires, with his imagination and poetic language, he does bring back before the modern reader's eyes the picture of a time inhabited by various forms of living beings long-passed. His perceptions about man's animal past and the cycles of the geological time, along with his respect for the natural history of man and other animals, all help humans to see more clearly their place among other forms of life. These insights are more significant (and affect his readers more deeply) than his paleontological bone-huntings. The title of the volume, from the title of the poem in which Eiseley draws an analogy between the violence of the sabertooth and of mankind, reveals his warning not to forget men's lost animal environment, nor to ignore their responsibilities to other animals and the whole biosphere. In Eiseley's writing, anthropomorphism could be seen as an ecocritical move. So, in a sense, Eiseley makes great efforts to avoid anthropocentrism in his writings, though Eiseley cannot get rid of applying anthropomorphism in his animal poems, and "cannot cast thought in nonhuman shape."

In conclusion, voicing both fear and hope for the future of humanity, he believes that man contains the potential of transformation within himself, as promised in the quotation from Shakespeare that Eiseley bears in mind "what we wish will come" (NC 55). Like a shaman, Eiseley foresees the potential disaster of the extinction of his own kind. This is why he indicates that we should let divine animals guide us—either animal life or wise thinkers. In becoming-animal, the individual crosses the boundaries between humans and nonhumans. In Eiseley's eyes, language is not a barrier, and physical appearance is not the threshold; he enters the world of becoming-animal through his sympathy with other animals. So, in this sense, Eiseley's becoming-animal is driven by affect and the writer's creative powers or imagination function greatly in these becomings. Eiseley's writings about animals contribute to change man's anthropocentric view of nonhumans. His suggestion that "man could contain more than himself" (FT 176) demands man's immersion in the natural world. This is what I'll discuss in next section.

8.2. BLENDING THE CULTURAL AND THE NATURAL

External Nature and Interior World of Thought

In his essay "The Unexpected Universe," there is a paragraph in which Eiseley discusses mystery and the scientific mind. He begins by returning to a previous work: "a little book of essays" in which he poses the question,

> How Natural is Natural?—a subject that raised the hackles of some of my scientifically inclined colleagues, who confused the achievements of their disciplines with certitude on a cosmic scale. My very question thus implied an ill-concealed heresy. That heresy it is my intent to pursue further. It will involve us, not in the denigration of science, but, rather, in a farther stretch of the imagination as we approach those distant and wooded boundaries of thought where, in the words of the old fairy tale, the fox and the hare say good night to each other. It is here that predictability ceases and the unimaginable begins—or, as a final heretical suspicion, we may ask ourselves whether our own little planetary fragment of the cosmos has all along concealed a mocking refusal to comply totally with human conceptions of order and secure prediction. (UU 31)

Here Eiseley represents his own scientific inquiry as diverging from that of his scientific colleagues, who misjudge his question as "ill-concealed heresy." Though the incident is still in a personal tone, actually it pursues scientific considerations more than autobiography. When criticizing science in this essay, Eiseley does not conceal his ideas. At least in this passage, he points out that he does not belittle science but that science needs imagination and needs to break the boundaries between humans and nonhumans to reach a world where order, prediction, and regularity come under suspicion. The original German phrase "the fox and the hare say good night to each other" refers to a wilderness devoid of human traces. That's where Eiseley believes "the unimaginable begins" and "secure prediction" comes to a halt. Later Eiseley declares, "No longer, as with the animal, can the world be accepted as given. It has to be perceived and consciously thought about, abstracted, and considered. The moment one does so, one is outside of the natural; objects are each one surrounded with an aura radiating meaning to man alone" (UU 32). The obvious meaning is that once man thinks about the objects around him, the world surrounding him is no longer the natural one. The implicit meaning is that when human beings established their cultural world, the natural world was then no longer the pure realm of nature. In contrasting man with "the animal," Eiseley suggests first that animals accept the world as given (even the human world that animals have to coexist with); and second, he suggests that in earlier times human beings were with the animals and simply accepted the world as given without reflecting on it. Thus, modern man inevitably confronts a gap between the natural world and the cultural world.

Though this passage begins with personal experience, it quickly goes on to discuss man's conception of objects, which then allows the reflection on the difference between the natural world and cultural world to emerge. The essay is not strictly a scientific essay, giving facts and hypotheses; instead it moves to metaphysical ideas like that of "a universe ... being woven together by unseen forces," and of man using "primitive magic" to connect himself with his surroundings (UU 32). This small paragraph is like a small piece of splintered glass that reflects and lets shine out Eiseley's ideas and hopes of reaching a place where a combination of science and imagination, humanity and animality can coexist.

Eiseley brings together the culture of the modern scientific world, the culture of the indigenous people, and the culture of animals in a reflection on geological time. In his poem, "The High Plains," he finds "antique barbed wire," "mammoth teeth," and "flint knives" together, "lying mixed on the hardpan" (NA 55). The wind (an element of nature) that treats similarly a man-made material forged from metal, the fossils of an ancient extinct animal, or the hand-hewn tools of the indigenous people seems to whisper an important message to Eiseley. Grouped together, the debris of different cultures has something to tell the observer. Both "the literate" and "the illiterate" leave "artifacts" that make impressions in the earth. Their "final purpose" and the "final perspective" (NA 55) refers to the end of each limited life, either that of human beings or more-than-humans. Eiseley emphasizes that each form of life, as fragments of nature, are only passing moments in the vast scope of geological time; and in the face of that time, the history of humans or the history of animal life should be judged similarly. At the sight of these ruins mixed together, a man may gain a clearer perspective of himself, just as Eiseley does.

A perspective on oneself or on the rest of life around one can be better gained by taking a wider view. Eiseley relates a story showing how humanity requires self-transcendence. He says, "Buddha is reported to have said to his sorrowing disciples as he lay dying, 'Walk on.' He wanted his people to be free of earthly entanglement or desire. That is how one should go in dignity to the true harvest of the worlds. It is a philosophy transferred from the old sun civilizations of earth. It implies that one cannot proceed upon the path of human transcendence until one has made interiorly in one's soul a road into the future" (IP 81–82). Eiseley reveals the importance of interior development for humans to survive. He then examines the modern, man-made civilization, and says, "A scientific civilization in the full sense is an anomaly in world history. The civilizations of the sun never developed it" (IP 82). Eiseley suggests that the scientific civilization of his time is not a product of the natural world. "Sun civilizations" may refer to civilizations in which people cultivate the correspondence of the outer and inner worlds. Based on the understanding of the ancient "sun civilizations," Eiseley gives his prescription for humanity—maybe to build up a new kind of civilization—to reconcile the split between the natural world and the cultural world:

> [T]he necessity for him consciously to reenter and preserve, for his own safety, the old first world from which he originally emerged. His second world, drawn from his own brain, has brought him far, but it cannot take him out of nature, nor can he live by escaping into his second world alone. He must now incorporate from the wisdom of the axial thinkers an ethic not alone directed toward his fellows, but extended to the living world around him. He must make, by way of his cultural world, an actual conscious reentry into the sunflower forest he had thought merely to exploit or abandon. He must do this in order to survive. If he succeeds he will, perhaps, have created a third world which combines elements of the original two and which should bring closer the responsibilities and nobleness of character envisioned by the axial thinkers who may be acclaimed as the creators, if not of man, then of his soul. (IP 154–55)

In Eiseley's text "the axial thinkers" refer to "the creators of transcendent values," namely, "Christ, Buddha, Lao-tse, and Confucius" (IP 147), who "encouraged the common man toward charity and humility. They . . . bespoke man's purpose to subdue his animal nature and in so doing to create a radiantly new and noble being" (IP 148). Eiseley emphasizes Emerson's perception that "Nature is 'the immense shadow of man,'" and says "We have cast it in our image" (NC 143). Between the exterior nature and interior thought of man, Eiseley suggests a third world that reconciles the first world of nature and the second world of culture. It shall be a world in which man bears the best characteristics of a human being—"responsibilities and nobleness"—an ethical attitude toward the whole community he lives in and shares with various living beings. He imagines a path toward self-transcendence and a journey of the soul that man needs for his and his own kind's future. It is a road toward the creation of a new man, a new self.

Response and Responsibility to Living Things

Eiseley expresses his empathy for animals in what Donna Haraway calls "embodied mindful encounter[s]" with other species.[23] The poet's attentiveness to other-than-human subjects affords him the kind of encounters that Haraway describes:

> To hold in regard, to respond, to look back reciprocally, to notice, to pay attention, to have courteous regard for, to esteem: all of that is tied to polite greeting, to constituting the polis, where and when species meet. To knot companion and species together in encounter, in regard and respect, is to enter the world of becoming with, where who and what are is precisely what is at stake. . . . I am not a posthumanist; I am who I become with companion species, who and which make a mess out of categories in the making of kin and kind. Queer messmates in mortal play, indeed.[24]

Haraway emphasizes the importance of "regard" (both observation and consideration), "respect," "response" to, and responsibility for other animals. Like Haraway, Eiseley also blurs these categories by showing his regard and respect for more-than-humans. In a previous chapter I've discussed Leopold and Eiseley, showing how the two ecological writers present their critiques of men's recklessness and irresponsibility in building their human and cultural world and in looking at nature only as a resource to be exploited.[25] Hélène Schmutz argues that "Leopold's land ethic opens up a breach in western anthropocentrism, and questions the clear division between man and nature."[26] Indeed, Leopold's land ethic shows that "morally, man is responsible for the protection of the community of the living to which he belongs."[27] Eiseley eagerly embraces the same moral position through his writings. Leopold, Eiseley, and Haraway all clarify that humans can be responsible and noble human beings by assuming their responsibilities toward other species.

There is an incident in Eiseley's essay "Man in the Autumn Light" that illustrates his love for other species. One snowy night, Eiseley's speaker heads for the "remaining fragment of woodland" nearby his house. He finds the tracks that "people had crunched by on their way to the train station, but no human trace ran into the woods. Many little animals had ventured about the margin of the trees, perhaps timidly watching; none had descended the path" (IP 128). Through observing the impressions on the snow, the speaker sees that the paths traced by humans and animals have not crossed, either because people are busy heading for the train station or because the animals are too afraid to come across. However, the speaker "swung aside into the world of no human tracks" (IP 128). With the help of the starlight, there he finds "a still-living Christmas tree hurled out with everything dispensable from an apartment house at the corner of the wood. I stroked it in wordless apology" (IP 130). Though the domain was seemingly untouched by humans, the speaker still finds the tree abandoned by a human family. The word *still-living* shows Eiseley's emphasis on the significance of a living being though it is of another form of life—a tree. He even sends a "wordless apology" to it—maybe for man's casualness in abusing the resources in nature.

Meditating on man as the earth's destroyer, and with a feeling of loneliness, the speaker "yearned silently toward those who would come after me if the race survived" (IP 133). Is he so disappointed in his own kind—the world eaters and planet spores—that he already anticipates a new humanity ("if the race survived") to come? Maybe he is setting up the image of a new kind of human in the action that he takes: "In the deepening snow I made a final obeisance to the living world. I took the still green, everlasting tree home to my living room for Christmas rites that had not been properly accorded it. I suppose that the act was blindly compulsive. It was the sort of thing that Peacock in his time would have termed the barbarism of poets" (IP 134). Through the act of bringing the dying tree home, at least, the man shows the respect for another form of life in nature. What's more, the tree becomes "everlasting"; maybe to the man who loves nature and respects its vastness both in time and space, the tree becomes a symbol of the "everlasting" life of the biosphere. He seems to extend the Christian concern for the immortal soul to the tree: "Christmas rites had not been properly accorded." This description of the Christmas tree contains both irony and humor, since the poet's cultural tradition permits men to damage a living life in the natural world. This behavior of bringing home the tree seems to be "compulsive," but it is poetic though maybe barbaric; it comes from a man's animal instinct (a desire for the green world—the tree is "living green" [IP 130]—to offset the world of snow) as well as from the goodness in humanity (the man's empathy for the tree's suffering caused by his cultural tradition).

Eiseley is very passionate and brings feeling to his discipline and shows his love for nature, especially for animals. He combines the curiosity of scientist with the compassion of a poet and humanist. He suggests that "a love for earth, almost forgotten in man's roving mind, had momentarily reasserted its mastery, a love for the green meadows we have so long taken for granted and desecrated to our cost" (IP 156). Eiseley encourages man to love the earth, the real and only home that man sprung from but has casually abused; and to love "the green meadows we have so long taken for granted" because "there is nothing very 'normal' about nature" (IJ 63). Without the grassland, the earth would be a barren planet, and the flowers would not have come to change the world and create the conditions for animal life. "Without the gift of flowers and the infinite diversity of their fruits, man and bird, if they had continued to exist at all, would be today unrecognizable" (IJ 77). Then it is humanity's brotherhood, the other animals, to whom Eiseley expresses his love. For him, "the love that transcends the boundaries of species was the highest spiritual expression he knew" (LN 80). In the preface of his first volume of poetry, *Notes of an Alchemist*, Eiseley says, "there were animals I cherished and of which I have left some account in prose. My love for these creatures was recorded privately in poems which I no longer bothered to publish" (NA 11). In his poem, "Magic," Eiseley states that "I / love forms beyond my own / and regret the borders between us" (NA 65). Though his scientific essays often conceal his love for other species, we can find poems where he voices his love for them clearly.

We can also sense Eiseley's love for earth, for the green world, and for animals in regarding his reactions to them in his anecdotes. Eiseley sometimes sees himself as a messenger who warns animals away from dangerous men who follow and kill them. There are several kinds of reactions to animals, but normally he stays still or moves in silence to get out of the scene. Either he chooses not to trouble them, to leave them alone, or sometimes he intervenes for the purpose of saving a potential life. For example, witnessing a snake trying to steal eggs from a mother bird "might have been worth scientifically recording" (FT 174), but Eiseley's speaker drives the snake away (without hurting it) to save the bird and her eggs because he "thought of the eggs somewhere about, and whether they were to elongate and writhe into an armor of scales, or eventually to go whistling into the wind with their wild mother" (FT 174–75). Given a choice between letting the snake consume the eggs and allowing them to hatch, he sides with the avian mother. There are several anecdotes in which Eiseley's speaker sacrifices the scientific objectivity that would bring him fame and, instead, prefers not to trouble the animal life that he values for its potential existence. Searching for the reason Eiseley maintains this sympathy and respect for animals, I guess it comes from the combination of his scientific knowledge of evolution theory and the wisdom he has gained by seeing the world from the perspective of romantic nature writers. For example, once in a pine woods walk, he finds himself in "the brown needles and the fallen cones, the stiff, endless green forests [that] were a mark that placed me in the Age of Dinosaurs." And then he sees a green lizard and "reined in with the nostalgic intent, for a moment, to call him father" (FT 163). This reaction is based on his knowing about evolution theory and also a romantic heart. However, there is something more important than the love of animals that makes Eiseley decide to behave like this. Whether he is saving the eggs for the mother bird or calling the lizard father, Eiseley tries to earn "a greater, more comprehensive version of myself" (FT 176). In respecting and responding to other animals, he thinks or feels better about himself as a human being. The love for animals can also be seen from Eiseley's choice of words to describe them. He usually employs affectionate terms, for example, *my muskrat* (FT 156) or positive adjectives like *friendly* and *innocent*. For him, men are often too greedy and not guiltless, but animals ask little and remain blameless.

In conclusion, Eiseley's writings reveal the image of a man who intends to enter the mode of becoming-animal in his relations with other animals—a man who possesses both scientific knowledge and the warm heart of a poet. The combination of the two characteristics that reside in him allows him to see clearly and wisely man's place in the biosphere. He offers his suggestions for humanity—man should look inside of himself, his soul, and find his kinship with other forms of life. An awareness of the scientific age and the problems it has brought makes this nature writer imagine a third world that contains the first world and the second. It is a world where the split between nature and culture, the past and the future, humans and nonhumans can be reconciled, a world in which mankind would immerse themselves in the natural world and thus assume the responsibility and nobility of which human beings should be capable.

Eiseley reveals that man cannot live only in the second world—the cultural world he creates. Through his revelation of his philosophy of man's transformation, we can see his efforts to blend the cultural and the natural in hope for a new humanity. He earns the title of "sorcerer" since his writings well illustrate Deleuze and Guattari's becoming-theory in which they argue a writer is a sorcerer when he writes like an animal. Eiseley declares his passion for other forms of life and his desire to cross the boundaries between them. However, Eiseley's interest in man's metamorphosis comes from not only from applying poetic license; he sympathizes with animals and finds in that cross-species emotion the basis of an ethical approach to life forms. The scientific knowledge and wisdom gained from romantic naturalists prepare Eiseley to discover the magic residing in animal life and nature. He believes in the potentialities of humans and nonhumans to transform in time. Concerned about other animals, he emphasizes, like Donna Haraway in her writing about companion species, man's respect for and responsibilities to other animals. It is interesting to find that in his poems Eiseley announces his love for animals openly, whereas this often is concealed in his essays.

NOTES

1. Deleuze and Guattari, *Thousand Plateaus*, 247.
2. Deleuze and Guattari, *Thousand Plateaus*, 240.
3. Deleuze and Guattari, *Thousand Plateaus*, 258.
4. "Hofmannsthal, or rather Lord Chandos, becomes fascinated with a 'people' of dying rats. . . . Then a strange imperative wells up in him: either stop writing, or write like a rat" (Deleuze and Guattari, *Thousand Plateaus*, 240).
5. See my discussion in "Double-Faced Mankind" in 4.2. A New Jeremiad: Dreams and Prophesies of Disaster.
6. See my discussion in "Wild Animals Nearby" in 6.1. Strange Proximities—Encounters with Animals.
7. Reiss, *Dolphin in the Mirror*, 238.
8. See my discussion in "Wild Animals Nearby" in 6.1. Strange Proximities—Encounters with Animals.
9. See my discussion in "Objectivity and Detachment" and "Hunting, Collecting, and Living" in 2. Eiseley's Critique of Science.
10. In his essay "The Last Magician," Eiseley remembers the importance of his tutor, Frank G. Speck, to whom he dedicates *The Invisible Pyramid* and says at the beginning of the book, Speck to him is "The Last Magician."
11. See my discussion in 4.2. A New Jeremiad: Dreams and Prophesies of Disaster.
12. Nizalowski, "Eiseley and Jung," 292.
13. See my discussion in "Overspecialization and Single-Minded" in 2.1. Scientific Method—Detachment and Overspecialization.
14. Deleuze and Guattari, *Thousand Plateaus*, 244–245.
15. Deleuze and Guattari, *Thousand Plateaus*, 245.
16. Hurth, "A Comme Animal."
17. Deleuze and Guattari, *Thousand Plateaus*, 54.
18. Deleuze and Guattari, *Thousand Plateaus*, 292.
19. See my discussion in "Fragile Wildlife" in 6.1. Strange Proximities—Encounters with Animals
20. Deleuze and Guattari, *Thousand Plateaus*, 239–240.
21. Angyal, *Loren Eiseley*, 122.
22. Angyal, *Loren Eiseley*, 122.
23. Haraway, *When Species Meet*, 23.
24. Haraway, *When Species Meet*, 19.
25. See my discussion in "The Ecological Implications of Eiseley's Thought—Connections to Rachel Carson and Aldo Leopold" in 2.2. Scientific Authority and the Destructiveness of Technology.
26. Schmutz, "Posthumanism," 65.
27. Schmutz, "Posthumanism," 62.

Conclusion

A Writer for the Twenty-First Century

Eiseley witnessed and worried over the ever-widening split between science and the humanities in the modern era. The exploration of his scientific influences and poetic influences reveals the intellectual resources that nourish his philosophy throughout his writings; he brings together scientific knowledge and humanistic wisdom in approaching the natural world. Eiseley's observations about those scientific forefathers who possessed artistic qualities as well as his literary inspirations, who remained observant and explicit instructors for their descendants, foreshadow the kind of science Eiseley dislikes. He believes that in applying scientific findings to the living world, his contemporaries denatured our planet and created a world that was becoming hostile to living things.

In exploring Eiseley's writing style I have tried to illustrate how he works to reconcile the split between science and the humanities in his writing on science, man, and nature. He is a hybrid essayist who looks at science in a new way, romancing the discipline by infusing it with poetry. He manages to combine history, geological events, fiction, science, and meditation together in poetic form. Eiseley admires and wants to emulate the true poet—one who holds onto the past, while looking at the present and into the future. As an ecologically minded humanist, he wants to be a prophet who sees both the environmental and cultural dangers threatening humanity.

Eiseley also reveals the split in time that characterizes the modern era, and he warns of the danger posed to the earth by the lack of balance between scientific pursuits of his future-oriented society and the rhythms of the natural world. With immense imagination in exploring humanity's antiquity, Eiseley argues that our species, though we come from nature, have forgotten our animal past and our real home, thus dismissing the complexity and mystery in nature and life. He tries to change modern society's limited anthropocentric attitude toward nature. Suggesting that the resolution lies in the lessons of the past, Eiseley helps modern people widen their vision of nature and time and see the meaning of living in mortality as well as living with a sense of infinity.

Eiseley's writings encourage his readers to see clearly and wisely man's place in the biosphere and immerse themselves in the natural world. Eiseley explores two paradoxes in the relationship between humans and other animals: first, although men may find animals familiar, there is a world to which animals have access but from which humans feel excluded; second, although man divides humans from animal life, Eiseley believes that we are netted together and emphasizes the continuity of animal life in human beings. On the one hand, he tries to reawaken in his readers a sense of awe at the strangeness in nature and animal life; on the other hand, he wants to suggest that we should reconnect to animals and to the animal in ourselves. An awareness of both would work to establish man's ethics towards nature and animal life. Man must learn to respect the mystery and unknown in nature and life and to respond to and take responsibilities in the encounters with the rest of life. Eiseley shows how the split between humans and more-than-humans can be reconciled through a sympathy with other life forms that is the key to entering the world of becoming.

In short, in describing the problems of the bifurcation in modern thought, then in developing the consequences of the different types of splits, and finally in revealing Eiseley's resolution of the divisions, this book has tried to advance toward a reconciliation of the split between science and art, humanity and animality, as well as the split in time, in the hope of finding a path for a new humanity in a new world.

Eiseley's ideas seem even more pertinent for the twenty-first century than for his own. He anticipated contemporary ideas like the twenty-first-century realization that we have entered the Anthropocene era or that we need environmental humanities as a new discipline that responds to the moral issues involved in environmental problems. Also, Eiseley's writings promote multidisciplinary thinking since they combine science, history, philosophy, and poetry. He anticipated the interdisciplinarity widely practiced at the present time; for example, the ecocriticism on animals practiced by Donna Haraway and Frans de Waal. I believe in the future, and that those who follow Eiseley in writing across disciplines on science, nature, man, and animal life will be increasingly numerous. His talent as both a true scientist and a poetic humanist will be recognized increasingly. What's more, Eiseley's warnings to his readers still remain valid. Like his contemporaries Rachel Carson and Aldo Leopold, Eiseley cautions us about the dangers to the planet. His proposals for ethical attitudes toward nature and its other-than-human inhabitants are still valuable to us, since we face problems like the cruelty to experimental animals, species extinction, industrial waste, and technological destructiveness to the natural world. His vision still applies to the world we live in at present and even for the future.

Bibliography

Abram, David. *The Spell of the Sensuous: Perception and Language in a More-than-Human World*. 1st ed. New York: Vintage Books, a division of Penguin Random House LLC. 1997.

Angyal, Andrew J. *Loren Eiseley*. Boston: Twayne, 1983.

Beaulieu, Alain. "The Status of Animality in Deleuze's Thought." *Journal for Critical Animal Studies*, 2011. www.criticalanimalstudies.org/wp-content/uploads/2009/09/JCAS-2011-Vol-X1-Issue-1-2Continental-Philosophical-Perspectives-complete-up.pdf.

Bennett, Jane. *Vibrant Matter: A Political Ecology of Things*. Durham: Duke University Press, 2010.

Blake, William. *Blake's Poetry and Designs: Authoritative Texts, Illuminations in Color and Monochrome, Related Prose, Criticism*. Edited by Mary Lynn Johnson and John E. Grant. New York: Norton, 1979.

Calarco, Matthew. *Zoographies: The Question of the Animal from Heidegger to Derrida*. New York: Columbia University Press, 2008.

Carson, Rachel. Letter to Loren Eiseley. 4 Nov. 1960. MS. Jane Pope Geske Heritage Room of Nebraska Authors, Bennett Martin Public Library, Lincoln, Nebraska. The Gale E. Christianson Collection of Eiseley Research Materials.

Chesterton, G. K. *The G. K. Chesterton Collection [50 Books]*. Catholic Way Publishing, 2014.

Christianson, Gale E. *Fox at the Wood's Edge: A Biography of Loren Eiseley*. Lincoln: University of Nebraska Press, 2000.

Deleuze, Gilles, and Félix Guattari. *A Thousand Plateaus: Capitalism and Schizophrenia*. Translated by Brian Massumi. Minneapolis: University of Minnesota Press, 1987.

Derrida, Jacques. "The Animal That Therefore I Am (More to Follow)." Translated by David Wills. *Critical Inquiry* 28, no. 2 (2002): 369–418. doi.org/10.1086/449046.

Eiseley, Loren C. *All the Strange Hours: The Excavation of a Life*. New York: Scribner, 1975.

———. *Another Kind of Autumn*. New York: Scribner, 1977.

———. *Darwin's Century: Evolution and the Men Who Discovered It*. New York: Anchor Books, 1958.

———. *The Firmament of Time*. Lincoln: University of Nebraska Press, 1999.
———. *Francis Bacon and the Modern Dilemma*. Lincoln: University of Nebraska Press, 1962.
———. "The Illusion of the Two Cultures." *American Scholar* 33, no. 3 (1964): 387–99. www.jstor.org/stable/41209201.
———. *The Immense Journey*. New York: Random House, 1957.
———. *The Innocent Assassins*. New York: Scribner, 1973.
———. *The Invisible Pyramid: A Humanist Account of the Space Age*. London: Rupert Hart-Davis, 1971.
———. *The Lost Notebooks of Loren Eiseley*. Edited by Kenneth Heuer. Boston: Little, Brown, 1987.
———. *The Night Country*. Lincoln: University of Nebraska Press, 1997.
———. *Notes of an Alchemist*. New York: Scribner, 1972.
———. *The Star Thrower*. Orlando etc.: A Harvest Book, 1979.
———. *The Unexpected Universe*. Orlando: Harcourt Brace and Company, 1985.
Franke, Robert G. "Blue Plums and Smoke: Loren Eiseley's Perception of Time." *Western American Literature* 24, no. 2 (1989): 147–50. www.jstor.org/stable/43024222.
Goebel, James R. "Uncanny Meat." *Caliban* 55 (2016): 169–90. doi.org/10.4000/caliban.3438.
Gottlieb, Roger S., ed. *The Oxford Handbook of Religion and Ecology*. New York: Oxford University Press, 2006.
Haraway, Donna J. *Simians, Cyborgs, and Women: The Reinvention of Nature*. New York: Routledge, 1991.
———. *When Species Meet*. Minneapolis: University of Minnesota Press, 2008.
Harding, Wendy, and Jacky Martin. "Oscar, Derrida's Cat, and Other Knowing Animals." *Transatlantica* 2 (2011). doi.org/10.4000/transatlantica.5627.
Hurth, Dominique, trans. "L'Abécédaire De Gilles Deleuze / A Comme Animal." After 1968. Maastricht, NL: Jan van Eyck Academie, February 4, 2010. www.after1968.org/app/webroot/uploads/ABCDelAnimal.pdf.
Lejeune, Philippe. *On Autobiography*. Edited by Paul John Eakin. Minneapolis: University of Minnesota Press, 1989.
Leopold, Aldo. *A Sand County Almanac: And Sketches Here and There*. New York: Oxford University Press, 1949.
Lynch, Tom, and Susan N. Maher, eds. *Artifacts and Illuminations: Critical Essays on Loren Eiseley*. Lincoln: University of Nebraska Press, 2012.
Mackenthun, Gesa. "Hidden Cities in the American Wilderness: The Cultural Work of a Romantic Trope." *Miranda* 11 (2015). doi.org/10.4000/miranda.6954.
Momaday, N. Scott. "The Spiritual Mountain." Essay. In *Mountains Figured and Disfigured in the English-Speaking World*, edited by Françoise Besson, 44–58. Newcastle upon Tyne: Cambridge Scholars Publishing, 2010.
Nelson, Brandon. "Walking in the Footsteps of Loren Eiseley Scientific Discoveries in Western Nebraska." *ESU13*, n.d. www.esu13.org/vimages/shared/vnews/stories/5e30648edf693/WalkingInTheFootstepsOfEiseley_Poster.pdf.

Nizalowski, John. "Eiseley and Jung: Structuralism's Invisible Pyramid." Essay. In *Artifacts & Illuminations: Critical Essays on Loren Eiseley*, edited by Tom Lynch and Susan N. Maher, 271–92. Lincoln: University of Nebraska Press, 2012.

Otto, Rudolf. *The Idea of Holy: An Inquiry into the Non-Rational Idea of the Divine and Its Relation to the Rational*. New York: Galaxy Books, 1958.

Pitts, Mary Ellen. *Toward a Dialogue of Understandings: Loren Eiseley and the Critique of Science*. Bethlehem: Lehigh University Press, 1995.

Quinodoz, Jean-Michel. *Reading Freud: A Chronological Exploration of Freud's Writings*. London: Routledge, 2005.

Reiss, Diana. *The Dolphin in the Mirror: Exploring Dolphin Minds and Saving Dolphin Lives*. Boston: Houghton Mifflin Harcourt, 2011.

Schmutz, Hélène. "Is Aldo Leopold's 'Land Ethic' an Early Form of Posthumanism?" *Caliban* 55 (2016): 53–68. doi.org/10.4000/caliban.3226.

Shklovsky, Victor. "Art as Technique." Essay. In *Russian Formalist Criticism: Four Essays*, translated by Lee T. Lemon and Marion J. Reis, 3–24. Lincoln: University of Nebraska Press, 1965.

Sörlin, Sverker. "Environmental Humanities: Why Should Biologists Interested in the Environment Take the Humanities Seriously?" *BioScience* 62, no. 9 (2012): 788–89. doi.org/10.1525/bio.2012.62.9.2.

Thoreau, Henry David. *Early Spring in Massachusetts*. Edited by Harrison G. Blake. Boston: Houghton, Mifflin, 1893.

———. *The Illustrated "A Week on the Concord and Merrimack Rivers."* Edited by Carl F. Hovde. Princeton: Princeton University Press, 1983.

———. *Journal, Volume 1, 1837–1844*. Edited by John C. Broderick. Princeton: Princeton University Press, 1981.

———. *Journal, Volume 2, 1842–1848*. Edited by John C. Broderick. Princeton: Princeton University Press, 1984.

Waal, Frans de. *The Ape and the Sushi Master: Cultural Reflections by a Primatologist*. New York: Basic Books, 2001.

White, Gilbert. *The Natural History of Selborne*. London: J. M. Dent, 1906. Introduction by Bertram C. A. Windle.

Wilson, Edward O. *Biophilia*. Cambridge, MA: Harvard University Press, 1984.

Wordsworth, William. *William Wordsworth: The Prelude: A Parallel Text*. Edited by J. C. Maxwell. Harmondsworth: Penguin, 1971.

Worster, Donald. *Nature's Economy: A History of Ecological Ideas*. Cambridge: Cambridge University Press, 1994.

Index

aesthetic, 14, 16, 114
ancestral, 14, 35, 97, 140, 154, 156, 157
animal life, 3, 4, 137, 148, 155, 156, 159, 160, 161, 163, 165, 172, 176, 179, 180, 181, 190, 192, 195, 196
animality, 3, 18, 63, 172, 183, 186, 191
Anthropocene, 2
antiquity, 16, 87, 102, 115, 121, 132
authority, 27, 43, 59, 70, 71, 145
awe, 1, 13, 19, 40, 41, 70, 107, 115, 116, 122, 138, 140, 159, 164, 165, 166, 169, 171, 172

Bacon, Francis, 7, 8, 9, 10, 11, 12, 13, 14, 16, 24, 38, 42, 43, 44, 64, 70, 92, 124, 125
becoming, 11, 18, 32, 41, 88, 101, 105, 109, 125, 138, 144, 157, 159, 170, 172, 175, 181, 182, 183, 184, 185, 186, 187, 188, 189, 190, 193, 196
belief, 17, 24, 56, 73, 81, 83, 99, 102, 104, 110, 111, 114, 121, 122, 123, 151, 152, 162, 170, 172, 187
Bible, 37, 58, 59, 70, 89, 120, 155
biodiversity, 104, 105, 111, 113, 115, 116, 132
biosphere, 18, 23, 58, 113, 116, 153, 162, 163, 177, 179, 181, 185, 189, 194, 196

Blake, William, 63, 79, 81
bond, 1, 32, 35, 90, 109, 112, 145, 148
border, 51, 162, 183, 185, 186, 195

Carson, Rachel, 52, 53
Carson, Jaqueline, 174
changeling, 87, 91, 92, 93, 95, 102, 115, 177
childhood, 2, 62, 69, 73, 77, 78, 79, 80, 81, 82, 95, 98, 117, 123, 139, 150, 153, 161, 187, 188
Christian, 80, 92, 107, 109, 162, 170, 174, 194
coexist, 16, 27, 76, 110, 121, 122, 132, 163, 191
companion, 9, 15, 80, 95, 99, 117, 138, 142, 143, 146, 151, 172, 182, 193, 196
conflict, 37, 81, 104, 105, 125, 130, 132
consciousness, 2, 20, 23, 52, 91, 107, 118, 149, 176
contact, 19, 20, 45, 68, 95, 114, 127, 137, 140, 142, 143, 145, 153, 155, 173
creative, 8, 16, 19, 67, 71, 76, 77, 82, 93, 161, 164, 190
cruelty, 31, 32, 100, 147, 148

cultural world, 12, 24, 28, 53, 75, 76, 87, 92, 93, 94, 101, 106, 108, 183, 185, 186, 191, 192, 193, 196

Darwin, Charles, 8, 9, 10, 12, 13, 14, 15, 16, 17, 18, 22, 23, 24, 31, 41, 66, 80, 88, 89, 90, 92, 93, 112, 161, 164, 165
death, 18, 20, 44, 50, 52, 55, 62, 65, 69, 80, 81, 91, 95, 96, 98, 99, 102, 104, 105, 113, 116, 117, 118, 119, 120, 123, 128, 129, 131, 143, 156, 159, 172, 173, 174, 175, 176, 177, 178, 180, 182, 186
Deleuze, Gilles, 3, 139, 142, 144, 173, 181, 182, 183, 185, 186, 187, 188, 196
Derrida, Jacques, 3, 149, 167
deterritorialization, 181, 186
dimension, 8, 19, 20, 50, 79, 82, 89, 107, 109, 110, 111, 121, 122, 161, 166, 172, 186
discipline, 7, 8, 11, 12, 22, 43, 59, 61, 83, 109, 190, 194
division, 7, 40, 46, 55, 139, 156, 172, 193
domestic, 14, 31, 38, 137, 138, 139, 142, 143, 145, 146, 153, 156, 157, 173

ecocriticism, 2
ecological, 2, 3, 50, 53, 54, 55, 56, 58, 72, 77, 81, 89, 97, 108, 114, 160, 193
Eden, 17, 154, 155
Emerson, Ralph Waldo, 18, 73, 184, 192
endangered, 50, 54, 143, 184
environmental humanities, 83
ethic, 29, 31, 32, 37, 38, 45, 52, 53, 54, 55, 56, 57, 79, 114, 181, 187, 192, 193, 196
evil, 13, 46, 62, 80, 81, 105, 132, 155
experimental, 1, 9, 17, 30, 31, 32, 42, 72, 76, 117

extinction, 39, 48, 49, 52, 53, 59, 71, 87, 91, 97, 106, 107, 114, 115, 116, 119, 126, 131, 132, 190

first world, 124, 133, 185, 192, 193, 196
Freud, Sigmund, 40, 144, 154

genetic, 2, 34, 41, 115, 126, 127, 183
genius, 2, 8, 9, 10, 15, 17, 19, 20, 22, 23, 24, 39, 58, 93, 184
geological time, 9, 106, 116, 118, 124, 125, 132, 161, 162, 189, 191, 192

Haraway, Donna, 2, 29, 31, 32, 33, 35, 117, 142, 151, 181, 193, 196
Homo sapiens, 35, 47, 48, 50, 58, 61, 88, 91, 94, 96, 98, 101, 112, 115, 125, 126, 130, 131, 132, 175, 177
Hudson, W. H., 19, 73
humanistic, 17, 22, 24, 27, 33, 39, 70, 82, 83, 104, 121, 126
humanity, 2, 3, 7, 10, 12, 13, 23, 24, 27, 28, 30, 31, 32, 36, 37, 38, 39, 42, 45, 46, 47, 49, 52, 55, 59, 61, 62, 63, 66, 70, 72, 75, 76, 80, 83, 87, 88, 92, 93, 94, 97, 100, 104, 105, 107, 111, 113, 114, 117, 127, 130, 131, 132, 140, 147, 148, 160, 161, 167, 174, 175, 176, 177, 178, 179, 180, 183, 188, 189, 190, 191, 192, 194, 195, 196

ice age, 76, 96, 97, 99, 100, 106, 127, 128, 132, 140, 143, 144, 155
identification, 49, 51, 182
illusion, 47, 104, 109, 110, 112, 161, 162, 163, 166, 170
immortal, 81, 120, 170, 194
Industrialization, 52, 106
infinite, 38, 55, 99, 104, 161, 195
inner world, 2, 19, 20, 28, 32, 53, 71, 93, 99, 181, 185, 192
innocence, 2, 78, 79, 80, 81, 150, 153, 189
instinctive, 90, 91, 92, 109, 149, 150, 159, 171

Index 207

kinship, 41, 49, 95, 117, 153, 160, 184, 188, 196

language, 12, 36, 44, 73, 74, 75, 76, 77, 82, 137, 140, 141, 148, 149, 150, 151, 152, 153, 156, 157, 161, 181, 182, 183, 184, 186, 189, 190
Latour, Bruno, 2, 115
life forms, 2, 45, 47, 48, 49, 50, 56, 57, 69, 88, 90, 94, 110, 112, 115, 120, 146, 148, 149, 156, 157, 160, 161, 162, 164, 172, 177, 178, 179, 187, 196
loneliness, 10, 21, 68, 92, 93, 137, 147, 148, 150, 153, 155, 156, 157, 194
love, 2, 16, 33, 35, 40, 53, 55, 56, 58, 65, 70, 94, 113, 140, 141, 145, 153, 175, 182, 193, 194, 195, 196
Lynch, Tom, 174

Melville, Herman, 19, 22, 23, 185, 186
metaphysical, 3, 33, 34, 42, 70, 82, 119, 191
moral, 11, 23, 37, 43, 44, 46, 47, 53, 59, 114, 156, 193
mortality, 78, 104, 117, 119, 155, 159, 174, 175, 176, 177, 178, 180
Mother Nature, 92, 95, 115
mystery, 8, 13, 18, 19, 33, 38, 40, 41, 48, 61, 70, 76, 101, 102, 105, 107, 132, 142, 164, 166, 169, 171, 172, 187, 190
mythology, 65, 128

naming, 83, 153
natural world, 1, 2, 3, 8, 10, 12, 14, 16, 19, 20, 27, 28, 34, 36, 37, 41, 42, 45, 46, 47, 49, 50, 52, 54, 57, 59, 62, 65, 66, 70, 80, 83, 92, 93, 94, 95, 96, 101, 102, 103, 104, 110, 114, 115, 122, 124, 125, 130, 132, 133, 140, 141, 143, 148, 151, 152, 154, 156, 159, 161, 163, 165, 169, 171, 172, 173, 180, 184, 185, 190, 191, 192, 194, 196

numinous, 40, 41, 122

paradox, 62, 64, 74, 81, 83, 91, 96, 110, 123, 137, 164
philosopher, 2, 3, 11, 17, 18, 33, 35, 50, 75, 81, 82, 117, 146, 149, 181
philosophical, 3, 16, 17, 31, 41, 55, 56, 58, 61, 68, 70, 74, 81, 137, 147, 156, 160, 163, 164, 172, 176, 181, 185
poetry, 1, 3, 24, 61, 65, 68, 70, 71, 74, 75, 76, 77, 81, 189, 195
power, 2, 13, 16, 17, 19, 20, 22, 24, 27, 28, 32, 36, 37, 40, 42, 43, 44, 45, 46, 47, 53, 58, 59, 63, 64, 67, 71, 73, 74, 75, 78, 81, 90, 92, 94, 95, 100, 101, 102, 105, 107, 109, 113, 116, 117, 120, 122, 123, 124, 125, 128, 130, 131, 138, 142, 145, 146, 148, 149, 150, 151, 153, 159, 160, 162, 164, 165, 169, 172, 173, 178, 182, 183, 185, 186, 187, 190
preternatural, 72, 164

reconciliation, 1, 27, 46, 181, 185
regressive, 102
responsibility, 2, 21, 24, 29, 36, 37, 38, 44, 49, 181, 183, 193, 196

second world, 8, 24, 38, 124, 133, 174, 185, 192, 193, 196
self-awareness, 20, 21, 23
Shakespeare, 23, 184, 190
shaman, 102, 116, 182, 184, 185, 190
soul, 20, 21, 43, 46, 51, 105, 152, 155, 192, 193, 194, 196
space, 2, 8, 10, 18, 19, 27, 35, 43, 44, 46, 50, 58, 69, 73, 75, 76, 77, 83, 93, 95, 96, 97, 101, 110, 139, 155, 157, 161, 167, 186, 187, 194
species, 18, 32, 34, 35, 39, 48, 49, 50, 53, 54, 57, 63, 74, 87, 88, 89, 90, 91, 92, 97, 98, 104, 107, 110, 112, 113, 114, 115, 116, 119, 126, 130, 131, 137, 141, 149, 151, 152, 153, 154, 155, 156, 160, 162, 164, 168,

171, 179, 182, 184, 185, 187, 188, 193, 195, 196
spiritual, 8, 12, 20, 43, 56, 108, 120, 128, 170, 185, 195
split, 1, 7, 12, 24, 29, 61, 62, 83, 109, 132, 133, 179, 181, 185, 192, 196
strangeness, 1, 20, 34, 38, 45, 61, 91, 100, 145, 162, 164, 165, 179
suffer, 9, 10, 15, 31, 32, 36, 114, 122, 178, 194
supernatural, 41, 93, 100, 121, 122, 159, 169, 170, 171, 172

sympathy, 2, 28, 29, 32, 39, 94, 125, 126, 132, 144, 154, 156, 163, 175, 178, 179, 180, 190, 195

Thoreau, Henry David, 7, 8, 15, 17, 18, 19, 20, 22, 23, 24, 33, 53, 71, 73, 93, 98, 162, 166, 185
totem, 92, 102, 121, 122, 152
transcendentalism, 33

Uexküll, Jakob von, 154
umwelt, 154, 159
uncanny, 34, 40, 89, 100, 159, 169, 171, 172

About the Author

Qianqian Cheng obtained her PhD in English from the University of Toulouse-Jean Jaurès, France. She has taught English at the University of Shanghai for Science and Technology and Chinese at the University of Toulouse. She has published articles on animal studies as well as on Loren Eiseley.

www.ingramcontent.com/pod-product-compliance
Lightning Source LLC
Chambersburg PA
CBHW061444300426
44114CB00014B/1829